FORENSIC PSYCHOLOGY

THE BASICS

This text provides an engaging overview of the core topics within Forensic Psychology, guiding the reader through this exciting and popular discipline. Combining a discussion of theory with information about the role of a professional forensic psychologist, it addresses such key issues as:

- Police psychology
- Psychology of crime and delinquency
- Victimology and victim services
- Legal psychology
- Correctional psychology.

With a glossary of key terms, case studies and suggestions for further reading, this is an informative study guide for anyone approaching the academic study of Forensic Psychology for the first time.

Sandie Taylor has 20 years of experience teaching Forensic, Criminological and Investigative Psychology at both graduate and undergraduate level at the University of West London, Bath Spa University and the University of South Wales.

THE BASICS

ACTING
BELLA MERLIN

AMERICAN PHILOSOPHY
NANCY STANLICK

ANCIENT NEAR EAST
DANIEL C. SNELL

ANTHROPOLOGY
PETER METCALF

ARCHAEOLOGY (THIRD EDITION)
CLIVE GAMBLE

ART HISTORY
GRANT POOKE AND DIANA NEWALL

ARTIFICIAL INTELLIGENCE
KEVIN WARWICK

THE BIBLE
JOHN BARTON

BIOETHICS
ALASTAIR V. CAMPBELL

BODY STUDIES
NIALL RICHARDSON AND
ADAM LOCKS

BUDDHISM
CATHY CANTWELL

CHRISTIANITY
BRUCE CHILTON

THE CITY
KEVIN ARCHER

CONTEMPORARY LITERATURE
SUMAN GUPTA

CRIMINAL LAW
JONATHAN HERRING

CRIMINOLOGY (SECOND EDITION)
SANDRA WALKLATE

DANCE STUDIES
JO BUTTERWORTH

EASTERN PHILOSOPHY
VICTORIA S. HARRISON

ECONOMICS (THIRD EDITION)
TONY CLEAVER

EDUCATION
KAY WOOD

ENERGY
MICHAEL SCHOBERT

EUROPEAN UNION (SECOND EDITION)
ALEX WARLEIGH-LACK

EVOLUTION
SHERRIE LYONS

FILM STUDIES (SECOND EDITION)
AMY VILLAREJO

FINANCE (SECOND EDITION)
ERIK BANKS

FOOD ETHICS
RONALD SANDLER

FREE WILL
MEGHAN GRIFFITH

GENDER
HILARY LIPS

GENOCIDE
PAUL R. BARTROP

GLOBAL MIGRATION
BERNADETTE HANLON AND
THOMAS VICINIO

GREEK HISTORY
ROBIN OSBORNE

HUMAN GENETICS
RICKI LEWIS

FORENSIC PSYCHOLOGY

THE BASICS

Sandie Taylor

Routledge
Taylor & Francis Group

LONDON AND NEW YORK

First published 2015
by Routledge
2 Park Square, Milton Park, Abingdon, Oxon OX14 4RN

and by Routledge
711 Third Avenue, New York, NY 10017

Routledge is an imprint of the Taylor & Francis Group, an informa business

British Library Cataloguing in Publication Data
A catalogue record for this book is available from the British Library

Library of Congress Cataloging in Publication Data
Taylor, Sandie.
Forensic psychology: the basics / Sandie Taylor.
pages cm. – (The basics)
Includes bibliographical references and index.
1. Forensic psychology. I. Title.
RA1148.T39 2015
614'.15 – dc23
2014046359

ISBN: 978-1-138-02158-7 (hbk)
ISBN: 978-1-138-02160-0 (pbk)
ISBN: 978-1-315-69574-7 (ebk)

Typeset in Bembo
by Taylor & Francis Books

I would like to dedicate this book to Professor Lance Workman for all his support during this entire project

CONTENTS

LIST OF FIGURES

ACKNOWLEDGEMENTS

I would like to acknowledge Professor Lance Workman for reading all chapters and making useful suggestions and helpful corrections. I would also like to thank my two editors, Iram Satti and Siobhan Poole, for all their help and for being such good editors.

FORENSIC PSYCHOLOGY AND THE ROLE OF THE FORENSIC PSYCHOLOGIST

Interestingly, the word 'forensic' derives from the Latin word *forensis*, which when translated into English means 'of the forum' – the central area of ancient Rome where the city's law courts were held. Since then, the term 'forensic' has evolved to include scientific principles and practices applied within a legal context, and as such is a recognised specialised area that links psychology and law. An excellent way of introducing what forensic psychology entails and what a forensic psychologist does is by using the example of a personal account, in this case practising forensic psychologist Dr Eric Mart.

DR ERIC MART SPEAKS

Forensic psychology is a speciality area of applied psychology. Forensic psychologists work at the intersection of the legal world and clinical psychology. They provide assessments and expert testimony in a variety of types of cases and some also provide court ordered treatment in clinics and prisons. I work in a variety of forensic areas, but much of my practice involves evaluating persons accused of criminal offenses to see if they are competent to stand trial, evaluating defendants to see if they are legally insane (not guilty by reason of insanity) and evaluating convicted sexual

> offenders to see if they are eligible for commitment as sexually violent predators. I also perform personal injury, child custody, and fitness for duty assessments.
>
> (Cited by McKay and McKay 2009)

What should be immediately apparent to the reader is the diversity of work carried out by forensic psychologists. Much of this work arises out of the core areas taught in most forensic psychology courses. These core areas include:

- Police investigations
- Psychology of crime and delinquency
- Victimology and victim services
- Legal psychology
- Correctional psychology.

While this list provides us with some insight as to what forensic psychology entails, Blackburn (1996) gives us a succinct working definition, stating that forensic psychology is:

> ... the provision of psychological information for the purpose of facilitating a legal decision.
>
> (Blackburn 1996, p. 7)

The British Psychological Society (BPS) expands on this, defining forensic psychology as follows:

> Forensic Psychology is devoted to psychological aspects of legal processes in courts. The term is also often used to refer to investigative and criminological psychology: applying psychological theory to criminal investigation, understanding psychological problems associated with criminal behaviour and the treatment of those who have committed offences.
>
> (British Psychological Society 2013)

This will provide the backbone for our discussion of forensic psychology. First, however, we will explore the history of forensic psychology and how it developed into a discipline in its own right.

THE HISTORY OF FORENSIC PSYCHOLOGY

An important question to consider is that of when forensic psychology actually began. While the term 'forensic psychology' is a relatively recent one, the roots of the science date back at least 100 years. The development of forensic psychology has been helped along by influential figureheads who used their research findings and experience as evidence in a court of law.

Figure 1.1 highlights four key figureheads whose testimony, research and publications have impacted on the development of forensic psychology as a respectable discipline and helped shaped the role and status of what forensic psychologists do within a legal framework. From evidence presented by figureheads such as Schrenk-Notzing and Marston, for example, research determining whether a defendant has provided a false confession is now within the domain of forensic psychology. Forensic psychologists have developed ways (albeit not foolproof) of distinguishing different types of confession, including false confessions. This is important and would have been a blessing, for example, during the Salem witch trials of 1692, where 19 women were accused of practising witchcraft and were forced to confess by being tortured. It is the role of the forensic psychologist in British and American society to ascertain whether a confession is false or true and, if false, why it was falsely made.

Another important role for the forensic psychologist derived from past developments is the determination of whether a defendant is fit to stand trial and the decision as to whether an insanity plea is appropriate. If we go as far back in history as 1772 BC, for instance, the insanity defence was mentioned in Hammurabi's code, the legal code of ancient Mesopotamia. The Romans also had an equivalent concept, *non-compos mentis*, used to describe an individual who had little mental control over their behaviour and therefore could not possibly be guilty of a crime. In the past, the determination of insanity has generally been based on biblical tests of 'knowing good from evil' or on the 'wild beast test'. The wild beast test was applied in the British case of *Rex* v. *Arnold* in 1724. Under the rules of the test, a defendant considered to be unaware of what he was doing was considered to behave like a wild beast and therefore should be acquitted. In a similar vein, the Criminal Lunatics Act of 1800 decreed that a mentally ill defendant should be acquitted on grounds of insanity and detained in an

Key figureheads	Contribution towards the development of forensic psychology
James McKeen Cattell 1895	He asked students at Columbia University to respond and rate their degree of confidence in the answers they gave to a series of questions. He found many inaccuracies in the responses provided, and that correctness and confidence were unrelated – some students were overly confident in their incorrect answers while others had little faith in their correct answers. By doing this experiment he highlighted the problems associated with jury perceptions of confident eyewitnesses with accuracy.
Albert von Schrenk-Notzing 1896	He testified at a murder trial providing evidence of the detrimental effects **suggestibility** has on witness testimony. He referred to mainstream psychological research on memory to argue how pre-trial media coverage could confuse witnesses into believing they had seen what was reported in the press when they had not. This is an error of perception resulting in the falsification of information. His testimony highlights the relationship between psychology and law as his expert advice arises from within a legal context used to inform the courts of a legal decision.
Hugo Münsterberg 1908	He published 'On the Witness Stand: Essays on Psychology and Crime' where he discussed the flaws of eyewitness memory, the role of hypnosis within a legal context and the detection of false memories. Investigators trying to establish the number of shots fired during the assassination of President Kennedy referred to Münsterberg's research some 60 years later.
William Marston 1917	He established the link between systolic blood pressure and lying. After he testified in the case of *Frye* v. *US* (1923), the acceptance of expert witnesses in court judging the psychology of testimonial reliability had begun. His work also led to the development of the polygraph.

Figure 1.1 Key figureheads that helped to shape forensic psychology

institution until considered fit for release into society. To ascertain a defendant's mental state required expert knowledge about the human mind – a role seemingly fit for a forensic psychologist. This ability to ascertain the mental state of a defendant was put to the test when, in 1843, Daniel McNaughton shot the secretary of the Prime Minister instead of his target the Prime Minister, whom he believed was persecuting him. He was clearly deluded and was deemed insane, which meant he was not accountable for his actions. This case led to the introduction of the McNaughton Rules (to the U.K. in 1843 and the U.S. in 1851), which holds that a person found insane cannot be guilty of a crime they have committed. To this day, forensic psychologists are called upon to assess the mental state of a defendant and ascertain fitness to stand trial using the insanity plea.

Another role of the forensic psychologist derived from past developments, this time in psychology itself, is the use of assessments. Of particular importance are intelligence and personality tests used to assess normal mental or cognitive functioning (see Chapters 3 and 5). Tests using questions and problem-solving tasks to assess intelligence were first used in 1889 by Alfred Binet and later in the work of David Wechsler, who developed the Wechsler Adult Intelligence Scale in 1921. Such tests as these and personality tests like the Minnesota Multiphasic Personality Inventory (MMPI), developed in 1939 by Starke Hathaway (a psychologist) and J.C. McKinley (a psychiatrist), remain widely used as assessment tools by forensic psychologists today.

It is clear from these examples that the contributions of past research, testimony and publications have helped to shape forensic psychology as a discipline and define the role of forensic psychologists. In fact, they have helped to create two types of forensic psychologist with very different roles – the academic and the practitioner. The academic and practitioner and their varying roles will be our next topic of consideration.

HOW HISTORY HAS SHAPED FORENSIC PSYCHOLOGY: ACADEMIC AND PRACTITIONER

Forensic psychologists – whether academics or practitioners – are interested in the same theories, issues and subject matter but deploy their skills rather differently. The difference in the acquired skill base for academics and for practitioners of forensic psychology primarily derives from their working environments, what their aims and objectives are, and their daily job activities. This difference can be traced back historically to the different pathways taken. There are those, for example, who have taught and researched forensic psychological phenomena (i.e. primarily the academic) and those who have applied their knowledge of forensic psychological phenomena to contexts deriving from their work environment (i.e. primarily the practitioner). This, however, does not preclude the academic from acting as a professional expert in a court case, or the practising forensic psychologist from imparting knowledge to students at university. Academics who teach forensic psychology tend to have a range of different training backgrounds, qualifications and experiences of the area. Practitioners, on the other hand, are expected to undergo specialised training and experience, leading to a Diploma in Forensic Psychology which allows them, in the U.K., to become Chartered Forensic Psychologists. In the U.S., certification as a Diplomate in Forensic Psychology is awarded by the American Board of Professional Psychology (ABPP). According to the Division of Criminological and Legal Psychology (DCLP) Training Committee 1994, there are numerous skills and a range of knowledge that a forensic psychologist must possess before he or she is allowed to have Chartered status – which, in the U.K., means that they can qualify as a practising forensic psychologist (see Figure 1.2).

Conceptual understanding of work within a legal structure

Understanding of achievements gained through psychological application within a legal and clinical context

Understanding of what type of psychology is relevant to offenders, witnesses, victims and investigators

Understanding of forensic psychological applications in areas of assessment and how assessment should be approached; investigation and court procedure; making decisions of guilt or innocence and whether treatment or rehabilitation is appropriate; professionalism at all times and how to apply this in a report and testimonial presentation

Practical experience in one or more sub-areas of forensic psychology

Figure 1.2 Skills of a practising forensic psychologist

These skills and the outlined knowledge base are also required for forensic psychologists practising in the U.S.

These skills are important, enabling a practising forensic psychologist to operate within the context of a legal structure and to apply their specialised expertise in a variety of situations. Their specialised expertise is diverse but there are two areas that are fundamental to the role of the forensic psychologist which we will consider in the next section.

FUNDAMENTAL EXPERTISE ACQUIRED BY FORENSIC PSYCHOLOGISTS

Forensic psychologists perform a variety of roles, most of which involve two fundamental skills – those of assessment and therapeutic intervention.

ASSESSMENT

Assessment has become an important aspect of a forensic psychologist's work. It is increasingly used to inform them of an appropriate course of action, such as which therapy would best suit an offender with specific needs or what areas of problem behaviour can be improved using therapeutic intervention. Offenders are normally assessed on entering the correctional system (i.e. prison, probation or a special hospital) and when they are ready to leave (i.e. to be released into the community or reduced supervision), but can also be assessed during periods of psychological crisis (e.g. when there are relationship problems, a death in the family or recurring mental illness). In the U.S. this assessment can include the determination of competency to be executed in death penalty cases. The following are common areas of assessment:

- Custody issues
- Competency to stand trial
- Risk of danger to self or others
- Lethality/dangerousness
- Insanity
- Vulnerability
- Personality (i.e. antisocial).

THERAPY

There are many different types of therapeutic intervention available to forensic psychologists; such therapies, however, have to be relevant in the treatment of offenders. Psychotherapy is commonly used because it is concerned with the treatment of behavioural problems exhibited by individuals. These problems can present wide-ranging symptoms such as anger management issues, communication difficulties and anxiety. These have to be taken into consideration when determining the best psychotherapeutic approach, whether this is delivered in an individual, group, family or couples format. Forensic psychologists endeavour to use therapeutic techniques that have been empirically tested and are known to work in the treatment of specific problems. Behavioural treatments can be designed to deal with issues of anxiety, hence the use of relaxation techniques. Hypnotherapy can also be used to treat anxiety problems and has also been useful in the treatment of memory problems, in the management of addictive behaviours and in enhancing cognitive performance. However, it is to the 'talking' therapies, or psychotherapy, that many forensic psychologists resort. Psychotherapy draws upon different theoretical areas from psychology. Some of the most effective psychotherapies that forensic psychologists use are described in the Box, pp. 8–9.

MAIN THERAPIES USED TO TREAT PROBLEM BEHAVIOUR

Cognitive therapy: used as a means of identifying automatic thoughts that interfere with an individual's perceptions, and often distort their understanding of information. This approach enables the individual to identify the occurrence of these thoughts and to evaluate their causation. With the help and guidance of therapists, these dysfunctional and often disabling thoughts and beliefs (i.e. cognitions) can be challenged and responded to appropriately.

Behavioural therapy: used as a means of changing or modifying behaviour through the alteration of environmental factors responsible for initially causing the onset of problem behaviour. It is through the repeated presentation of the anxiety-provoking **stimulus** (i.e. an object, person or situation) that an individual can become desensitised (i.e. comfortable with) to the feared stimulus. It is these changes to the environment which alter behaviour, and the underlying thoughts and emotions underpinning the behaviour.

Cognitive-behavioural therapy (CBT): as the name suggests, this approach combines cognitive with behavioural therapy. CBT focuses on the environment, behaviour and cognition in a highly structured, ordered and goal-directed way. The contribution of thoughts in the causation of an individual's symptoms is addressed by changing them. Another element of CBT is a problem-solving aspect, where offenders are taught new skills to help resolve any interpersonal problems. This is achieved through using the stages of CBT, whereby problems are defined; goals are set; a schedule imple-mented to help change behaviour and thoughts; and the outcomes evaluated for schedule effectiveness.

Interpersonal therapy: used to address problems with relationships with others, which can be due to, for example, social skill deficits, or disputes over changes or transitions in one's own role within a family (e.g. the individual suddenly finds that they are no longer head of the family, or has difficulty coping with grief that affects relationships).

Family therapy: this involves all family members and is used to correct the dynamics of dysfunctional relationships occurring as a consequence of distorted communications. This might involve helping family members come to terms with and learn about their loved one's condition (e.g. coping constructively with a mental illness such as schizophrenia).

Psycho-education: used to inform individuals about their diagnosis or condition and its treatment. Such individuals are taught how to identify early signs of relapse and what preventative measures to adopt. As this might be a long-term problem it is important that strategies are in place to enable individuals to cope with prolonged behavioural and emotional difficulties. Psycho-education therapy extends to family members, as their cooperation in helping sufferers to comply with treatment reduces the risk of relapse.

PROFESSIONAL PRACTICE

Professional practice is of particular importance to practising forensic psychologists, who not only owe a level of professionalism and reliability to their 'clients' but also have a duty to maintain the standards of their profession, and need a method of protecting themselves against malicious allegations. Professional practice encompasses a wide number of issues, which we will cover next.

PROFESSIONAL SKILLS

Professional skills involve a rather eclectic and diverse set of abilities. One important skill for the forensic psychologist, however, is the ability to problem solve. As difficult decisions are often made under changing and challenging situations, forensic psychologists need to have good effective problem-solving abilities, which are required for the determination of appropriate treatment programmes and choices of assessment. Decisions based on professional judgement must conform to the stipulated Code of Practice determined by the professional body representing the forensic psychologist. This means that decisions deemed to be suitable for the individual must be within the context of an ethical and acceptable solution under the Code of Practice. The professionalism of the forensic psychologist should foster skills such as competency in what they do and confidence in their knowledge and practice-based abilities – it is this which leads to good judgement and decision making. When an offender presents symptoms of disordered thought, for example, it is the forensic psychologist's responsibility to make a clear assessment of what is causing the problem and decide what the best treatment available is. To make such a judgement requires competency and confidence in the knowledge and experience acquired over the years.

Professional skills also involve the ability to identify issues which might require advice and guidance from other agencies. Knowing the parameters of a situation is useful in determining the extent of relevant input the forensic psychologist can make. Being aware of legal boundaries and clinical research can help inform decision making, but might also highlight limitations of a forensic psychological approach, leading to guidance and cooperation being sought from health professionals, councils, counsellors and other relevant professionals and agencies. An offender on probation might need forensic psychological input to help with issues of anger management – so they might be required to attend anger management sessions. However, if these issues stem from problems associated with living conditions such as housemates taking drugs, then the solution to this situation is beyond the capabilities of the forensic psychologist but within the remit of the council or housing association.

There are likely to be ethical dilemmas which forensic psychologists need to recognise through skills of reflection, supervision and consultation with peers. Help and advice can come from a variety of sources in addition to working peers. The Division of Forensic Psychology's (DFP) website provides a resource for subject knowledge and skills for forensic psychologists, and is renowned for its promotion of the profession (British Psychological Society 2015). The DFP disseminates information on current developments in the field, as well as advice and training opportunities for forensic psychologists.

CHOICE OF INTERVENTION USED

Decisions concerning the nature of offender treatment and rehabilitation programmes develop from years of experience. These are helped by appropriate assessment and one-to-one interviews with offenders as a means of establishing details of their mindset, upbringing and psychological vulnerability. Such attention to detail can also be used by the penal system to establish the best location for the prisoner. A prisoner assessed as psychologically vulnerable might, for instance, be best placed closer to home or even in an alternative institution to a prison. Information about the offender is pertinent in tailoring the best type of treatment and/or rehabilitation for the individual concerned.

WRITING REPORTS

As part of their daily routine, forensic psychologists need to be able to keep appropriate records of individuals they see. These records should be written using appropriate language that is mindful and respectful. Furthermore, the content reported should be respectful to the individual concerned, and this means that information must also be recorded, processed and stored in confidence to prevent any unconsented disclosure. Records of how and when events occurred, such as what happened during a session, must be clearly documented, but only with the consent of the individual. Forensic psychologists are expected to be in a position to produce formal written reports which could be used to help write policies and strategies for improving forensic psychological services. Occasionally, a report is written to the court which provides information to lawyers defending or prosecuting individuals with an offence history.

AWARENESS OF ETHICS

Ethics can be succinctly defined as a 'science of morals or rules of behaviour' and forensic psychologists are no exception to upholding the ethics of their profession. Psychologists uphold standards of professionalism set by their representing body, the British Psychological Society (BPS), or the American Psychological Association (APA) in the U.S., which promotes ethical behaviour, attitudes and judgements. The Royal Charter of the BPS specifies a Code of Conduct, first introduced in 1985. In connection with this, the Ethics Committee is used in the process of ethical decision making. It is therefore the Code of Ethics and Conduct which guides all members of the BPS on professionalism. In the U.S., it is the American Psychological Association (APA) that provides the Ethics Code for practising forensic psychologists. Other countries, such as Australia, New Zealand and Canada for example, have Codes of Ethics and Conduct stated in their respective psychological bodies.

The Code of Ethics is highly structured and rule-bound and adheres to four ethical principles – respect, competence, responsibility and integrity – which, combined, act as guides to ethical decision making and behaviour based on ethical reasoning (see Figure 1.3).

In 1992, a survey was conducted to assess the range of ethical dilemmas forensic psychologists encountered in their practice and, interestingly, there was much similarity in the problems faced by those practising in Britain (surveyed by the BPS), the U.S. (surveyed by the APA) and Sweden (surveyed by the Swedish Psychological Association or SPA).

Ethical principles	What they entail
Respect	Psychologists should value the dignity and worth of all individuals; be mindful of client perceptions of the authority and influence the psychologist wields; respect the rights and privacy of others including issues of confidentiality and self-determination (i.e. clients wanting to do things for themselves); and respect the need for consent to disclose any confidential information.
Competence	Psychologists should strive to develop and maintain high standards of competency in their work. They should also recognise their limitations in knowledge, skill and experience.
Responsibility	Psychologists should value and uphold their responsibility of care to their clients and in so doing prevent harm, misuse and abuse. This extends to their research participants.
Integrity	Psychologists should value fairness, honesty, clarity and accuracy in all that they do. They should endeavour to maintain the integrity of the profession.

Figure 1.3 The four ethical principles

THREE STUDIES BASED ON POPE AND VETTER'S 1992 SURVEY QUESTIONNAIRE

Confidentiality was the most commonly reported ethical dilemma – 18 per cent (APA), 17 per cent (BPS) and 30 per cent (SPA). This tended to relate to incidents of child sexual abuse and indiscretion of peers. The second dilemma commonly reported by the APA and SPA was conflicting relationships, where the professional boundaries with a client were compromised in some way (17 per cent and 18 per cent respectively). For the APA, payment issues were placed third, at 14 per cent. This concerned poor insurance cover of the client, attaining money from appointments missed, and the reduction of fees. This figured low in the BPS survey; this is likely to be a direct consequence of having a free National Health Service which covers referrals to forensic psychologists. Other ethical dilemmas included:

- Academia, teaching and training
- Research
- Conduct of colleagues
- Sexual issues
- Assessment
- Harmful interventions
- Competence.

(Pope and Vetter 1992)

There have been some cases in the past where forensic psychologists and psychiatrists alike have had to defend themselves against client allegations of unprofessional conduct. A case in question is that of *W* v. *Edgell* in 1990 (cited in Dolan, B. 2004). Dr Edgell was a psychiatrist treating a detained patient. The Mental Health Tribunal wanted a report from Dr Edgell concerning the suitability of patient W for release. The report contained confidential information about W's level of dangerousness that would ultimately have prevented any possibility of his release. This information was passed on to his Medical Officer without W's consent. In effect, Dr Edgell had passed on damning confidential information about W without any consent for disclosure and it was for this reason that W took Dr Edgell to the Court of Appeal. However, his claim was dismissed on grounds that Dr Edgell acted in a professional manner and pitted confidentiality against public interest. He knew that this type of information would have been withheld at the tribunal hearing, resulting in the release of a dangerous man. W had been detained in a special hospital as he was diagnosed with paranoid schizophrenia, and was convicted of manslaughter on five counts.

WORKING WITH OTHER AGENCIES

It is important that forensic psychologists cooperate with other related agencies and professionals such as lawyers, judiciary, police, and probation and prison officers. This is because the services that forensic psychologists offer sometimes involve the help of other agencies. Offenders in prison, for example, are subjected to a daily routine determined by the prison system and prison officers who are there to enforce it. Therefore, forensic psychologists have to negotiate suitable times and dates with prison officers for meeting their clients. Simple requests such as running group therapy in prisons require clearance with those in charge. This extends to other agencies too, such as probation officers who supervise those on a probation order. Offenders need to report to their probation officer on a daily basis in some cases, and probation officers therefore need to be kept informed of any treatment their clients are receiving or rehabilitation programme that they might be signed up to. In the case of lawyers, there are various roles that the forensic psychologist might have, such as informing the defence lawyer of any psychological issues their client might have that could influence the case. The discussion of sensitive information about a defendant's state of mind requires cooperation with lawyers and negotiating the boundaries of what is permissible evidence in court. Attending court requires cooperation with the judiciary and an understanding of what is considered to be permissible expert evidence – hence forensic psychologists need to be fully aware of how the legal system operates.

Working with other agencies can be difficult at times, as there might be incongruent professional codes of conduct. While a lawyer, for example, might want as much information as possible about an individual, it is not necessarily in the best interests of the forensic psychologist to disclose confidential reports concerning their client. Due to professional codes of conduct, especially that which concerns the disclosure of confidential information without the client's consent, forensic psychologists can be left in a tricky situation. This can cause a great deal of distress in situations where the non-disclosure of such information could result in a mentally unstable and dangerous offender being released from a psychiatric unit and being free to reoffend. This dilemma was seen in the case of Dr Edgell which we have already considered. By divulging confidential information without the consent of his patient, Dr Edgell was contravening the professional codes of conduct. The patient filed a report to the Court of Appeal, but lost the case. It appears to be a judgement call on the part of the professional, so while codes of conduct are there to prevent misconduct there has to be flexibility in the system to allow experts to make decisions in cases that could be potentially dangerous to the public if information is withheld.

WHAT CAN FORENSIC PSYCHOLOGISTS DO FOR OTHER AGENCIES?

LAWYERS

- They can help witnesses to prepare for giving evidence in court by improving their testimony presentation skills.
- They can help convince the jury by providing advice on case presentation and evidence and opening/closing statements.
- In the U.S., lawyers hire forensic psychologists to advise on jury selection.

JUDICIARY

- They can help the court to comprehend and evaluate the evidence presented. For example, they can explain the consequences of their findings from psychological assessment.
- They can testify regarding a host of issues such as child custody, competency to stand trial, predicting dangerousness and mental illness (and whether prison or a mental hospital is more appropriate), criminal responsibility, appropriate treatment and/or rehabilitation, and criminal profiling.

POLICE

- They can offer advice on appropriate interrogation techniques and interviewing skills. For example, from sound psychological theory on how memory operates best, experienced forensic psychologists have devised the cognitive interview technique which many police forces now use.

- They can help in police investigations using criminal profiling techniques. For example, research regarding offender profiling has provided interesting information which links crime scene and victim details to the likely behaviour and motivation of the perpetrator.

PAROLE BOARDS AND MENTAL HEALTH REVIEW TRIBUNALS

- They can offer expert advice concerning the offender's state of mind. For example, based on their assessments forensic psychologists can make predictions about the offender's likely future behaviour and provide this invaluable advice to parole boards.

WORKING WITH OFFENDERS AND VICTIMS

Forensic psychologists work on a one-to-one basis with offenders who are on probation, in prison or on parole. Often, they are expected to write a report concerning the offender's state of mind and whether they are likely to reoffend. This is done through administering psychological assessments such as the MMPI and tests for cognitive function. Other tests might be administered for likelihood of suicide and dangerous behaviour. In the case of victims, interviews and other psychological tests might be undertaken to ascertain how affected they are by their experience of being a victim. Depending on the findings, victims can be offered relevant counselling and therapeutic intervention. Different types of intervention are available, depending on the nature of need, for offenders and victims alike. Rehabilitation and treatment is offered to offenders in prison or high security hospitals.

SPECIALISED SKILLS FOLLOW THE SUBDIVISIONS OF FORENSIC PSYCHOLOGY

The skills of practising forensic psychologists follow the aforementioned sub-divisions (police investigations; psychology of crime and delinquency; victimology and victim services; legal psychology and correctional psychology), which will be briefly described here and developed further in following chapters. It is important to note, however, that within any of these areas, forensic psychologists are expected to not only be well informed and on top of any new findings and research developments but to also be a part of the research process itself. This is undertaken by conducting surveys, experiments and treatment trials, all subject to ethical approval, as a means of contributing towards the existing body of knowledge within forensic psychology. Through the DFP, new information about current developments within forensic psychology can be disseminated and used in the training of forensic psychologists. The areas of opportunity for research are diverse and include:

- Jury decision making
- Effects of juror personality traits and demographics on decision making
- Eyewitness reliability under stressful conditions and poor visual circumstances
- Developments of professional practice
- Offender management
- Interview techniques
- Identifying vulnerable suspects
- Validity of treatment interventions
- Reliability of confessions
- Criminal prediction and profiling.

POLICE INVESTIGATIONS

The help and support provided by forensic psychologists in police investigations is diverse. They liaise with other professionals such as hospital and university staff, social workers, probation and prison officers, as well as representatives from judicial and legal systems. In crisis situations where negotiations for hostage release are required, forensic psychologists can advise police on the best 'talk-down' strategy. This advice extends to strategies and tactics for interrogation procedures and judgements of confession reliability. They also work with police in the preparation of psychological assessments of offenders in criminal cases and provide behavioural analyses of crimes and criminals in the search and apprehension of repeat offenders such as serial killers.

PSYCHOLOGY OF CRIME AND DELINQUENCY

Forensic psychologists may also work as academics teaching university students interested in the application of psychology to crime and delinquency. In this context, they use psychological theory to explain and account for why individuals commit crime and how psychology can contribute towards criminal investigations. They are involved in training potential forensic psychologists within an educational establishment, but at the same time have links with practising forensic psychologists so that students can attain practical experience. Academics keep pace with new developments in overlapping areas such as the law and its impact on forensic psychology, and further help in the creation of an informed up-to-date research-based culture within forensic psychology.

VICTIMOLOGY AND VICTIM SERVICES

Victimological information and evidence are important for cases taken to court because they are used in the evaluation of victims, their circumstances and jury decision making. It is for these reasons that data must be obtained objectively by forensic psychologists. Information should be relevant to the case for it to be admissible in a courtroom and provide an evidence-based construction of the criminal event. Furthermore, victimological data helps a jury and judge to visualise demographical information concerning the victim (such as age, gender, height, hair type, status) in a bid to understand more about the perpetrator's mindset. This is particularly useful, for example, in the detection and apprehension of stalkers.

LEGAL PSYCHOLOGY

In the role of providing expert opinion and advice, forensic psychologists inform mental health review tribunals, court cases and parole boards of the mental state of the individual concerned. As part of this they perform assessments and write formal reports which may directly or indirectly inform policy makers of best ways to improve current legislation. This helps to provide a link between psychological knowledge and any new developments in the rule of law. This is one reason why it is good for forensic psychologists to improve the professional practice of their discipline by conducting research. They may also be involved in training and mentoring new trainee forensic psychologists. It is common for forensic psychologists to work alongside lawyers to help prepare witnesses for cross-examination in court and to anticipate likely questions. Frequently, forensic psychologists are asked to testify in court cases as an expert witness. It therefore pays to be research active and on top of any new theoretical and practical developments in the discipline and in related and overlapping areas.

CORRECTIONAL PSYCHOLOGY

Forensic psychologists specifically work with offenders who are imprisoned, on parole or on probation. In this context they act as assessor, evaluator and treatment provider, which means they devise treatment and/or rehabilitation for offenders in high security hospitals, prisons and mental health residential units. The evaluation of offenders provides information that is supportive of professionals working within both civil and criminal justice, prison officers and social systems such as the welfare department. Treatment and rehabilitation provided to offenders is designed to encourage positive change in their social behaviour and thinking patterns. To do this successfully, forensic psychologists conduct specialist risk assessments for violent and dangerous offenders and other assessments to identify particular problem areas of behaviour and thought which can be identified for treatment. Forensic psychologists working in this area offer advice to a variety of people (such as psychiatrists, an offender's key worker, prison and probation officers), taking the offender's best interest into consideration. This includes advising on issues such as the most suitable location for the offender concerned, and initiatives to reduce the stress experienced by prisoners and those staffing prisons. In a similar vein to forensic psychologists working in legal psychology, those working in correctional psychology can also be called upon as an expert witness and are encouraged to be research active.

Forensic psychologists often choose to work within one of these sub-areas of forensic psychology. While there can be some movement from one sub-area to another, forensic psychology practitioners tend to specialise in one. This means years of gaining experience, which is one reason why they tend to remain practising in their selected specialism. Although academic forensic psychologists are well attuned to these different sub-areas and are able to lecture across these quite easily, they also tend to focus on one area when conducting research. There are other disciplines which overlap with forensic psychology that are concerned with similar concepts and have a common interest. Psychology overlaps extensively in terms of the theoretical approaches to understanding human behaviour; in fact, many of the theories that forensic psychologists use are derived from psychology per se. Other areas such as the judicial and legal systems have a common area of interest, which is to see that trials are conducted fairly and that the right individual is found guilty and punished for his or her crime(s). Furthermore, through briefs based on social research, or *amici curiae* ('friend of the court' briefs), judges and other members of the judiciary are often kept informed of research conducted by forensic psychologists. This can be very useful, for example, in the understanding of how memory works, especially for eyewitnesses who often observe criminal events under stressful conditions. Criminology, crime scene investigation and forensic science are other areas that also deal with criminal events, although very differently, and therefore overlap with forensic psychology in trying to understand what happened during such an event. For example, forensic psychologists specialising in offender profiling try to establish what happened during a criminal event, but specifically from the perspective of the perpetrator and the perpetrator/victim relationship. In the next section these overlapping disciplines will be examined in more detail.

DISCIPLINES OVERLAPPING WITH FORENSIC PSYCHOLOGY

PSYCHOLOGY

There is much overlap between forensic psychology and psychology, so much so that in 2001 the American Psychological Association officially recognised forensic psychology as a specialism of psychology. In the U.K., the BPS outlines eight practising areas of psychology: clinical, counselling, educational, forensic, health, neuropsychology, occupational, and sport and exercise. Only seven of these are recognised by the Health and Care Professions Council (HCPC), which includes forensic psychology but excludes neuropsychology (on the grounds that it is a sub-division of clinical psychology and is therefore indirectly included), and contained within new statutory legislation introduced in 2009. In the case of both the academic and the practising forensic psychologist, they can choose which specific areas they wish to specialise in by considering the various sub-divisions within psychology per se – the sub-divisions from which these specific areas within forensic psychology originally derive. The academic forensic psychologist might, for example, be more engaged in theories from developmental, biological, cognitive or social psychology, whereas the practising forensic psychologist might specialise more in theories derived from applied areas of psychology such as clinical, investigative and police or prison psychology, depending on the nature of their working environments. However, even these applied areas of psychology draw upon theories and data from mainstream psychology (see Box, pp. 22–3).

HOW DO MAINSTREAM AND APPLIED PSYCHOLOGY HELP INFORM THE FORENSIC PSYCHOLOGIST?

Developmental psychology: can provide information about juveniles and delinquency by focusing on issues specific to this group and behaviour. Frustration and aggression are common problems associated with delinquency and the developmental changes that occur within individuals of this age group.

Biological psychology: can offer explanations of criminality by considering the inheritance of a criminal mindset and temperament, or the effects of brain injury during childhood.

Cognitive psychology: considers how people make decisions about what they have seen and remember of a criminal event. Much research in this area addresses the reliability of eyewitness testimony and how witnesses decide what they have actually seen based on their perceptions of different situations and people. It also focuses on how interviews impact on memories of events and decision outcomes.

Social psychology: focuses on the interaction between jurors and how this impacts on their group decisions. Other research in this area has focused on what are called extra-legal defendant characteristics (i.e. physical and social aspects of the defendant that should have no bearing on evidence presented in court), which can be influential in juror decision making.

Clinical psychology: this specialises in the assessment of clients with mental health issues which interfere with behaviour. Predictions of future criminal and/or dangerous behaviour can be made through clinical interview and assessment.

Investigative psychology: involves the linkages of information about the crime scene, victim and perpetrator that can be used by police to apprehend criminals.

Police psychology: focuses on stress reduction among police officers and recruitment assessment.

Prison psychology: involves the assessment of a prisoner's readiness for release or parole, and the nature of supervision required. While in prison, the identification of specific needs can be assessed to determine appropriate treatment and rehabilitation.

JUDICIAL AND LEGAL SYSTEMS

Given that it is important for the court to establish the likelihood of a defendant making a false confession, one role of the forensic psychologist is to advise on the false confession phenomenon. In recent years, research by forensic psychologists has established the different motives for falsely confessing, distinguishing between those who choose to lie, those who are forced to lie and those who have wrongly come to believe that they committed the crime. This is an area where research in forensic psychology has helped police and the legal profession to understand the effects of interrogation on certain individuals and has led to new legislation such as the U.K. Police and Criminal Evidence Act 1984 (PACE). Furthermore, advice on effective and ethical methods of interrogation and obtaining evidence from suspects and witnesses alike has led to interview initiatives such as the cognitive interview and PEACE (an acronym for planning and preparation, engage and explain, account, closure, evaluation).

Forensic psychologists have been involved in stress reduction for police and prison officers, and in the recruitment of individuals who have the appropriate skills and temperament for tolerating the events that go with these jobs. The forensic psychologist's skills in offender and geographical profiling have helped police in their investigations, through narrowing the likely physical and mental traits of the suspect based on research showing the co-occurrence of crime scene and victim traits with **modus operandi** (MO), suspect traits and the type of crime committed.

As expert witnesses, forensic psychologists can be called on to advise a court on the defendant's state of mind through clinical assessment and judgement. This work can help inform judges when passing a sentence, since it allows them to take into account, for example, the level of security warranted and the type of incarceration required. Additionally, forensic psychologists advise the judiciary of appropriate treatment intervention and rehabilitation.

OTHER DISCIPLINES

A forensic psychologist is not a criminologist, a crime scene investigator (CSI, also known as a scenes of crime officer or SOCO) or a forensic scientist. Despite the commonality of subject content addressed by these three disciplines they are radically different. Many television programmes have depicted the forensic psychologist as a person who has access to the crime scene, analyses details of the crime scene and victim, and then provides police with information about the likely culprit. *Cracker*, a British drama in the 1990s, is an example of this kind of media portrayal of the forensic psychologist. To disambiguate forensic psychology from other disciplines it is important to understand the differences. We will begin with criminology, which does overlap with forensic psychology in the nature of theoretical understanding.

CRIMINOLOGY

Forensic psychology clearly overlaps in intellectual content with criminology, especially where theoretical explanations of criminality are concerned. Cesare Lombroso (1876, 1899), considered to be the 'daddy' of criminology, advocated the view that criminals possessed an appearance that distinguished them from non-criminals – they were hirsute (hairy) and had physical features such as joined-up eyebrows, a heavy brow and pronounced forehead, warts and extra fingers, which Lombroso described as atavistic characteristics or a throwback to primitive man. These features correlated with the presence of a criminal mindset. This theory has now been discarded, as have other such approaches linking physical attributes with certain behavioural traits. In the 1940s, William Sheldon, a psychologist, advocated the view that certain body-types are linked to specific behavioural traits (Sheldon 1942). According to Sheldon, the body-type most likely to indulge in criminal behaviour is the 'mesomorph'. This type is based on physical and personality traits listed by Sheldon (hard, muscular body, thick skin, adventurous, desire for power and dominance, indifferent to wishes of others, competitive and pursues risk and chance).

In the late 1700s, Cesare Beccaria advocated the view that humans had free will, which was governed to a large degree by pleasure seeking and pain avoidance. Individuals inclined towards criminality, Beccaria (1764) claimed, are more inclined to look out for their own personal satisfaction. This means that they will commit deviant acts that contravene the law in pursuit of their pleasure and happiness. Beccaria supported the use of punishment that was proportionate to the seriousness of the deviant and illegal act to deter the perpetrator and others from repeating the same crime. These issues are very much the same as those faced by forensic psychologists today.

Adolphe Quetelet, in 1831, documented the extent of crime using official crime statistics. Crime statistics are useful indices for geographical profiling used by forensic psychologists today, but were used by Quetelet to ascertain social factors relating to crime. He found robust relationships between gender, age and crime, and demonstrated the effects of poverty, climate and alcohol consumption in exacerbating criminality. Social factors such as these are still apparent in explanations for criminal behaviour presented by forensic psychologists.

While the theoretical content may overlap, the role performed by the criminologist is very different from that performed by the forensic psychologist. Criminologists are not involved with assessing the mind of an offender, nor do they provide therapy and other treatment interventions. Criminologists are more likely to be involved with providing advice about complicated types of crime such as fraud. They might provide expert evidence in court concerning the legalities of complicated cases such as fraud, corporate crime and drug cartels.

CRIME SCENE INVESTIGATION (CSI)

Scenes of crime officers (SOCOs) or, as they are more commonly known, crime scene investigators (CSIs) work on their own, wear protective garments and gather physical crime scene evidence that is packaged and given to the forensic scientist to examine in a forensic laboratory. CSIs have a number of defined roles that are very different from the role of forensic psychologists. They need to be skilled at photography and using video-recording equipment to record evidence at the crime scene and on the victim. They need to be able to find and recover physical evidence without causing contamination. Finger and palm print recovery is important evidence for the forensic scientist. Storing physical evidence without contaminating it is a skill that the CSI has to acquire. They also look for other relevant information that could be physical evidence of the crime event, and help to establish the MO of the criminal and other details of how the act was committed. For example, tyre marks, broken glass and footprints near to the crime scene are all examples of physical evidence that could help establish the means of entry to and escape from the crime scene. With their expertise in gathering evidence, they are also expected to provide police with advice concerning the crime and crime scene. There are currently about three thousand operational CSIs in the U.K.

FORENSIC SCIENCE

The foundation of forensic science rests on the value of 'trace evidence', on which Edmond Locard based his contact trace theory in 1910. This simply means that "a criminal will always carry away with him some trace from the scene of his crime and leave some trace of his presence behind" (see Lane 1992, p. 1). Therefore, the role of the forensic scientist is to establish this trace evidence and link it to the perpetrator. The CSI provides the physical evidence; the forensic scientist investigates the significance of the physical evidence using a variety of laboratory-based techniques. In the case of deceased victims, a pathologist will perform an autopsy to ascertain the cause of death and find evidence that might link the victim to a potential murderer. In the forensic laboratory a variety of biological and chemical tests are performed. Biological tests involve the examination of hair and fibres, insect infestations, DNA profiling and body fluids. Chemical tests, on the other hand, examine items such as paint and glass, shoeprint impressions, tool marks, and drugs and alcohol. Medical forensic examinations, in addition to establishing the cause and time of death, might involve performing facial reconstructions, forensic dentistry and anthropological reconstructions (i.e. piecing bone fragments together to reconstruct the victim's skeleton).

Forensic science and CSI approaches to understanding crime are very different from that of the forensic psychologist. Forensic science requires knowledge of scientific methods derived from biology, chemistry, physics and medicine, unlike forensic psychology, which deals in behavioural models of criminal behaviour.

SUMMARY

This chapter has been concerned with introducing the discipline of forensic psychology and the role of the forensic psychologist, in an effort to overcome the confusion many people experience between this and other disciplines that also deal with crime. Forensic psychology deals with many areas of crime, criminal behaviour and criminality, but does so using a behavioural approach which perceives criminals as having a behavioural problem deriving from deviant ways of thinking and perceiving the world. The forensic psychologist taps into these thoughts, perceptions and behaviours using a variety of clinical assessments, and then uses the results of these assessments to identify problem areas that can be changed through the implementation of appropriate treatment interventions. Whatever the forensic psychologist does is based on sound evidence derived from empirical clinical effectiveness research, and on professional guidance and ethical standards of practice stipulated by the representing professional body – these being, in the U.K., the BPS and the HCPC.

RECOMMENDATIONS FOR FURTHER READING

Adler, J. and Gray, J.M. (2010). *Forensic Psychology: Concepts, Debates and Practice* (2nd edn). Cullompton: Willan Publishing.

Davies, G.M. and Beech, A.R. (2011). *Forensic Psychology* (2nd edn). Chichester: Wiley.

2

THEORIES OF CRIMINAL BEHAVIOUR THAT HELP INFORM PRACTICE

As we discovered in Chapter 1, forensic psychology developed as a discipline in its own right as an offshoot from mainstream psychology. It is therefore not surprising that many of the theories of crime and criminal behaviour have evolved from those commonly used in psychology. The theories used in cognitive psychology, for instance, can offer explanations of how individuals make decisions – which factors influence our reasoning capability and how motivations and perceptions can impair decision making. We saw how social psychology can provide a framework for understanding how jurors might make decisions about defendants. Social psychology also adds to this area by addressing how stereotypes and biased perceptions can cloud our reasoning ability. This comes into its own when decisions about a defendant's guilt are based on whether, for example, they look physically unattractive and are therefore more likely to be perceived as threatening. Stereotypes of physically attractive individuals are positive whereas unattractive individuals generally receive negative weightings.

Theories from mainstream psychology have been adapted to explain criminal behaviour. Theories provide a working paradigm, which means that they come with a set of assumptions leading to a defined methodology. This can be seen in the behaviourist approach to understanding behaviour. Advocates of **behaviourism** understand human behaviour as a set of responses to **stimuli** that initiate a particular way of behaving. Responses to stimuli beyond one's conscious control are easily accounted for using biological concepts, such as a biological drive of hunger causing the salivary glands to release saliva at the sight of food. Behaviour under the conscious control of an individual is less easily explained in this way, but behaviourists do so by introducing the notion of associative learning. They believe that responses to stimuli that are learned occur through association, so that when a sex offender becomes excited at seeing pornographic images of children this pleasurable feeling is put down to seeing children in compromising situations. This association becomes reinforced further through the sexual arousal that viewing pornography brings and it is this which guides the individual's future behaviour. The underlying assumption of the behaviourist approach, therefore, leads to a working method for changing behaviour – simply disrupting the cycle of association. Hence, therein lies the treatment intervention strategy. The main theoretical approaches which offer a working paradigm for under-standing offending behaviour include evolutionary psychology, biopsychology, cognitive and behavioural psychology, environmental and situational theories in psychology, socio-cultural and finally biopsychosocial psychology (see Figure 2.1). We will consider each in turn in this chapter.

Beginning with evolutionary psychology, we will explore how this can be perceived as an overarching discipline from which sub-divisions

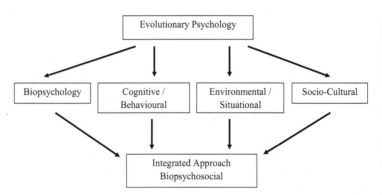

Figure 2.1 The main theoretical approaches for understanding offending behaviour

of psychology known to influence forensic psychology might arise. Why should this be so, you might ask? A good question, which we will explore in due course. Needless to say, not all psychologists agree that the evolutionary approach is the way forward for psychology. Indeed some have been quite critical of this approach (Buller 2005). Despite this, evolutionary psychology is currently making a great deal of headway that may ultimately help to integrate the approaches outlined in Figure 2.1 (Buss 2012; Workman and Reader 2014). The biopsychosocial perspective is an example of an integrated approach which attempts to bring together these sub-divisions in an effort to demonstrate how important the different areas are in explaining criminality – the whole is greater than the sum of the parts. First, however, we need to understand just exactly what evolutionary psychology is.

WHAT IS EVOLUTIONARY PSYCHOLOGY?

Evolutionary psychologists are interested in how the mind developed, from our ancestral past to current modern day humans. They examine past environmental pressures that led to the universal human nature – in other words, what our ancestors were up against and how they managed to overcome environmental adversities by adapting to the elements of the day rather than fighting them. To explain this, evolutionary psychologists defer to the principles outlined by Charles Darwin's theory of evolution. An explanation of evolutionary psychology has been well defined by Workman and Reader: see Box, pp. 31–2.

WORKMAN AND READER DESCRIBE EVOLUTIONARY PSYCHOLOGY

Evolutionary psychology is a relatively new discipline that applies the principles of Darwinian natural selection to the study of the human mind. The principal assumption of evolutionary psychology is that the human mind should be considered to be an organ that was designed by natural selection to guide the individual in making decisions that aid survival and reproduction. This may be done through species-specific 'instincts' that

> enabled our ancestors to survive and reproduce and which give rise to a universal human nature. But equally the mind is an organ which is designed to learn, so – contrary to what many people think – evolutionary psychology does not suggest that everything is innate.
>
> Workman and Reader 2014, p. 1

Darwin (1859) introduced the concept of **natural selection** to explain how genetic variation can help to enable species to adapt to their environment. Individuals within a given population will vary genetically and as a result some will be better suited to current ecological pressures. It is these individuals with the appropriate **adaptations** that will produce larger numbers of surviving offspring. This raises the question of where the genetic variation comes from. There are two main sources of variation in sexually reproducing organisms – **mutation** and **recombination**. In the case of mutation, specific genes will differ from those of the parents due to spontaneous biochemical change (due, for example, to background radiation). In contrast, recombination consists of the changing of gene combinations that occurs during the process that we call sex. Hence, natural selection is based on how well specific gene combinations 'fit' their environment. We can think of the currency of natural selection as differential reproductive success.

You may ask what this has got to do with forensic psychology or human behaviour. Darwin believed that natural selection plays an important role in the evolution of human behaviour. The human mind operates mechanistically, argued Darwin, which means it can be studied by reducing it to the workings of the brain. It is therefore the brain that is responsible for our behaviour, and as it is an organ like any other organ in the body it is affected by the pressures of natural selection. This means the mind and behaviour are products of evolution by natural selection. In recent years many cognitive psychologists have begun to make use of Darwin's ideas in order to explain human cognitive processes such as perception, memory, thought and language. Since natural selection is based on reproductive success we have to realise that evolution does not necessarily lead to morally correct behaviour. According to evolutionary psychologists, some criminals may be using different strategies to the rest of us to pass on copies of their genes. A system where most individuals play by the rules with regard to moral conduct leaves itself open to infiltration by freeriders (i.e. those who engage in criminal activity). It is well established within evolutionary theory that there may be more than one solution to an adaptive problem (Maynard-Smith 1993). Hence, freeriding criminals may be maintained in a population where the vast majority act honestly. Note that this perspective assumes that genetic differences between individuals may, in part, account for differences in moral behaviour.

Darwin realised that natural selection could not explain why there are gender differences across many different species, including humans. He therefore introduced the concept of **sexual selection**, which provides an account of how the behaviour of each gender might have an impact on the behaviour of the other (Darwin 1871). Sexual selection can be defined as:

Darwin's second mechanism of evolutionary change. Sexual selection 'selects for' characteristics that help an individual gain access to mates.
(Workman and Reader 2014, p. 484)

The process of sexual selection can be illustrated by the expenditure of time and effort males use to attract a female. This uses much energy and can be costly to the male especially if she turns him down or he gets involved in a fight with another male also competing for her attention. Males must therefore have characteristics or traits that females find appealing in order for them to be considered as suitable sexual partners. It is these very characteristics or traits that are selected for as a consequence of female choosiness. A large, muscular male, for instance, puts out the signal that he is strong and would be able to take care of his partner and their offspring. In this respect he would be a good example of an individual who is likely to survive and provide healthy genes for her offspring – hence 'survival of the sexiest' (Workman and Reader 2014).

Evolutionary psychologists use sexual selection to explain aggressive behaviour. Cross-culturally, males are more likely to commit aggressive acts than females, as the statistical data bears witness – regardless of whether it is grievous bodily harm or homicide (Archer 2004; Campbell 2013). Although John Archer is a social psychologist, he has combined sexual selection theory with social explanations of why females are less aggressive than males. There are primarily two social approaches: social role theory and biosocial theory. Social role theory assumes that gender roles are shaped by society through the process of socialisation (i.e. where parents and others bring their children up to adopt the values, beliefs, morals and attitudes representative of the society they are a part of). In the case of applying social role theory to gender differences in physical aggression, it is suggested that girls are socialised to respond less aggressively than boys. The biosocial theory sees the divide in gender roles as being a result of physical sex differences which are biologically determined. These physical differences then cause us to gravitate towards gender roles promoted by society. Archer considered sexual selection, social role and biosocial theories singularly to ascertain which of the three best accounts for the data on male and female aggression. He concluded that sexual selection best accounts for the gender difference in aggression, as explained in the Box, pp. 34–6.

SEXUAL SELECTION EXPLAINS GENDER DIFFERENCES IN AGGRESSION, SAYS JOHN ARCHER

John Archer (2004) divided aggression into three ascending levels: indirect, direct verbal and physical. In the case of physical aggression there is actual contact violence towards another individual. Direct verbal, also known as psychological, aggression involves the use of language to portray aggressive thoughts aimed at hurting a person's feelings. Indirect aggression is designed to harm another person's reputation through, for example, the spread of negative gossip. He found that physical aggression was a strategy used more often by men, whereas indirect aggression was more often adopted by women. With regards to direct verbal aggression, the evidence is blurred across gender.

In an attempt to determine what causes these differences between the genders, Archer considered the age trends in gender differences in physical aggression (i.e. development). One of the assumptions made from both the social role and biosocial perspective is that children are born psychologically gender neutral. This implies that differences in aggression should be minimal at this time and will increase as a consequence of socialisation. The evidence for this does not hold up, because differences in aggression occur from an early age, thus suggesting sexual selection had its hand in priming males to behave aggressively from birth. Archer also looked at what he called mediators of aggression. By this he meant the underlying causal factors of aggression (i.e. hormones such as testosterone) or situational factors (i.e. emotions of anger or fear relating to aggression). Interestingly, Archer found that females injected with testosterone showed less fear and empathy, which are normally factors that reduce aggression. Testosterone is a hormone particularly associated with males which can increase aggressive behaviour. This furthers the sexual selection argument in explaining gender differences for aggression. Archer was also interested in within-gender individual differences for physical aggression. In the case of males, there are two reproductive strategies which can be used – the first is where he spends his time in a monogamous relationship helping to raise his children (i.e. the dad), the second where he attempts to inseminate as many women as possible while failing to provide any parental input (i.e. the cad). It is the 'cad' strategy which is most likely to lead to aggressive confrontations with other competing males. This is less likely to happen in females, as they are responsible for giving birth, and as a consequence would be less likely to engage in many different relationships – their options are therefore restricted. The fact that Archer found greater variability in levels of aggression in males than in females suggests that sexual selection is at work here, due to the existence of these two strategic extremes for men. Another factor Archer considered is the variation in gender differences in aggression due to environmental conditions. Archer argued that males become more aggressive when they fail to obtain a mate because of some environmental factor blocking their path. This holds up to a sexual selection argument. The social role theory arguing that emancipated women (i.e. those with good career prospects) become less subservient towards males and more aggressive unfortunately does not hold up on its own.

While in all of these areas sexual selection theory provides a better explanation for gender differences in aggression, Archer does not dismiss gender roles as a partial explanation for such differences. Rather he views it as a layer on top of differences driven initially by sexual selection. Hence, Archer does not reject biosocial theory out of hand.

Males have higher levels of testosterone than females. It plays a major role in shaping the sexual behaviour of males but also increases the tendency for males to behave aggressively. Boyd (2000) used the evolutionary perspective to explain the effects of testosterone on young men in a study conducted in the U.S.A, Canada and the U.K. The findings showed that violence increased at 15 years of age, peaking at 20 and then declining from 30 years onwards. Boyd suggested that a higher level of testosterone was a good measure of homicide, as both boys and girls showed similar rates of homicide at pre-pubescence which increased twofold for boys once they reached 13 years and was four times higher at 16 years of age (i.e. when levels of testosterone increased). This coincides with sexual competition for females and accounts for the potential for violence.

EVOLUTION – THE GRAND UNIFYING THEORY

It has been argued that Darwin offered a grand unifying theory, which is why apparently disparate theoretical approaches within psychology can come together. This implies that all areas can be related to natural and sexual selection – Darwin's mechanisms for evolutionary change. This is best explained through using examples of antisocial behaviour such as psychopathy. Forensic psychologists encounter many offenders who are antisocial by virtue of their criminal conduct – committing crime – but there are offenders who are assessed as having Antisocial Personality Disorder (APD) and in some cases the extreme form of APD known as psychopathy. Psychopathic offenders are characterised by lacking empathy, being self-serving and self-centred, having a disregard for the rights of others, showing no feelings of guilt or shame and acting callously towards other people, often causing them harm and suffering.

It is often difficult to detect a psychopath until it is too late, and just as tricky to apprehend criminal psychopaths who are likely to have a string of offences in tow before they are identified. Evolutionary psychologists ask whether the traits expressed by psychopaths have an adaptive value. For Trivers (1972, 1985), an important factor underpinning much of our social behaviour is reciprocation, where our social exchanges rest on the assumption and expectation of receiving a future gift or help in response to having provided aid to the person in question. A society founded on this principle is a positive thing, as everyone benefits from such a reciprocal outlook. Unfortunately, there will always be individuals who fail to follow the rule, and in doing so take advantage of cooperative reciprocating citizens by being non–reciprocators – in other words cheaters, users or freeloaders (see Box, pp. 37–8).

NATURAL AND SEXUAL SELECTION – A CASE OF PSYCHOPATHY

It is argued by some evolutionary psychologists that non-reciprocation is a dominant trait of psychopaths. They also argue that a freeloading strategy is more likely to occur in males because of sexual selection. Sexual selection, introduced by Darwin as another mechanism for evolutionary change, selects those characteristics that increase an individual's chances of gaining access to mates. Hence, having more of a masculine build might have been very useful for a male in our evolutionary past in attracting a female who would be looking for a strong male likely to survive and ensure her and their offspring's survival. This might have involved warding off predators and other males. Females in our evolutionary past were more likely to choose males who were strong, good fighters and quick to defend them and their offspring. This accounts for why males are more aggressive and prone to aggressive outbursts than females. The crime statistics support this, showing that more men commit violent and aggressive crime than women, and that there are higher rates of criminal psychopathy among men than women. In relation to individuals with psychopathic traits, it might have paid them to be freeloaders among a population of reciprocators. For one thing, they would have been difficult to detect. There is evidence from twin and adoptee studies to show that psychopathy has a high level of heritability. Also, the risk of developing psychopathy increases fivefold for first-degree male relatives of psychopaths – hence 1 in 50 people are psychopaths. This makes it easy for psychopaths to remain undetected in a population where more people are reciprocators than not.

Evolutionists argue that genes are selected within populations and passed on if they out-compete other genes that lead to less successful strategies. This implies that the gene manifests itself through behaviours that have some adaptive value for the individual. Being a non-reciprocator might be one form of adaptive behaviour that enables the individual to father many offspring before being detected as a 'cad'. Mealey (1995) suggests some extreme behaviours (such as psychopathy) can be maintained in a population provided they occur at a low frequency. This is important because if they rise above a certain level they become easier to detect and hence counteract.

Given the reputation of psychopaths for non-reciprocating behaviour and taking advantage of others, evolutionary psychologists have developed Mealey's hypothesis further by suggesting two theories to account for how psychopaths manage to go unnoticed. The first is the balancing theory, which predicts they are more likely to go undetected in densely populated cities where there are fewer face-to-face interactions with their potential victims. In smaller social settings, balancing theory predicts that psychopathy occurs less frequently. Furthermore, balancing theory states that there is an interaction between genes inherited for psychopathy and specific environmental conditions such as those supporting selfish behaviour which enhance the expression of psychopathic traits. The second is the contingent shift theory, which is similar to the balancing theory minus the assumption that genes for psychopathy must be present. This theory assumes that we all have the propensity to develop psychopathy given the right environmental conditions. Therefore, individuals brought up in neglecting and rejecting families, or who have experienced childhood abuse, are more prone to developing psychopathy.

As we can see, an evolutionary psychological approach to understanding human behaviour is diverse and is the only grand unifying theory that purports to bring together the various subfields of psychology. It can be used to explain criminal behaviour and provides a good infrastructure for other areas of psychology to develop from. For example, biopsychology is a natural stepping stone from evolutionary psychology. This is because it provides an explanation of the effects our biochemistry, genes and brain have on our behaviour on a day-to-day basis. For instance, it helps us understand the effects of hormones on our behaviour with a 'here-and-now' timeframe and a proximate focus (i.e. a means-to-an-end focus). In contrast, evolutionary psychology informs us of why we have these hormones and offers an explanation of how hormones came to be. Evolutionary psychology provides a longer timeframe and an ultimate focus (i.e. an explanation over a geological timeframe).

WHAT IS BIOPSYCHOLOGY?

There are three major areas of research in biopsychology:

1. Physiological/biochemical
2. Genetics
3. Brain structure and function (i.e. neurocognitive).

PHYSIOLOGICAL/BIOCHEMICAL

It is assumed that our behaviour and experiences arise out of activity in the nervous system. Intimate experiences like our thoughts and feelings stem from electrochemical events occurring at a micro-level between nerve cells (or neurons) of the brain. Neurons communicate with other neurons via chemical transmitters known as neurotransmitters. There are many different types of neurotransmitter but their role in acting as a vehicle for transmission from one neuron to another has important consequences for our behaviour. It is important that there is a balance of these chemicals in the brain, because an imbalance can result in the over- or under-activity of the targeted areas of the brain. The repercussions of this are altered thought, emotion and behaviour, which can lead to criminality.

Psychologists focusing on physiological and biochemical processes, therefore, explain behaviour as a consequence of brain and neural activity. There are many different structures of the brain responsible for cognitive functioning that interconnect to share information and produce an overall response. In the case of communication, the speech centres interconnect with areas concerned with thought and memory. If there is a learning disability for communication, then it is likely to result in poor comprehension and interpretation of what other people are saying – which could ultimately lead to an aggressive response if, for example, a joke is misconstrued as an insult. Behaviour can be dramatically changed by, for example, sex hormones like testosterone, renowned for increasing risk-taking.

High levels of testosterone in the brain were found to be related to aggression and impulsivity in adult males (Coccaro et al. 2007). Testosterone appears to have a direct link with provoked aggression – where a situation causes an individual to feel aggrieved. Other studies have shown high levels of testosterone in aggressive prisoners and violent rapists. Levels of testosterone and the neurotransmitter serotonin during childhood are good predictors of later violence (Raine et al. 1997). In a study of 4,462 males, the factor which correlated with delinquency and aggressive behaviour was high levels of testosterone. Serotonin levels have been found to influence aggression also. Low levels of serotonin in the brain (as measured in the cerebrospinal fluid), for instance, have been associated with impulsive aggressive behaviour, but not premeditated violence (Halpern 1997). High levels of blood serotonin also appear to be a characteristic of violent males (Moffitt et al. 1998).

There have been interesting findings concerning the hormone cortisol. Cortisol is produced as the body's mechanism to deal with stressful conditions – it raises blood pressure and heart rate. It reminds us that we are in a stressful situation and need to feel stressed in order to be ready to deal with the situation in an appropriate way, such as escaping from the stressor. Children with Oppositional Defiant Disorder (ODD), which is similar to a childhood form of psychopathy, exhibit lower cortisol levels than children without this condition (van Goozen et al. 1998). The study by van Goozen and her colleagues investigated this difference by taking measurements of blood pressure, heart rate and cortisol levels under both stressful and non-stressful conditions. They showed that cortisol levels increased under stressful conditions when the child was considered to be highly aggressive, disruptive and anxious but, interestingly, decreased in children classified as highly aggressive and disruptive only. This pattern fits in with antisocial adults, who exhibit low levels of cortisol under stressful situations, suggesting that their physiological responses to stressful situations are different to the norm and explaining why they fail to show signs of anxiety. These findings overall suggest that psychopathic tendencies have a physiological basis and that this commences at an early age.

GENETICS

The influence of genes on behaviour is normally researched by looking at twins, adoptees and family history. The reason that studies of twins, adoptees and families are paramount in the investigation of genetics and understanding the impact that the genes inherited from our parents have on our behaviour is linked to the different degrees of genetic relatedness. By focusing on one behaviour or trait, it is possible to trace the genes involved – especially now that the Human Genome Project has completed mapping our entire genetic code. Biopsychologists agree that brain development is in part due to our genes, which thereby indirectly influence our behaviour. How genes influence our behaviour is an important question. The widely held view among biopsychologists is that many of the symptoms of schizophrenia, such as delusions, hallucinations and disordered thought and communication, are related to the inheritance of faulty genes. It is believed that these faulty genes impact on the development of the nervous system, causing it to malfunction in ways consistent with the symptoms seen in schizophrenia. This can equally be applied to the understanding of criminality – why individuals behave in a criminal way. This area of research has become known as behavioural genetics. Not everyone, however, accepts behavioural genetics in the study of criminality. Professor of Law and of Biological Sciences Owen Jones (2006) was surprised to find the misunderstandings of behavioural genetics that some people have.

PROFESSOR OWEN JONES EXPLAINS

First, I attended the 1994 conference on genes and crime, at which interrupting protestors famously chanted, 'Maryland conference, you can't hide; we know you're pushing genocide.' Two signs illustrated their concerns. One read: 'Jobs, Not Prozac.' The other read: 'This Conference Predisposes Me to Disruptive Behavior Disorder.' ... the yawning gulf between what I or anyone else was actually saying (or about to say) and the preempting assumption about what we must mean, intend, and advocate was breathtaking.

(Jones 2006, pp. 81–2)

To understand the important link between family relatedness and criminal behaviour, the case of 'Landrigan', whose real name was Billy Hill, highlights the influence of our genes on disordered behaviour (Jones 2006). Billy Hill's mother abused alcohol and drugs during pregnancy and his father went to prison. At six months old he was adopted by the Landrigan family and attained a new identity as Jeffrey Landrigan. Landrigan was a troublesome child, a trait which continued into adulthood when he was convicted for murdering his friend and imprisoned in Oklahoma. Interestingly, while he was serving his sentence his biological father was on death row in Arkansas prison. Landrigan escaped but was later convicted of another murder. The court described him as a man who was amoral and devoid of remorse. This case is interesting because his attorneys wanted a resentencing hearing based on evidence that Landrigan had a genetic predisposition for 'disordered behaviour'. They argued first that he sustained *in utero* poisoning as a result of his mother abusing alcohol and drugs during pregnancy, and second that this and her subsequent rejection of him during his childhood led to his later drug and alcohol addictions. It was deemed that 'Landrigan's behaviour and activities from infancy into childhood, and through adulthood, were not the products of "free will" as society defines this term because Landrigan lacked the ability to make non-impulsive, considered choices about his life's path' (Brief of Petitioner-Appellant, Landrigan II; supra note 2 at 6–7).

This was rejected, but at a later hearing other factors were introduced such as his sustained organic brain damage and his unlucky genetic and *in utero* environmental interaction. This modified argument by Landrigan's attorney, however, failed to prevent his execution, which was carried out by lethal injection on 26 October 2010.

Another family link with antisocial behaviour was that of the Jukes (see Box, pp. 43–4).

THE JUKES FAMILY, STUDIED BY RICHARD DUGDALE (1877)

In 1877, Dugdale published his findings about the Juke family, who for generations had been well established criminals and well known to the police. Dugdale addressed the question of whether heredity or one's environment caused, or at least contributed towards, criminality. Using a survey approach, he looked at issues relating to heredity, income, intelligence, education and criminality across generations of the Juke family. Dugdale found a connection between crime and poverty and assumed that prostitution and illegitimacy would have led to offspring who were neglected and uneducated, without knowledge of their parents. He traced members of the Juke family as far back as the 1700s and managed to tease out the legitimate from the illegitimate children. The first Juke member had legitimate and illegitimate children and his two boys married his daughters incestuously. Dugdale focused on these lineages only, resulting in there being 709 family members in the Jukes studies (540 were of Juke blood and 169 were from family reconstitutions). Out of the 535 children born, 335 were legitimate, 106 illegitimate and 84 unknown. Dugdale concluded from his data that:

1. Heredity played a major role in physical and mental capacity
2. Moral behavioural conduct was mainly shaped by the environment

3. The environmental context caused the development of lifestyle habits which could potentially become hereditary, such as pauperism
4. Heredity tends to produce an environment aiding in the perpetuation of that heredity
5. The environment influences an individual's path in life, which makes heredity an organised consequence of an unchanging environment.

Many people are uncomfortable with the idea of there being a gene or a number of genes influencing the way we behave, or that genetics can be used to help explain why some violent individuals are capable of murder. The concept of some people having a genetic predisposition towards criminality has a sense of determinism which takes away the notion of free will. It should be pointed out, however, that even hardened geneticists believe that the environment plays a strong hand in determining the expression of genes. There is, nevertheless, mounting evidence that certain genes can predispose an individual to lead a criminal lifestyle. A study by Brunner et al. (1993) linked a mutated gene (MAO) to aggressive criminal behaviour in the male line of a Dutch family. This mutated gene was responsible for decreasing the amount of monoamine oxidase A (MAOA) produced, a deficiency resulting in low levels of serotonin (5-HIAA), which as we have seen is associated with impulsive aggressiveness. MAOA deficiency was used to explain the levels of aggressive behaviour in the history of the family. Having the mutated form of the MAO gene was used to explain why psychopathic murderers can kill using extreme violence. The case of Bradley Waldroup supports the mutated MAO gene theory. He murdered his wife's friend and attempted to murder his wife using extreme violence. Once caught, he faced a murder charge but, because he committed murder in Tennessee, it was also a State Capital case that carried the death penalty. Waldroup tested positive for the mutated MAO gene, thus arguably demonstrating his predisposition to be violent. Despite the pervasiveness of the mutated gene MAO (also known as warrior gene) theory as an explanation for extreme violence, Professor James Fallon has concluded that it does not act on its own, but rather that there is a gene–environment interaction.

NEUROSCIENTIST PROFESSOR JAMES FALLON ASKS, 'WHAT MAKES A MURDERER?'

Fallon (2011) demonstrated how PET scans of individuals with various mental health issues and personality disorders can be separated by virtue of brain structural and functional differences. In particular, he identified a group of brain scans that were very different from the rest but which also had features that were similar to each other. There were abnormalities in two main areas of the brain – the orbito-frontal cortex and the amygdala. Both of these areas are concerned with impulsive behaviours and the processing of emotions. Interestingly, these scan abnormalities were exclusive to the group of psychopaths who were murderers. These findings suggested that there was a biological basis for their need to kill. He also found that these murderers had the mutated MAO gene, which purportedly predisposes an individual to aggressive, violent and dangerous behaviour. Fallon was interested in whether the mutated MAO gene and the structural and functional abnormalities found in the brain combine to create a murderer.

Fallon analysed his own brain scan blindly and found that he too had these anomalies. He later discovered that he also had the mutated form of the MAO gene and yet he had never murdered anyone. Why he was not a murderer was the obvious question to ask. After searching his family tree, he found that his cousin had murdered her parents and that there were a total of 16 murderers in his family line. The fact that Fallon had never murdered anyone suggests that there is another piece to the puzzle and that that piece is 'nurture'. Nurture refers to an individual's upbringing and events that occur in their immediate environment (which in this case, presumably, trigger the genes). The likelihood of becoming a murderer is increased when the genes interact with having an abusive childhood. This is becoming increasingly apparent when the childhoods of psychopathic murderers are analysed. In the case of Fallon, he had a wonderful upbringing and was a happy child, but not so for Waldroup (see p. 44), who was severely abused and punished as a child. This gene-environmental interaction resulted in Waldroup's escape from the death penalty and the commutation of his sentence to involuntary manslaughter. This has opened up a whole can of worms for juridical systems as to what constitutes admissible evidence in court.

BRAIN STRUCTURE AND FUNCTION (THE NEUROCOGNITIVE APPROACH)

In the past, biopsychologists attached electrodes to different parts of the scalp to 'read the mind'. These electrodes recorded brain activity in the form of brain waves caused by the firing of neurons in the brain. There are different types of brain waves linked to varying levels of consciousness. For example, 'alpha waves' are seen in an alert brain and are characterised as small, frequent waves. Brain waves were tracked and recorded by using the electroencephalogram (EEG). During the 1950s, the Canadian neurosurgeon Wilder Penfield electrically stimulated parts of the cerebral cortex (the outer layer of the brain) of patients he was operating on to see how these areas related to their behaviour – such as moving an arm up or down or recalling vivid memories. Although still used, EEGs have largely been replaced by advanced technologies such as CT (Computerised Tomography), MRI (Magnetic Resonance Imaging) and PET (Positron Emission Tomography) neuroimaging techniques. MRI scans record structures of the brain while PET scans take measures of brain activity. With recent developments in scanning technology, fMRI scans can also measure brain function and have largely replaced PET scans. Scans using fMRI technology have provided biopsychologists with valuable information about psychological disorders such as schizophrenia and depression, but are also of importance to forensic psychology and the study of criminal behaviour. It has been reported that as many as 47 per cent of males and 21 per cent of females among prison populations have a psychopathic disorder (Fazel and Danesh 2002), and that three in four prisoners are psychopaths and that one in four is at the borderline cut-off point (Hobson and Shine 1998). It is no wonder that biopsychologists are eager to get inside the brain of the psychopath and have turned to scanning techniques in order to achieve this.

SCANNING THE PSYCHOPATH'S BRAIN

Using PET scans, Raine et al. (1998) were able to differentiate between two types of murderer based on their brain scan. The two types of murderer considered were those who kill in the heat of the moment (or affective murderers) and those who plan their kill (or predatory murderers). Raine and his colleagues were able to show that affective murderers had a reduced prefrontal lobe arousal pattern which prevented them from controlling and regulating their emotions. This suggested that a brain deficit such as this is associated with impulsive violent criminal acts. Symptoms of prefrontal lobe dysfunction include an inability to plan ahead and to make connections between actions and their consequences. Other researchers have found that the prefrontal area of the brain is important in cyphering thought, while the amygdala, another area of the brain found to be flawed in structure and function in psychopaths, plays a central role in processing emotion and interpreting fear (Blair et al. 1999). An abnormal amygdala, as seen in many psychopaths, is held to be responsible for their inability to control emotion and behaviour and to feel empathy for others (Yang et al. 2009; Shamay-Tsoory et al. 2010).

So how does a biopsychological approach help the forensic psychologist? First, there are many parallels that can be drawn with an evolutionary psychological approach. From this we can see why there should be differences between males and females concerning criminal behaviour. Biopsychology provides us with a greater understanding of what these differences are in terms of hormones such as testosterone, framed within an evolutionary account – sexual selection provides the explanation for the way that differences in testosterone between men and women arose, for example. This knowledge provides the forensic psychologist with insight as to why violent criminals are more likely to be men. Given the differences between men and women, this information can be used to anticipate under what conditions men are likely to have violent outbursts. This can be useful information in understanding the triggers and how these can be avoided – something that can be considered when developing treatment interventions. Furthermore, knowledge of how upbringing and other environmental factors, such as abuse, impact on our genes can be put to good use when treating children showing early signs of ODD. There is also the development of drug therapy, which forensic psychologists can make use of in conjunction with behaviourally oriented treatment interventions. For instance, it is possible to reduce the level of circulating testosterone using anti-androgen drugs like cyproterone acetate (CPA) and the hormone medroxyprogesterone acetate (MPA). Both reduce erection, deviant sexual arousal and the frequency of sexual fantasies. Clearly, such interventions have both personal and social repercussions for these individuals and their families. In many cases, however, they may offer a successful solution to problem behaviour.

Our next theoretical approach, cognitive and behavioural psychology, also provides valuable information for the forensic psychologist about the thought patterns and behaviours of offenders. It has a working paradigm and approach to assessment and treatment which research shows to be successful in the treatment of the many symptoms exhibited by offenders.

WHAT IS COGNITIVE AND BEHAVIOURAL PSYCHOLOGY?

Both cognitive and behavioural psychology have offered invaluable information to forensic psychologists by establishing the workings of the mind and how this influences behaviour respectively. It is best, however, to discuss the two disciplines separately and then combine them in an effort to understand a unique therapy which has made a substantial contribution to the treatment of offenders.

COGNITIVE PSYCHOLOGY

Cognitive psychology has provided a working methodology for understanding how human perception, memory, thought and language operate. Research findings are diverse, but have been helpful in distinguishing between 'normal' and 'atypical' cognitive function. All of the above four facets of cognitive psychology have contributed towards understanding offenders. Some of these will be considered in later chapters, but for our purposes here two areas will be briefly addressed: memory and thought in decision making.

MEMORY AND THOUGHT

Since the addition of working memory (WM) to the existing model of sensory, short-term and long-term memory (Baddeley and Hitch 1974), there has been an abundance of research over the years investigating the impact of poor working memory on performance and decision making. This has included research into the working memory of offenders. WM is the equivalent of short-term memory (STM) and has the role of transferring information to long-term memory (LTM). Baddeley and Hitch proposed that, in order to do this, information needs to be maintained and manipulated using some kind of rehearsal strategy by means of a phonological loop (see Figure 2.2). The phonological loop can therefore be regarded as a go-between for WM and LTM. Phonology, as the name suggests, is essentially concerned with the rehearsal of verbal information such as words, numbers and prose, whereas the visuo-spatial sketchpad is the pictorial equivalent. The final component of WM is the central executive (CE), a mechanism responsible for directing our attention and initialising a plan of action. The CE enables us to shift perspective on a problem and to plan a strategy outlining goals of

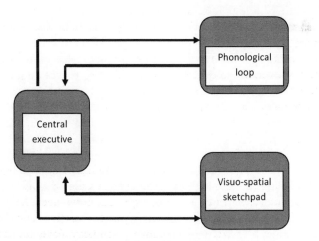

Figure 2.2 Diagram of Baddeley and Hitch's model of working memory

action at the same time as considering more than one parameter of a problem. It also enables us to execute the steps of a plan, monitor the outcomes of these steps and detect and correct any errors. Monitoring the outcomes involves the ability to incorporate new information and, equally important, to filter out any interference. There is a limiting factor, which is the amount of information that the phonological loop can process at any given time. If there is too much information then an individual can experience cognitive overload, leading to poor decision making.

Studies show that antisocial youths have impaired WM function and that physically aggressive boys perform poorly on tests of WM, in particular those relating to the CE (Moffitt and Caspi 2001; Séguin et al. 1999). One test in particular is the evaluation of prospective outcomes involving simple cost–benefit analysis. An example of this kind of test might involve making a decision as to whether it is worth pursuing a crime when the reward is low but the risk of being caught is high. In one study, physically aggressive boys were found to be poor at making rational decisions.

Other studies have found that young offenders presenting with substance abuse symptoms had problems with CE functions such as planning, risk assessment and making rational decisions. It has also been shown that young offenders make more risky decisions, supporting the notion of their inability to perform risk assessment tasks. American psychologists Kahneman and Tversky have spent many years studying decision making. One of their particular interests is the effects of cognitive overload in the processing of information and the consequences this has for decision making. They introduced the notion of heuristics to explain the quick, simple, 'rule of thumb' decision making that most of us use. The use of heuristics in decision making relies on very little information – a simple frequency-of-occurrence calculation – which means that there is less chance of cognitive overload. Kahneman and Tversky (1979) introduced Prospect Theory, based on how people use heuristics in their decision making. For example, the decision choice of an offender to burgle a house versus a commercial property could rest on a rule of thumb demonstrating a history of being caught by the police for breaking into commercial properties. This history of capture under these circumstances would lead to a simple frequency calculation of the number of times he or she burgled a house and was caught versus the frequency of capture for breaking into commercial properties. If frequency of capture for breaking into a commercial property exceeds that for burgling a house, then the dominant option for future reference would be to avoid commercial properties and select residential ones. However, memory of previous events can be misrepresented, allowing errors and biases to cloud 'rational' judgement.

A different approach to understanding thought processes which influence behaviour and can lead to inappropriate decision making is cognitive distortion. This is widely documented in relation to sex offenders who exhibit inappropriate sexual behaviours that are driven by deluded thought processes (cognitive distortions). A rapist might believe, for example, that women deceive men about their true sexual desires or that using force will make them more receptive to having sex. These cognitive distortions are used as an excuse for their behaviour which further reinforces the association between thought and behaviour.

HOW DO COGNITIVE DISTORTIONS FORM? MANN AND BEECH ANSWER

Mann and Beech (2003) describe how sex offenders acquire negative stereotypes of women and children which are then used to interpret how women and children behave. Perpetrators, furthermore, have beliefs about how others should behave, which guides their own behaviour in situations where they feel threatened. A good example of this in action is when a man who has beliefs that justify rape coupled with low self-esteem experiences public humiliation by a female colleague. This situation challenges his cognitive distortions of women and might ultimately result in him searching for a potential victim to rape. These belief schemas, as they are referred to by Mann and Beech, can be changed through cognitive therapy. Cognitive therapy challenges these strongly held cognitive distortions by a process of restructuring them. This procedure is full of confrontation and challenges to the existing unfounded beliefs held. The irregularities of thinking are constantly pointed out to the offender in an attempt to make them realise the flaws in their patterns of thought.

If cognitive psychology focuses on the way we interpret and store information, then behavioural psychology is strictly concerned with what is overt – in other words, behaviour that can be seen and requires little if any verbal explanation.

BEHAVIOURAL PSYCHOLOGY (ALSO KNOWN AS BEHAVIOURISM)

Introduced in 1913 by John Watson as a means to understanding human behaviour, this approach considers the acquisition of behaviours through a process of conditioning. Conditioning, according to Watson, is a consequence of the way we interact with our environment. This was demonstrated in an experiment where a toddler immortalised as 'Little Albert' was subjected to a loud noise above his head and out of sight, every time he stroked a white furry rabbit. The fear of the noise became associated with stroking the rabbit such that he became frightened of the animal. Watson later incorporated the findings of Ivan Pavlov's experiments on dogs. Pavlov (1927) showed that dogs could learn to associate a neutral stimulus such as the sounding of a bell with food, provided the bell rang just before the food was presented. Eventually the dogs would react to the sound of the bell alone by salivating in anticipation of food. Pavlov called this classical conditioning. He also demonstrated that the salivation in response to the bell could be undone, through a process of extinction – that is, by repeatedly sounding the bell but failing to provide food, the association could be broken and the salivation which is a natural response to food would eventually stop. This demonstrates that associative learning could be used to change the behaviour of sex offenders and other types of criminal. Associative learning is an important facet of behaviourism which Watson considered to be the underlying mechanism for constructing our behaviour.

Another aspect of conditioning, known as operant conditioning, was introduced by Burrhus Skinner (1953). In this form of conditioning, behaviours are acquired using reinforcement and punishment schedules. Behaviour is repeated when there is a positive reinforcement such as feeling aroused, which in itself is a rewarding outcome. Punishment is designed to attenuate the behaviour by either removing the rewarding outcome immediately after the occurrence of the behaviour or substituting it for an unfavourable outcome.

There are many types of behavioural modification treatment which have changed the behaviour of offenders using either classical or operant conditioning methods. One form of classical conditioning approach, called aversion therapy, was used to change the behaviour of a violent criminal in Stanley Kubrick's film *A Clockwork Orange*.

AVERSION THERAPY IN *A CLOCKWORK ORANGE*

This is a film about a gang of delinquent youths who are led by a psychopath into committing violent sexual acts. The main character, Alex, murders a woman in her mansion home, bludgeoning her to death with a statue, and is apprehended by the police, charged and sentenced by the court to 14 years in prison. After serving two years, the Minister of the Interior arrives at the prison looking for participants for an aversion therapy treatment designed to rehabilitate criminals. Alex volunteers and is drugged, strapped into a chair, his eyelids propped open while he is forced to watch images of violence. The timing of viewing the images of violence and receiving drugs which cause nausea is crucial, leading Alex to associate being sick with seeing violence. In this way, his feeling of arousal from violence is replaced with feeling sick. After two weeks of this treatment, Alex is put on show to demonstrate that he is 'cured'. At a staged fight he is shown to be unable to fight back, and he becomes sick when he sees a topless woman. When released, he finds himself homeless. Various events lead him to the house of one of his victims, where he is eventually locked in the upstairs bedroom for singing the song 'Singing in the Rain' (which he would sing while attacking his victims). He awakes to hear Beethoven's Ninth Symphony being played, which causes him to experience extreme pain, as he was accidentally conditioned to be sick to this music. After jumping out of the window to avoid hearing the music, he regains consciousness in hospital, whereupon he discovers that he no longer has an aversion to violence.

The principles of behaviourism were used in the aversion therapy adopted in the film. Stanley Kubrick demonstrated how associative learning could be used to substitute socially inappropriate behaviours for behaviours considered to be acceptable by society.

COGNITIVE-BEHAVIOURAL PSYCHOLOGY

Cognitive and behavioural psychology combine to form a successful therapeutic approach with the objective of replacing deviant cognitions and behaviour with appropriate and socially acceptable ones. This successful therapeutic intervention is called cognitive behavioural therapy or CBT. There are many objectives defining the different stages of the therapy but one of the first is to identify distorted thinking and deviant behaviour. Cowburn (1990) outlined the aim of CBT in relation to sexual offending as:

> [T]o recognise the role of sexual fantasy, how to control and modify it; to understand the behaviour cycle and how to interrupt it; to identify high-risk situations; to become more aware of the victim's perspective in sexual offences; to improve social skills and self-control.
>
> (Cited by Barker and Beech 1993, p. 41)

These aims are achieved by restructuring offenders' distorted cognitions and eliminating deviant behaviour through the identification of triggers (or precursors) for the behaviour. This is encapsulated in the SORC framework, where S refers to antecedent stimuli, O to organism variables, R to response variables and C to consequent stimuli. What this implies is that behaviour can be best understood through analysing the relationship between preceding and consequent events or stimuli. In the case of the preceding stimuli, events occur which trigger the individual into behaving a certain way, which for paedophiles might be seeing a child walking in the street. There are consequences which follow an individual's response (i.e. consequent stimuli) to an antecedent stimulus, such as following and befriending a child seen walking in the street. The relationship between these two forms of stimulus is what contributes towards the initiation of the behaviour and its continuation. The SORC framework helps in providing CBT with a focus for disrupting the connection between antecedent and consequent stimuli.

A CLOSER LOOK AT THE SORC FRAMEWORK

Antecedent stimuli – these are triggers causing the individual to react in a specific way to a stimulus (e.g. getting a buzz from thinking about stealing a car).
Organism variables – these include physiological factors such as inherited dispositions (e.g. a violent temperament) and learned habitual behaviours (e.g. arousal to pornographic materials).
Response variables – these include an individual's responses to a targeted stimulus (e.g. always feeling excited by driving a stolen car).
Consequent stimuli – the repercussions of a response made to the antecedent stimulus (e.g. joyriding in a stolen car).

The next approach – environmental and situational psychology – is different from cognitive-behavioural approaches generally, but shares with them the importance of identifying triggers, as described in the SORC model, that could potentially cause an individual to commit a criminal act, such as finding an open ground floor window and climbing inside with the intention to burgle. In this case an open window acts as a trigger for a criminally inclined individual to enter someone's home and steal items that can be sold for money. If this happened during the day then by providing a service of community-based vigilance such as 'Neighbourhood Watch', the incident might have been averted.

WHAT IS ENVIRONMENTAL AND SITUATIONAL PSYCHOLOGY?

Environmental psychology is concerned with how environmental factors such as noise pollution and street space and design impact on the way we behave. It is well known that noisy environments affect our emotions and behaviour by motivating us to move away from the source of noise as quickly as possible, and in so doing avoid contact with other people (which might involve deliberately ignoring others and refusing to offer help). The design of cities and towns in the past might not have been conducive to engaging in communication with others, which is why city and town planners have introduced more spaces as meeting points for pedestrians. Just as designs for cities and towns can prevent people from communicating, they can also encourage hotspots for criminal activity. Dark, narrow streets with hidden doorways make good places for hiding and conducting illegal transactions. Environmental psychology has provided a different angle to understanding criminal behaviour by introducing three major approaches: situational crime prevention, urban design and planning, and social crime prevention.

A situational approach has its roots in interpersonal and personality theory, and social psychology. There has been an ongoing debate regarding whether personality is an unchangeable result of set traits (i.e. dispositional), or whether it is dynamic and changes depending on the situations individuals find themselves in (i.e. situational). For some psychologists, an individual's personality is considered to be consistent, which explains why, when making judgements about a person's behaviour, we can fail to consider any external factors that might be causing the behaviour – in other words, the situation. We generally perceive someone's behaviour as being a consequence of the individual's personality, which is why a person who acts aggressively is considered to be of an aggressive disposition. Hence we generally make internal attributions of cause, where an individual behaves aggressively because they are aggressive by nature. We can, however, make external attributions of cause, where the aggressive behaviour is a response to being provoked. Attribution theory, as this is known, comes from the social psychology of interpersonal relationships.

A situational approach is similar to an environmental one in understanding criminal behaviour as it also focuses on external factors that could be construed as contributing towards an individual deciding to commit a criminal act. There are different factors which are considered as part of a situational approach, including:

- Victim precipitation, used to describe how a victim's behaviour might be misconstrued by the offender
- Lifestyles that put victims at risk
- Alcohol and drugs that cause offenders to commit offences
- Offender cognitive distortions.

ENVIRONMENTAL APPROACH

The objective of environmental approaches is to reduce opportunities for crime to occur by making changes to the physical environment. This means that situational crime prevention and urban design and planning are geared towards modifying the environment to make it more 'people friendly'. Note that this is designed to encourage people to take pride in their immediate environment. Social crime prevention, alternatively, is more concerned with the underlying social and economic causes of crime which can puncture the very heart of a community. Problems such as the cohesion of the social fabric of a community are tackled through, for example, the implementation of legislation encouraging access to improved housing, jobs and services like health and education.

A situational crime prevention strategy first considers the nature of crime occurring in specific areas of a community and then attempts to identify the factors associated with these crimes. Very often, a criminal event occurs in a specific area because the offender:

1. Is motivated and ready
2. Is able to find a suitable target
3. Has no responsible guardian to prevent them from offending.

This is known as the routine activity theory and has been used to explain the role of society in creating opportunities for crime. Communities play a role in how offenders create opportunities for crime on a daily basis. It is assumed that by increasing community cohesion (through working cooperatively and by using more surveillance and security), the opportunities to commit crime will decrease. The reasoning for doing this is:

- To make the effort expended on offending much higher
- To make the risks of getting caught much higher
- To make the rewards for committing crime much lower
- To significantly reduce the situational factors influencing an individual to offend
- To significantly reduce the excuses used for offending.

Design and planning initiatives aim to develop an environment where opportunities for criminal behaviour are reduced. This might involve the regeneration of inner city slum areas or creating safer public spaces that provide natural surveillance. This could, for example, be in terms of creating thoroughfares that are spacious and well lit. Social crime prevention strategies, on the other hand, focus on ways of improving a community through developing and upgrading service infrastructures, such as supplying jobs to the area and creating wealth. Whereas social crime prevention focuses on improving the social situation of many offenders, treatment intervention programmes offered by forensic psychologists are designed to help offenders improve their social skills, self-esteem and ability to interact appropriately with other people.

SITUATIONAL APPROACH

The situational approach provides an explanation of why offenders (in particular sex offenders) attribute the responsibility for their own behaviour to the victim. It is more common than not for a rapist or paedophile to blame their victims for leading them astray. These perceptions are at the heart of victim precipitation accounts. Wolfgang (1958) coined the term victim precipitation to describe how a victim's behaviour might have influenced the offender's targeting choices. This view has been revisited and reconstructed as lifestyle theory, which has a passive or active edge. Passive precipitation describes victims as having characteristics which, in some way unknown to them, motivate or threaten the offender. Ted Bundy, a famous American serial killer, is a good example of a man who was motivated to kill his victims because they physically resembled his ex-girlfriend (who had previously rejected him). His victims had no idea that they were targeted for their physical characteristics. In contrast, active precipitation occurs when the victim has knowledge of acting provocatively, which might, for example, contribute towards their chances of being raped. In some rape cases, the defendant was found not guilty simply because the jury believed the victim had dressed suggestively to provoke a sexual response. Social psychologists found that this perceived style of dress encouraged jurors to form negative attributions towards the victim (Amir 1971, p. 259; Siegel 2006). Lifestyle theory can be extended to describe crime as being a consequence of an individual's preferred lifestyle putting them at risk – staying out late and socialising with younger men, for instance – but, in the case of rape, simply being female is probably the largest contributory factor, according to some social psychologists such as Anderson (2004) and Anderson and Swainson (2001).

Other situational theories regard the effects of alcohol and drugs as causal factors in accounting for rape and paedophilia. The evidence for this is limited, and a simple but important question which puts this argument to bed is: why don't all intoxicated men rape? A more viable situational approach concerns the attitudes held by offenders such as sex offenders. Cognitive distortions are considered as forms of offence-supportive cognitions. Studies have shown that paedophiles blame their victims for acting provocatively, but also that these were unsupported empty accusations. Ultimately the consensus is that victim precipitation derives from the offender's misinterpretation of victim behaviour, which does not exempt them from culpability. Situational factors can help to explain the interactional dynamics between victim and offender which can also be perceived within the context of socio-cultural approaches, considered next.

WHAT IS SOCIO-CULTURAL PSYCHOLOGY?

Socio-cultural psychology examines human behaviour and the deve-lopment of personality by considering the influence of society, social norms, socialisation, social groups, culture and subcultures. According to the socio-cultural approach it is society and culture that shape our behaviour and, more specifically, it is the instilment of social customs, beliefs, values and mores (and language), using the process of **sociali-sation**, which determine our personal identity. In a similar vein to social learning theory, the approach assumes that the personality we develop, the beliefs and attitudes we form and the skills we acquire are learned from observing other people. Furthermore, it assumes that it is difficult to understand a person without understanding the cultural context – this includes gender and ethnic identity.

Socio-cultural understandings of criminal behaviour have been explored from a multitude of perspectives. One perspective involves the educational system. Some researchers, such as Hirschi (1969), regard negative experiences in school as a catalyst for later delin-quency. Low academic achievement, and subsequent failures of school processes such as failing to engage delinquency-prone children, increases the likelihood of these children then playing truant and socialising with others who commit crime.

Another perspective is to consider the formation of groups and group identity. There has been much work in this area that has served to help forensic psychologists understand the mentality of gangs and delinquent subcultures. Interestingly, back in 1969, Matza advocated the view that delinquent gangs congregate in communities where there exists an already established deviant adult culture – such as where a family member has been in prison or currently has a criminal lifestyle and espouses criminal attitudes, beliefs and values (Matza 1969). According to the media in Britain, the new millennium has seen a spate of gang murders and murders of innocent bystanders using knives and guns. For example, Anuj Bidve was shot while walking with his friends in Salford in 2011. Five people were arrested for his murder; three of them were under 18. The Metropolitan Police reported 1,157 knife crimes in London alone in 2010–11. Delinquent gangs have their own attitude and belief systems that gel to form the norms of the group. In other words, these norms dictate how members of the group should behave, and if these groups are criminally inclined then the attitudes, beliefs, values and behaviour will be supportive of a criminal fraternity or sorority. Criminal or delinquent groups are often referred to as subcultures. A delinquent subculture offers its members an alternative source of status and a legitimate pathway to violence that would not be forthcoming were they not members and instead conformed to the dominant cultural views (i.e. society's rules). Membership of delinquent subcultures often offers a 'home' and cohesion to its members, something seemingly missing from their family background. Cloward and Ohlin (1960) studied juvenile delinquents from working class backgrounds in American society, arguing that they were more likely to become part of a criminal subculture, leading later into organised crime. Closely associated with criminal subcultures is the cycle of violence believed to be continued as a chosen lifestyle across generations of families. Youngsters are socialised into a subculture of violence where criminal attitudes and violent behaviour are considered the norm. This way of life has been traced back to urban slum areas where disorganised family life and unstable communities go hand in hand with poverty and lower class values supporting the use of violence.

Forensic psychologists are more likely to be involved with individual and family treatment intervention rather than situational and social approaches to crime prevention. Treatment interventions such as improving problem-solving and reasoning skills, and communication and person skills (including empathy), have developed out of socio-cultural psychology.

Each theoretical approach discussed thus far has different merits which can be successfully capitalised on using an integrated approach, discussed next.

WHAT IS THE INTEGRATED – BIOPSYCHOSOCIAL – APPROACH?

Integrated approaches to criminal behaviour attempt to triangulate different levels of theoretical explanation describing the same aspect of criminality. Triangulation has been defined as "the application and combination of more than one research perspective in the study of the same phenomenon" (Bailey-Beckett and Turner 2009, p. 2). Ward and Beech (2006) used an integrated approach to understanding sexual offending and have incorporated theoretical explanations from biopsychology (genetics and neurocognitive psychology) and socio-cultural approaches. By using the integrated approach to sexual offending they have enabled forensic psychologists to entertain different levels of explanation.

> ### DIFFERENT LEVELS OF EXPLANATION IN THE INTEGRATED APPROACH
>
> **Cognitive/Behavioural/Situational**: historical factors or static risk factors; dispositional factors or dynamic risk factors; contextual antecedents to violence; clinical factors
> **Neurocognitive/Clinical**: brain mechanism; neuropsychological; etiological and symptom expression
> **Evolutionary/Biopsychology/Socio-Cultural**: genetic and evolutionary; social learning (social, cultural, physical and individual environments)

It may be possible to obtain an informed prognosis and tailor treatment interventions for individual offenders using an integrated approach. In the case of sex offenders, the right treatment approach could help to alter distorted cognitions, emotions and behaviour. The evolution of brain development coupled with genetics and neurocognitive function may help explain brain differences and how these might contribute to criminality, but there are other important factors that contextualise the motivational and emotional reasons for committing criminal acts. For example, being brought up in a family where criminal values are the norm could be the motivator for committing crime. Environmental triggers, such as having a criminal family, help to perpetuate a criminal lifestyle. Clinical symptoms exhibited by offenders such as impaired social skills, cognitive distortions, empathy deficits and faulty reasoning and problem-solving abilities are also important to address, as they can be linked to socio-cultural factors (i.e. family background). Hence, criminal behaviour is a consequence of a combination of developmental, social, cognitive and behavioural, biological, environmental, situational and cultural factors which are ultimately brought together by evolutionary psychology.

SUMMARY

This chapter has been concerned with describing the main psychological theories that have offered a means to understanding criminal behaviour and the offender. Each theory provides the forensic psychologist with a research methodology and a therapeutic approach. Evolutionary psychology is considered by some to be an overarching approach that offers a framework into which the other areas of psychology can be weaved. Biopsychology offers physiological explanations and focuses on brain development through a gene–environment interaction. The breakthroughs in technology in this area are astounding and have enabled neurocognitive psychologists to 'read' the workings of the mind and spot the differences in brain structure and function in criminal psychopaths. Cognitive and behavioural psychology, individually and combined, have offered forensic psychologists a good understanding of the reasoning mind and behavioural output. When combined, cognitive and behavioural psychology provide forensic psychologists with a powerful antidote to some of the more deviant criminal behaviours that exist. Both environmental and situational approaches to understanding criminality have contributed interesting ideas to the mix of explaining criminality. The concept of victim precipitation is controversial and perhaps viewed as being politically incorrect, but recent understanding of serial killers and how they target their victims reopens the idea of passive victim precipitation. Socio-cultural approaches help to reinstate the importance of criminal attitudes and belief systems in the formation of delinquent subcultures, very much a problem in some areas of Britain today. The integrated approach can be used as a multilevelled strategy in the understanding of criminality and its causes. Furthermore, the integrated approach aims to reduce criminal behaviour by adopting many types of treatment strategy simultaneously – hence the term biopsychosocial.

RECOMMENDATIONS FOR FURTHER READING

Andrews, D.A. and Bonta, J. (2010). *The Psychology of Criminal Conduct* (5th edn). Newark, NJ: LexisNexis.

Jones, O.D. (2006). Behavioural Genetics and Crime, in Context. *Law and Contemporary Problems,* 69, 81–100.

3

FORENSIC MENTAL HEALTH AND CRIMINAL BEHAVIOUR

Some offenders experience mental health-related issues which interrupt their normal processing of thought and emotion. It is the thought–emotion interaction that is believed to influence the way we behave. The way that thoughts and emotions impact on our behaviour is of interest to psychologists, but also to forensic psychologists in their understanding of the relationship between mental disorder and criminal behaviour. The classification of mental disorder, based on the clustering of symptoms, is described in the Diagnostic Statistical Manual, or DSM for short. This is like a bible of psychological disorders and conditions regularly referred to by clinical psychologists. DSM is continuously being revised by the American Psychological Association in order to update it and, in so doing, create as accurate as possible a description of different psychological disorders. These psychological disorders can have a multitude of different explanations in terms of onset, development and cause. These include:

- Social
- Biological
- Physiological
- Genetic
- Individual differences such as personality and intelligence
- Developmental.

DSM is currently on the fifth version, only just published in 2013 (American Psychiatric Association 2013), which has seen many changes to the classifications of disorders. In DSM-IV-TR different types of schizophrenia were recognised (American Psychiatric Association 2000). Schizophrenia can be a devastating condition that interferes with an individual's thought and perceptual processing, causing delusions and hallucinations. The different types of schizophrenia in DSM-IV-TR reflected the nature of symptoms most commonly exhibited. In DSM-5, however, there is now just the description of schizophrenia. The classification of personality disorders, however, has remained unchanged. Mental disorders such as schizophrenia and personality disorders like Antisocial Personality Disorder (APD) or its extreme manifestation, psychopathy, tend to appear commonly in criminal populations. This means that forensic psychologists are very likely to come across offenders with either a mental or a personality disorder. While using DSM and other assessments makes it easier to identify these offenders, it can be more difficult to tailor an appropriate treatment to a hallucinating and deluded person with schizophrenia or a lying and manipulative psychopathic individual either of whom continues to offend.

Another category in DSM relevant to understanding criminality is learning disability. A learning disability can be regarded as a mental condition that causes learning difficulties – in other words, impairment of mind. In the U.K. it is these three classes of condition – mental illness/disorder, personality disorder and learning disability – that are formally recognised in the 2007 Mental Health Act (MHA). As forensic psychologists work within a legal context, the MHA is also used to guide their judgement as to when an offender comes under the jurisdiction of the MHA or, in the U.K., the 2003 Criminal Justice Act (CJA). When an offence has been committed by someone who might be diagnosed with one of these categories of condition, it may be difficult to determine the correct pathway to take – psychiatric institutionalisation (under the jurisdiction of the MHA) or imprisonment (under the jurisdiction of the CJA). If an offender commits a crime during a psychotic episode (e.g. hallucinating and hearing voices telling them to commit murder), should they be treated under the MHA or punished under the CJA? It becomes more difficult when decisions are confounded by the 'concept of dangerousness' – importantly, is this offender a danger to society?

Also of relevance in the U.K. in determining the nature of sentence an offender should receive is the 2008 Sentencing Guidelines Council guide to sentencing dangerous offenders. Forensic psychologists have an important role here as advisors to the court on the offender's state of mind at the time of the offence. Their informed judgement could influence the judge's decision about whether to sentence an individual to a term in a psychiatric prison ward or behind bars in prison. Being able to ascertain whether an offender is likely to be a danger to society is an important call for the forensic psychologist, which is why understanding the concept of dangerousness is so important. Forensic psychologists in the U.S. have the same decision dilemma, working under the auspices of their respective mental health acts and criminal justice laws.

Understanding the concept of dangerousness, however, is no easy feat. This is in part due to confusions over its legal and medical definition. Comprehending what dangerousness is and the implications it has for an offender are, after all, at the heart of understanding the decision about whether to institutionalise or to imprison a dangerous offender. The concept of dangerousness will be explored in the next section.

WHAT IS MEANT BY THE CONCEPT OF DANGEROUSNESS?

Within the context of a forensic setting, dangerousness can be considered as the extent of danger an individual convicted of serious violent crime poses to others. This can be extended to include society itself. More specifically, Bottoms and Brownsword (1982, p. 240) claimed that "Dangerousness has three constituent elements of the predicted act, viz. (i) seriousness; (ii) temporality, with two ingredients of frequency and immediacy (or recency); and (iii) degree of certainty about the future conduct." The second point Bottoms and Brownsword made will have an impact on the third point. For instance, if an offender constantly and continually poses a threat or danger to society, then their future conduct is assumed likely to continue along the same trajectory. This assumption, therefore, can be made with a high level of certainty. In the U.K., reference is made to dangerousness in Section 229(1)(b) of the 2003 CJA: that "the court must first decide whether there is a significant risk to members of the public of serious harm caused by the offender committing further specified offences". It continues that "there must be a significant risk of the offender committing further specified offences (whether serious or not), and there must be a significant risk of serious harm to members of the public being caused by such offences" (Criminal Justice Act 2003).

It appears from these two definitions that the element of causing harm to others, and the likelihood of this being repeated, is of importance to our understanding of dangerousness. Harm done to others, therefore, is at the heart of how an offender should be treated by the law, but the risk of causing more harm in the future is central to categorising an offender as dangerous. Moreover, it is important to determine why the individual is acting dangerously. This brings another level of complexity to the concept of dangerousness. What exactly are we talking about here? Is it the person who is defined as dangerous, or is it the acts they commit? This question is difficult to answer, as there is no distinct boundary between the two. This can be illustrated by the example of an offender who physically assaults a man, causing grievous bodily harm (commits a dangerous act), and then continues to threaten others around with a broken beer bottle (behaviour indicative of being a dangerous person). At what point does our offender become a dangerous person, given that no further criminal act has been committed? Also, is it fair to assume that he will commit another crime in the future − a prediction that is reminiscent of the film *Minority Report* (see Box, pp. 67–8).

AN INTERESTING PARALLEL WITH *MINORITY REPORT*

In England, 2005 saw the construction of a new unit in the grounds of Broadmoor Hospital called the Paddock Centre. Its purpose was to house and treat individuals considered to be dangerous who had a personality disorder. Individuals were admitted to the Paddock Centre if they were perceived as a danger to the public and suffered from more than two personality disorders as well as scoring high on Hare's Psychopathy Checklist (Hare 1991). Despite not having committed any crime, they were placed at Paddock

Centre as a means of 'preventive detention'. This means that they were 'imprisoned' because they had the propensity to be dangerous even though they had not broken the law. Preventive detention has been criticised for contravening the human rights of those detained. This is where the parallel with Steven Spielberg's film *Minority Report* can be clearly seen. The film is a futuristic portrayal of how individuals who have not yet committed a crime can be detected and apprehended as probable future offenders, based on the ability to read their minds. It is another form of the 'thought crime' that was also described in George Orwell's book *1984*. Both works of fiction are essentially depicting a world where it is a crime, resulting in preventive detention, to have thoughts against the State. In the U.S., preventive detention has been criticised by numerous civil rights litigators. Glenn Greenwald, for instance, made the following response to President Obama's speech in 2009: 'It's important to be clear about what "preventive detention" authorizes. ... Preventive detention allows indefinite imprisonment not based on proven crimes and/or past violations of the law, but of those deemed generally "dangerous" by the Government for various reasons' (Greenwald 2009). Interestingly, the Paddock Centre was closed in 2012.

Another difficulty for forensic psychologists is the ability to predict future dangerousness in offenders who have already committed a dangerous act. More will be said about this later, but just to demonstrate how difficult a task it is, consider which of the protagonists in the scenarios in the Box, Who is a Danger? (see pp. 68–9) are likely to be a danger to society by reoffending.

WHO IS A DANGER?

Case A involves two parents who were found guilty of murdering their six children by deliberately starting a fire. The plan was not to kill the children, who were sleeping in their beds, but rather to rescue them – but it all went terribly wrong. The father wanted to be seen as a hero. Both parents appealed to the public for support in finding the murderer; police, however, were not convinced by their faked emotions. It was established post-investigation that the father had a history of grievous bodily harm. Could the dangerousness of the parents have been predicted?

Case B worked in a nursing home for old people. She was overheard saying on many occasions that 'these people do not know what time of day it is' and that putting them out of their misery would be an act of mercy. Is she likely to be a danger to anyone?

Case C was in Broadmoor prison hospital in 1962 for poisoning his father. He later poisoned his stepmother, who died. He spent a total of eight years in Broadmoor before being discharged. Is he still a danger to anyone?

Case D was suspected of being a paedophile and, as a consequence, had to close his boys clubs. He had the desire to control others, especially the boys who had attended his clubs. Behind closed doors he had a collection of firearms. Is he likely to be a danger to anyone?

Case E went to Broadmoor for committing arson and assault. He had previously made indecent phone calls and indecently assaulted a woman. He was released from Broadmoor in 1983. Is he still a danger to anyone?

Case F, known as the 'Mad Bomber of New York', bombed areas of New York over a 16-year period. Bombs were left in busy areas where many people would be. He sent a letter to the police describing his annoyance with the Consolidated Edison Company. Later the hand-writing was compared with workers of the company, leading police to an ex-employee who was dismissed on grounds of ill health. Could his dangerousness have been predicted?

Case G involves an elderly man from Sun City, Arizona in the U.S. who shot his wife dead in 2012. She had suffered from multiple sclerosis for many years, and his health was failing. Is he a danger to society?

Dangerousness is difficult to assess when an individual has not committed a crime, but it can be even more problematic for forensic psychologists to ascertain the level of future dangerousness that a convicted offender poses. It poses a problem because if they make an incorrect assessment there are likely to be repercussions. Detaining an offender who is considered to be dangerous but in actual fact no longer poses a threat to society, for example, means that individual's civil rights have been contravened and a false-positive error made. Alternatively, releasing an offender who is still dangerous but exhibits no obvious sign of being so could result in a false-negative error, where the ex-offender commits another dangerous act such as murder. It is therefore the task of forensic psychologists to limit the number of false-positive and false-negative errors using good assessment strategies.

Regarding the cases in 'Who is a Danger?' – how well did you do? Case A refers to Mick and Mairead Philpott from England, who were charged with manslaughter and sentenced to imprisonment in 2013. Interestingly, there were many signs that Mick Philpott had a personality disorder, the traits of which were exhibited in his past behaviour. In 1978 he attempted to murder his girlfriend because she wanted to end their relationship (he also caused grievous bodily harm to her mother). He had been given a seven-year prison sentence but served less than three and a half years. In 1986, his wife accused him of being a controlling person and was relieved when he voluntarily left her. He also accrued a conditional discharge for head-butting a work colleague in 1991. Clearly, Philpott had a history of aggressive and violent behaviour, which he exhibited on many occasions and which would categorise him as a dangerous offender. Glenn Wilson, an evolutionary forensic psychologist, referred to Philpott as a "psychopath and exhibitionist with an antisocial personality disorder" (Wilson 2013). His lifestyle fitted that of a psychopath – many children with different women, controlling personality, use of violence, living on benefits and a parasitic approach to life. Signs of his dangerous nature were apparent long before he set fire to his house.

Case B is Beverley Allitt, who was employed at an English hospital called Grantham and Kesteven General Hospital in the children's ward. Between February and April 1991 she murdered three children and a baby. There were a further nine attempted murders, but fortunately these children recovered and survived. It was discovered that her past employment background had not been appropriately vetted, but that it provided evidence that she was a dangerous individual in the making; had it been investigated, the unfortunate deaths could have been avoided. Case C refers to Graham Young, who was supervised by a probation officer and a psychiatrist after his release from the famous English prison hospital Broadmoor in 1970. He found a job working in a warehouse that stored chemicals used in the photographic industry. It was there that he had access to thallium, which he used to poison and ultimately murder three work colleagues. He was a false-negative error, as he went on to reoffend in the same way as he had done before. Case D is the infamous 'Dunblane Primary School Killer' from Scotland. Thomas Hamilton went into the school and murdered 16 children and one teacher, leaving three teachers and seven children wounded. Despite his obsession with guns and his suspected paedophilia, assessing Hamilton as potentially dangerous would have been difficult given that he had no previous criminal record. The only predictable variable would have been his choice of place of murder – a school. Case E is that of Daniel Mudd who, after his release from Broadmoor, murdered a fellow resident at a mental aftercare hostel. He was considered to be a danger to society by medical professionals but was nevertheless released – a case of a false-negative error by the criminal justice system.

Case F was from America. His name was George Metesky and he was a dangerous man who had detonated home-made bombs in different areas of New York. He was a difficult man to locate, which explains why he was able to set bombs off in New York for over 16 years. He had an axe to grind with his previous employers but this, in its own right, should not have been responsible for his aggressive and dangerous behaviour. Predicting his dangerousness, however, was difficult given that he had no previous conviction for violence – and yet he was clearly a dangerous man.

Case G is also from America – his name is George Sanders. He was tried for murdering his wife but told the courts that she had asked him to kill her because of the pain she had endured from multiple sclerosis. Sanders shot her but she died two days later in hospital. Up until then Sanders had never had any experience with the criminal justice system and so was released on bail for $20,000 (a remarkably low sum for a murder suspect). In 2013, 86-year-old Sanders was given two years of probation for a mercy killing. Clearly, in this last case most people would not consider him to be a danger to the public.

Some of these cases were easier to assess for dangerousness than others, but a couple did not show up on the radar as there were no previous records of criminal activity. These cases demonstrate the difficulty that forensic psychologists are faced with when making decisions on an offender's future behaviour. This begs the question, however, of what the relationship between dangerousness and the law should be. Moreover, should dangerous offenders be considered sympathetically, as having a 'mad' sense of the world rather than one based on 'badness'? In the next section, the relationship between dangerousness and the law is examined by considering whether dangerous individuals deserve to be punished or treated. If punished, then what should be the nature of their sentence? If treated, is this the responsibility of the legal or the medical profession?

DANGEROUSNESS AND THE LAW

Implicit within the definition of dangerousness is the idea of committing serious offences which involve harming others – crimes of assault and violence, sex offending, manslaughter and homicide. These serious offences are considered to be **mala in se** crimes, that is, crimes that contravene the human moral code. These crimes are perceived as heinous offences which warrant severe punishments and detainment to protect members of society from potential harm. Punishments for these crimes in the U.K. and U.S. receive high-tariff sentences where detainment in prison is for a very long time. In the U.K., prior to the 2003 CJA, a life sentence was the only sentence reserved for dangerous offenders where the timeframe of imprisonment was undefined, dependent upon proof presented to the Parole Board that the offender no longer posed a threat to society and was safe to be released. In 2005, however, the 'Imprisonment for the Public Protection' (IPP) sentence was introduced so that judges could sentence dangerous offenders to an indeterminate stint in prison which, however, had a maximum tariff of no more than ten years. This meant that some dangerous offenders were sentenced using sentencing guidelines whereas others had an indeterminate

IPP sentence. This was seen to be inequitable and an infringement of offenders' rights by the current British government, which is why the Ministry of Justice abolished IPPs in 2012.

Decision making about what to do with dangerous offenders has a history of uncertainty and unfairness due to the problems involved in balancing how, and for how long, they should be detained to avoid false-positive and false-negative errors. Determining the most appropriate sentence for dangerous offenders is problematic but under the current Legal Aid, Sentencing and Punishment of Offenders Act (2012) in the U.K., the courts must impose a sentence of life imprisonment for offenders who have committed a second dangerous offence. An extended sentence can be imposed for certain violent and sexual crimes that the court considers to pose a serious threat of harm to members of the public. The extension should not exceed five years on top of the sentence for specified violent crimes, or eight years in the case of specified sexual offences. This means that the extended period should not exceed the maximum sentence set for such a crime. This was proposed under the Criminal Justice Act of 1991 (see Box, History of Proposed Legislation, pp. 73–5). In the U.S., indeterminate sentences for dangerous offenders that have no specified length of imprisonment are not allowed. Instead, dangerous offenders are given a determinate sentence which can be more than 30 years depending on the severity of violence used.

HISTORY OF PROPOSED LEGISLATION FOR DANGEROUS OFFENCES AND OFFENDERS IN THE U.K.

In 1975 the Home Office set up the Butler Committee, whose task was to devise a suitable sentence for dangerous offenders (Committee on Mentally Abnormal Offenders 1975). They proposed a reviewable open-ended indeterminate sentence which would be restricted to offenders convicted of crimes that caused serious harm to others – therefore including such offences as aggravated burglary (where the burglar also harms the occupier or occupiers), robbery, intended grievous bodily harm, arson, sexual offences, manslaughter and murder. The committee proposed that the release of such offenders would depend on issues concerning dangerousness, hence the length of detainment would be unspecified. Although unspecified, there would be a review conducted by the Parole Board once every two years and, even following release, statutory (compulsory as decreed by law) supervision for an unlimited duration.

The Howard League for Penal Reform organised a committee headed by Jean Floud in 1976. In the committee's report, known as the Floud Report, a double-track sentence was proposed for offences considered to be dangerous such as intended grievous bodily harm, sexual offences, manslaughter and murder (Floud and Young 1981). This was like having a sentence that was extended by four years. The idea behind the addition of four years was to serve the purpose of protecting the public from grave harm.

The 1991 Criminal Justice Act proposed that a dangerous offender should receive the same sentence for a crime as any other offender; however, if the crime was particularly violent then the top-end or maximum period of imprisonment was proposed, as long as it did not exceed the sentencing guideline. This type of sentence is a determinate sentence in that it has a set time period of imprisonment. It also ensures that dangerous individuals are punished more by taking the sentence up to the limit.

In 1997, the Crime (Sentences) Act proposed that High Court Judges should be free to give long but minimum sentences for serious offences and the mandatory life sentence for a second serious offence committed. This is similar to what happens in the U.S. where 'three strikes and you're out' legislation exists. In this case, if an offender commits two serious offences and a third non-serious offence (e.g. stealing a pizza), then a life sentence is justifiably enforced under this ruling.

Imprisonment for the Public Protection (IPP) was introduced in 2005, serving as a sentence for dangerous offenders. This meant that many prisoners who had served their time remained in prison, serving more years than their original sentence. This was changed in 2008 so that IPP was no longer used for offenders meeting the dangerousness criteria, but now there were pre-2008 offenders serving indeterminate IPP sentences and post-2008 offenders on determinate IPP who knew their release date.

Sentencing dangerous offenders becomes even more confounded when they are considered to have a mental disorder/illness. The question then is whether these offenders should be considered under the jurisdiction of the MHA, or of the CJA. Perhaps, in order to answer this question, we need first to consider whether dangerous offenders are any more likely to have a mental disorder than offenders who commit violent crimes but are not labelled as dangerous. Moreover, within any prison population, which type of offender is most frequently represented? These are important questions in need of further discussion – first, however, mental disorder/illness need to be defined.

WHAT IS MEANT BY MENTAL DISORDER/ILLNESS?

In the U.K., the MHA stipulated that:

'Mental disorder' means any disorder or disability of the mind; and 'mentally disordered' shall be construed accordingly.

(Mental Health Act 2007)

This is very different from the 1983 MHA, in which there were four types of mental disorder:

1. Mental illness (i.e. schizophrenia exhibiting psychotic behaviour)
2. Psychopathic disorder (i.e. disorder of mind resulting in aggressive and/or irresponsible behaviour)
3. Mental impairment (i.e. delayed or incomplete development of mind resulting in significant impairment of intelligence and social functioning linked with aggressive and/or serious irresponsible behaviour)
4. Severe mental impairment (i.e. delayed or incomplete development of mind resulting in severe impairment of intelligence and social functioning linked with aggressive and/or serious irresponsible behaviour).

(Mental Health Act 1983)

In the 2007 MHA these four categories were no longer defined or differentiated but were instead collapsed into one mass of conditions under the umbrella term of mental disorder. This means that at one level the identification of a mental disorder is less complicated but, at another, it is less precise in terms of the criteria that need to be met in order to ascertain what is wrong with the individual concerned. Couple this with the individual being an offender, and the lines of responsibility become even more blurred. Nevertheless, in the U.K., once a serious and dangerous offence has been committed, a process of cross-referencing with the Sexual Offences Act, Domestic Violence, Crime and Victims Act and the CJA is in place to help ascertain where responsibility for the offender lies. What does happen as a matter of course is that a decision is made concerning the accused's ability to stand trial – is he or she sane and therefore competent to be submitted to criminal court proceedings? A forensic psychologist might be involved in making this decision after performing a clinical assessment. If the accused is unfit to stand trial then one option is to transfer them immediately to a high security psychiatric hospital (e.g. Broadmoor) without prosecution. This could also occur during the process of a trial if the defendant suddenly becomes unfit to plead and in this case is also sent to a high security psychiatric hospital without a criminal record. In these latter two situations the defendant can plead insanity and is given a 'special verdict' of 'not guilty by reason of insanity'. The most likely defendant to receive such a verdict, according to Grubin (1996), is one suffering from schizophrenia. The special verdict can be traced back historically to 1843 (see Box, The Case of McNaughton, pp. 76–7).

THE CASE OF MCNAUGHTON

In the U.K., Daniel McNaughton was charged with manslaughter despite murdering Prime Minister Robert Peel's private secretary in 1843. The private secretary, Edward Drummond, died five days after he was shot by McNaughton. McNaughton's defence argued that he felt persecuted by the Tory government and was compelled to assassinate the Prime Minister, but he missed and the bullet hit Drummond instead. It was further argued by his defence counsel that he experienced delusions which interfered with his ability to control his behaviour. It was concluded by the medical professionals that he was in fact insane. It is for this reason that his trial was stopped by Lord Chief Justice Tindal. Instead a 'special verdict' was used for the first time, whereupon McNaughton was transferred to the State Criminal Lunatic Asylum at Bethlem Hospital under the 1800 Act for the Safe Custody of Insane Persons charged with Offences. To this day the McNaughton Rules apply in both the U.K. and the U.S. (although not all states legally recognise it – some follow less rigid guidelines set by the American Law Institute in 1962). They apply to offenders who are judged to be unable to control their impulse to act due to having a psychiatric disorder. The McNaughton Rules generate much controversy in both the U.K. and U.S., with some sceptics believing that all defendants who commit a crime should be found guilty, but perhaps that those with a severe mental disorder should receive a less punitive sentence. A verdict of 'guilty but mentally ill' was introduced in about 20 states in the U.S. This verdict can be taken into consideration when sentencing (a mitigating factor), to ensure that the individual receives the right treatment, rehabilitation and care while incarcerated in a prison hospital.

In the U.K., the 'House of Lords and Judges' Rules' of 1843 stated that the McNaughton Rules are there:

> To establish a defence on the ground of insanity it must be clearly proved, that, at the time of committing the act, the party accused was labouring under such a defect of reason from disease of mind, as not to know the nature and quality of the act he was doing, or if he did know it, that he did not know that what he was doing was wrong.
>
> (Cited in West and Walk (1977, pp. 74–81))

Clearly, Daniel McNaughton was suffering from a mental disorder, possibly schizophrenia (although this was not diagnosed at the time), which interfered with his thinking. There are many cases where serial killers, for example, have been found to have disordered thought. Many of these cases, however, pose difficulties for judge and jury because categorisation of mental illness is not a precise science. Hence prosecution and defence in a given case may bring separate experts (e.g. forensic psychologists and psychiatrists), who may differ in their view of diagnosis. In the U.S., such a case made the headlines worldwide and a film was released in 2003 called *Monster* which was devoted to the life story of female serial killer Aileen Wuornos. Wuornos prostituted herself for many years but it was only during 1989 and 1990 that she killed the seven men she had sex with. Wuornos claimed that she shot her victims in self-defence after they had either tried to rape her or succeeded in doing so. Psychiatrists for the defence testified that Wuornos was mentally unstable due to a personality disorder (i.e. APD). Interestingly, Wuornos made a plea of 'no contest', which derives from the Latin term *nolo contendere*, meaning that the defendant fails to admit to a charge or even to dispute it. Although this is not a guilty plea the consequences are the same, meaning that Wuornos could be charged for murder. A no contest plea is practised in most American states but is not used in the U.K. Wuornos pleaded guilty to the remaining murder charges, received six death sentences in total and was sent to 'death row' (where prisoners wait, sometimes for many years, for their date of execution). There were other clues to mental instability in the Wuornos case, such as inconsistent descriptions about how she murdered her victims and the fact that she recanted the claim of self-defence. Later, however, she claimed again, in confidence to filmmaker Nick Broomfield, that she had acted in self-defence (see Art of Crimes 2013). By this time Wuornos had been on death row for ten years and told Broomfield that she could no longer stand being there and wanted to die. In 2001 she stopped all appeals against her death sentence and claimed that she killed all seven men and would do it again if she were ever released. Wuornos continued by claiming she was competent and sane. Her defence argued that she was unstable but three psychiatrists claimed she was sane. Her belief that her head was being crushed by 'sonic pressure' and that she was being abused by prison staff to make her appear insane or to drive her insane are claims typical of a mentally unstable person. Nevertheless, she was executed in 2002. Hence, in this case, it appears that there was some dispute over whether to regard Wuornos as mentally unstable or as having psychopathy (i.e. 'mad' or 'bad' respectively).

In the U.K. between 1975 and 1980, Peter Sutcliffe, known as the Yorkshire Ripper, murdered 13 women and attempted to murder a further 7. His method of killing was to strike using a hammer, rendering the victim unconscious, and then using a knife or sharp implement like a screwdriver to mutilate the body. In 1981 he was convicted of murdering 13 women and at his trial pleaded not guilty to murder on grounds of diminished responsibility arising from a diagnosis of paranoid schizophrenia. The Sutcliffe case was infamous and at the time he was probably the most hated man in Britain, so it is not surprising that the jury rejected his defence. He was sentenced to 20 life sentences that were to run concurrently at HMP Parkhurst. Sutcliffe served less than three years at Parkhurst before being transferred to Broadmoor Hospital, under Section 47 of the MHA 1983, where he remains to this day. In the case of Sutcliffe there was no question of him not having a mental disorder, as he killed his victims during his psychotic episodes. During these psychotic episodes he heard the voice of God in his head instructing him to kill prostitutes – a symptom of his diagnosed schizophrenia.

There have been many broadly similar cases who are considered as dangerous offenders since both Wuornos in the U.S. and Sutcliffe in the U.K. The disputes over whether they have a mental illness, a psychopathic disorder or a mental impairment continue to be a focal point of discussion for many clinical and forensic psychologists. It is not always a straightforward diagnosis for those considered to be dangerous, as the examples in the Box, Mental Issues or Psychopathic Disorder? (see pp. 79–80), demonstrate.

MENTAL ISSUES OR PSYCHOPATHIC DISORDER?

Ian Brady and his accomplice **Myra Hindley** murdered five children during 1963–5 and buried their bodies on the Yorkshire Moors – hence they are known as the Moors Murderers. The youngest child was ten and the oldest 17 years. They murdered their victims after humiliating, torturing and raping them, capturing their crimes on audio tape. Neither showed any remorse at their trial nor apologised to the victims' parents. Brady had a past history of criminal behaviour known to the police in Scotland and commonly tortured animals as a child.

Rahan Arshad was sentenced to life imprisonment in 2007 after beating his wife and three children to death using a rounders bat. Arshad told the court that his wife had bludgeoned their children and on discovering this he killed her. His defence in court claimed that Arshad was jealous of his wife for having an affair. The reality, however, is that his jealousy caused him to murder his wife followed by his sleeping children, whom he carried one-by-one downstairs to kill.

In 2005 **Mark Hobson** was convicted of killing twins and an elderly couple. The evidence suggested that the four murders were premeditated, as he had written in a notebook details of what he planned to do and a shopping list containing items needed to execute his plan. During his trial it was revealed that he was both an alcoholic and heroin addict.

A businessman called Neil Heywood was found dead due to poisoning. **Gu Kailai** was accused of his murder and found guilty in 2012. Kailai escaped the death penalty, as she was suffering from anxiety, insomnia, depression and paranoia, all of which interacted with the cocktail of medications she was taking.

Anthony Arkwright committed three murders by mutilation in 1988. One of his victims was stabbed 70 times simply because he tried to 'scrounge cigarettes' from him. In addition to stabbing him, he gouged out the man's eyeballs and put unlit cigarettes into the empty eye sockets. In 1989 he was convicted and said to be an evil fantasist who wanted to be an infamous murderer.

Even though it is sometimes difficult distinguishing offenders with mental illness or impairment from those with psychopathic disorder, it is possible to make intuitive distinctions. Those of the examples above who have a psychopathic disorder include Ian Brady and Rahan Arshad. As for the remainder, Mark Hobson and Gu Kailai were under the influence of drugs which contributed to their behaviour. In the case of Anthony Arkwright there were other mental issues present, given his deluded desire to personify an evil murderer such as the U.K.-based 'Jack the Ripper' of 1888. Although the 1983 MHA used mental impairment and severe mental impairment as terms to describe an individual who has incomplete development of mind resulting in global intellectual and social function deficits, this is now more commonly referred to as learning disability. It has been estimated that offenders with learning disabilities in the U.K. make up between 1 and 10 per cent of the criminal population.

There is a problem with obtaining accurate statistics for the number of offenders with learning disabilities in prison, simply because not all will be processed through the criminal justice system – some will be diverted from the system. Mottram (2007) studied the extent of offenders with learning disabilities in three English prisons: a local prison, a women's prison and a young offender institution. Their IQ was assessed and it was found that it varied considerably from the average IQ of the general population. While it was found that learning disabilities occurred in 8 per cent of the general population, in the three prisons combined it was more like 32 per cent (breaking down this overall figure, 6.7 per cent were assessed as learning disabled and 25.4 per cent as borderline). In a population of 80,000 prisoners in England and Wales in 2007, 19,500 had learning disabilities of which 6,800 (7.6 per cent) had an IQ score of 70–4 (the average IQ is 100). Obtaining such figures in Scottish prisons is difficult, as formal assessment and diagnosis is performed rarely in secure settings (Loucks and Talbot 2007). It is possible, however, to obtain an estimation of the number of inmates in Scottish prisons with learning disabilities by translating research findings in England. When this is done using a prison population of 7,000 (as was in 2006–7), then it appears that on a daily basis in a Scottish prison as many as 500 have IQs bordering on learning disability, while 1,400–1,750 have significant enough learning disabilities as to require additional support (Loucks and Talbot 2007). In the case of Northern Ireland this translates to 105 prisoners on a daily basis with learning disabilities and 300–75 requiring additional support, in a prison population of 1,500 (Northern Ireland Prison Service 2007). Such findings suggest that offenders with learning disabilities might be struggling to cope and understand procedures of the criminal justice system, and unless their behaviour exhibits reason for concern, they are likely to remain unidentified (Murphy and Mason 2005). Of course, the deficits in cognitive and social behaviour vary widely depending on the nature and severity of the learning disability. Some prisoners, for instance, will have disruptive behaviours that include "misusing in-cell emergency call bells, kicking cell doors, damage to prison property, and shouting" (Loucks and Talbot 2007, p. 4). Others may physically assault prison guards or inmates.

It is clear that prison populations have a mix of dangerous offenders with varying degrees of mental issues traversing across the categories described in the 1983 MHA: mental disorder, psychopathy and learning disability. This requires us to consider in more detail the exact nature of the mental problems experienced by dangerous offenders in the prison population. Numerous studies over the years have indicated that psychopathic offenders, in particular, are over-represented in prisons – see Box, pp. 82–3.

WHAT THE RESEARCH ON THE NATURE OF DANGEROUS OFFENDERS DEMONSTRATES

Offenders diagnosed as having a psychopathic disorder, mental illness or learning disability were considered in a study by Robertson in 1981. Psychopaths, by far, committed more offences, received more sentences and spent far more time in prison than individuals in the other two groups.

In contrast, Spry (1984) considered offenders referred for psychiatric treatment. The percentage of those suffering from schizophrenia who had committed violent offences was much higher than the 1 per cent in the general population.

In 1986, Taylor reported that of the two-thirds of prisoners on a life sentence, 9 per cent suffered from schizophrenia and 13 per cent had depression, but 33 per cent had a personality disorder such as psychopathy.

Offenders with a mental illness who commit crimes such as murder, however, comprise a relatively small proportion of all murderers. In fact, the majority of homicides over a 38-year span were not committed by those with a mental disturbance (BBC News 1999, citing Pamela Taylor and John Gunn). Singleton et al. (1998) found that 7 per cent of male prisoners, 10 per cent of males awaiting trial (i.e. on **remand**) and 14 per cent of female prisoners had a psychotic illness. However, those who had an APD (i.e. psychopathy) represented 49 per cent, 63 per cent and 31 per cent respectively.

It has been estimated by Fine and Kennett (2004) that 50–80 per cent of prisoners have APD. They further estimated that of this range, 30 per cent have the more extreme form of psychopathy. In the U.K., criminal psychopaths are responsible for committing 50 per cent of serious and dangerous offences.

These findings suggest that offenders with psychopathic disorder are more likely to be dangerous than people with mental disorders or learning disabilities.

Assessing for mental illness, learning disability and psychopathic disorder is not an exact science, but there are ways and means of assessing offenders to reach a diagnosis. Assessment can be via clinical and statistical (actuarial data) prediction. It is important that forensic psychologists can also ascertain the extent of risk of reoffending. How this is done is discussed next.

ASSESSMENT OF DANGEROUSNESS AND RISK OF REOFFENDING

Identifying offenders who pose a risk to society in terms of their dangerousness is an important assessment which forensic psychologists perform. Being able to evaluate the likelihood of a dangerous offender reoffending, however, is a far more challenging task than their initial identification. There are two considerations used in the determination of dangerousness – whether an individual behaves violently or aggressively, and under what circumstances these behaviours are elicited. The circumstances of any given situation can act as triggers for violence and aggressiveness; it is the task of forensic psychologists to identify what these are. Clinical prediction is the most common route in the assessment of dangerousness and triggers for violence.

CLINICAL PREDICTION

The forensic psychologist relies upon years of experience of assessing different cases exhibiting similar or different behaviours to create a kind of 'clinical lore' or acquired knowledge. In their assessment of dangerous offenders, a range of factors is taken into account:

- Current offence
- Nature of current offence
- Criminal record
- History of criminality
- Family background
- Social background
- Childhood experiences and any oddities.

All of these details are recorded and kept confidential, as there is currently no law in the U.K. requiring forensic psychologists to inform police or service providers of an offender's intention to cause harm to others. This is not the case in the U.S., where forensic psychologists are subject to the Tarasoff Decision Rules of 1976. These are based on a case where Prosenjit Poddar murdered Tatiana Tarasoff because his infatuation with Tarasoff was unrequited. It was during a session with his therapist that he said he was going to kill her. The therapist reported this to the police, who interviewed Poddar but released him on the grounds that he promised to stay away from her. This case highlighted the importance of the therapist's decision to break the confidential code and report a potentially dangerous individual. Hence clinicians in the U.S. are now obliged to detain their clients if they suspect the possibility of future violence against another person. Although in the U.K. there is no such ruling, it has been pointed out by Dolan, M. (2004) that three circumstances exist where it is acceptable to breach confidentiality:

1. A client gives consent (limited to physical health issues)
2. The law requests information using a court order (here the clinician could be subpoenaed to disclose confidential information)

3. Release of information is considered to be in the public interest (disclosure will prevent harm to society per se rather than any particular person).

Note that this is still a long way from requiring a forensic psychologist to inform the police, or even to divulge information which could help in their investigations.

In the U.K., the General Medical Council Guidelines (GMCG) of 1993 released information concerning the issue of confidentiality in child abuse cases. In these cases, doctors who suspect that a child might be experiencing abuse are allowed to release confidential information provided it is disclosed to an appropriate person (e.g. a social worker or police officer). The reasoning for this is that a child might be incapable of providing or withholding consent for disclosure (General Medical Council 1993).

Confidentiality between offender and clinician is clearly important but this does beg the question of what exactly the nature of the information is that is to be kept confidential. In the case of dangerous offenders, there is a log of their past criminal conduct and a personal assessment based on interviews and tests determining their level of dangerousness, mental state and personality (see Box, Tests in Use by Clinicians, pp. 86–7). Based on the results of these assessments, it is possible to ascertain whether treatment or incarceration would be the best course of action to take in a bid to protect the public from potential harm. The whole assessment of a dangerous person revolves around the issue of risk – is this person safe to be let out into the community? The problem with clinical assessment is that clinicians can be duped into believing dangerous offenders have become reformed characters. This is especially true of criminal psychopaths, who are renowned for being manipulative, deceitful and convincing. The belief in accurate prediction of dangerous behaviour is considered by some to be a myth of the scientific expert. This was borne out by Peay (2002), who found that the subsequent behaviour of 65 per cent of dangerous offenders was predicted falsely. The two common errors made by clinicians were false positives (FPs) and false negatives (FNs). In the case of 65 per cent of dangerous offenders, many would have been victims of the FP, resulting in their being detained but failing to show behavioural indicators of future dangerousness. The FNs, however, are errors which clinicians should avoid as much as possible, as these can result in releasing a dangerous offender who later reoffends – perhaps committing another murder. Peay claimed that dangerousness is over-predicted by psychiatrists, finding for instance that only one in every three predictions is correct (Peay 2002). Despite this, other researchers put more weight on the importance of public protection than offender's rights (Glover 1999).

TESTS IN USE BY CLINICIANS

The Psychopathy Checklist (PCL-R) – a test developed by Robert Hare in 1991 used to predict violent reoffending and in the assessment of psychopaths.

The Revised Level of Service Inventory (LSI-R) – a test devised by Andrews and Bonta in 2006 used in the assessment of deviancy and rule violation, both factors used in the prediction of criminality.

Static-2002 – a test developed by Hanson and Thornton in 2003 which considers factors about the offender that are static – in other words they cannot be changed through therapeutic intervention (i.e. gender, age and criminal background). A total score is calculated which is compared to five categories of risk for reoffending. This test offers an accurate prediction of violent and sexual crimes.

The Historical-Clinical-Risk Management-20 (HCR-20) – a test designed by Webster et al. (1997) used to establish the risk of violence. It is based on 20 risk factors divided into three subscales: historical, clinical and risk management. The risk management scale helps inform clinicians of appropriate strategies and treatments as a means of reducing the risk of violent behaviour. A U.K.-based study of the effectiveness of the test showed the historical and risk management subscales to be useful in the prediction of further offending, but the clinical subscale to be less effective (Gray et al. 2008).

The Offender Group Reconviction Scale (OGRS) – a test used by the Probation Service in the U.K., developed by Copas and Marshall in 1998. There are seven items of information which, when combined, produce a risk score of reconviction. This includes items such as gender, current age, age of first conviction and the number of previous offences. OGRS-2 was introduced in 1999 and slightly improved the risk calculation score by its addition of social background factors.

Statistical or actuarial predictions are considered to be more reliable indicators in ascertaining the risk of dangerousness and reoffending. This, it has been argued by Pfohl (1979), is a consequence of employing approaches which consider an offender's past criminal behaviour rather than focusing on clinical aspects that rely on psychiatric models.

ACTUARIAL OR STATISTICAL PREDICTION

Dangerous offenders can be identified by using a number of factors known to reliably predict future violent and aggressive behaviour. An important factor shown to have a good prediction record is the offender's past behaviour. The statistical approach operates by grouping offenders according to their similarities, such as the type of crime they committed and when they first offended. By using the different groups of offenders based on the factors they have in common, it is possible to make predictions of high and low risk reoffenders. This assumes that an offender who has certain factors in common with a group of other offenders will behave in a similar manner. Palmer (2001) identified two types of factor that can be used as indicators for reoffending: static and dynamic. While static factors, such as age, gender, offence record and family background, cannot be changed, dynamic factors can be, by using appropriate interventions. Hence, an offender's social and psychological situation can be changed provided the right intervention is implemented. This might involve changes to friendships and maintaining a new job or learning to be more self-controlled.

Other forensic psychologists, such as Blackburn (2000), have classified risk factors into four groups:

1. Historical risk factors, such as offence history and life patterns of violence and aggressive behaviour

2. Cognitive and emotional attributes of the offender, such as how they react to social situations and solve problems
3. Clinical risk factors, including mental disorders causing episodes of violent behaviour
4. Personality disorder, which is considered apart from mental disorder and would commonly include offenders with Antisocial Personality Disorder or psychopathy.

Dynamic risk factors were added to this list by Gannon et al. in 2008. These include decision making, the emotions and thoughts underlying the decisions made, and the behaviours that follow these. Despite all of these different risk factors, the best predictors for reoffending were criminal history, the needs perceived by offenders, antisocial behaviour, age, gender and family background. It therefore makes sense to identify the best predictors to minimise errors (i.e. FPs and FNs) and maximise the number of hits (i.e. true positives, TPs, who are detained and would reoffend if released, and true negatives, TNs, who are released and do not reoffend).

HOW DOES DANGEROUSNESS RELATE TO TERRORISTS?

Due to events that have occurred during the last 15 years, terrorism has become a major issue in Britain and North America. Terrorism is an act where perpetrators resort to violence as a way of forcing governments into submission. Clearly, a terrorist fulfils the criteria of dangerousness. But are there risk predictors which can help to identify terrorist perpetrators (see Box, The Myth of the Mad Terrorist, pp. 88–9)?

THE MYTH OF THE MAD TERRORIST

There is little research to show that terrorists are mentally disturbed, which makes sense, as such an individual would be a liability to the cause (Horgan 2005). McCauley (1991) pointed out that terrorists are no more likely to suffer from a personality disorder such as psychopathy than any other individual. Furthermore, it is difficult to identify any specific psychological qualities segregating them from the general population (Taylor and Quayle 1994, p. 92). This is all very interesting but does not help us to understand why terrorists can commit multi-murder. It has been suggested that terrorists might be more likely to have traits such as risk-taking, wanting to engage in fast-paced activity and low self-esteem. They are 'stimulus hunters who are attracted to situations involving stress and who quickly become bored with inactivity' (Long 1990). According to Long, it is believed by some researchers that terrorists are neurotic or psychopathic and yet others claim that they can be understood by their political, economic and cultural environment. Griffin (2012) studied the terrorists which Egan (2013) summarised succinctly as 'idealist conservatives reacting violently to their way of life (and/or ideology) being threatened by the forces of modernisation' (p. 226). Because terrorists refuse to conform to changes in society that they disagree with, anyone else who does succumb to change is perceived as a traitor. This provides insight as to why they bomb the locations that they do – it is where the 'traitors' congregate in places such as shopping centres and major train stations.

The evidence suggests that having a strong group allegiance which supports one's political ideology is the best risk predictor for identifying terrorists. Low self-esteem, as suggested by Long, could be conceived as a psychological trait that encourages terrorists to bond so strongly with their group. Crenshaw (1985) suggested four factors that motivate terrorists to continue with their actions:

1. Provides an opportunity to terrorise
2. Being part of a terrorist group fulfils the need to belong
3. Being part of a terrorist group satisfies the desire for social status
4. Terrorism provides material reward.

Could this also be an important factor in the explanation of suicide bombers? An interesting study by Grimland et al. in 2006 looked at suicide bombers using psychological and non-psychological explanations. It is important to consider research showing the effects of group indoctrination on the psychology of an individual and, further still, the psychological need to be part of a group. This, coupled with other factors such as religion, political ideology, cultural traditions and nationalism, makes it clear that suicide bombing is to be considered as a weapon used to accomplish a mission of making a point.

Merari (2010) found that suicide bombers have traits typical of a dependent-avoidant personality (making them vulnerable to the influence of others) and traits of an impulsive-unstable personality (making them impulsive and self-destructive). The evidence available supporting a personality disorder, however, remains limited. What does appear to be consistent among terrorists is the need to be part of a group resulting from low self-esteem (Crenshaw 1985). Being strongly bonded in a group also creates an air of 'us against them' which enables hatred towards the enemy. The evidence, then, is very much against there being any psychological disturbance – so they are not mad, but rather individuals who succumb to indoctrination.

SUMMARY

This chapter has been concerned with understanding what dangerousness means in legal and medical terms, but defining and assessing dangerousness is riddled with problems. Are we assessing the person as dangerous or the criminal act as dangerous? This separation is not always easy to differentiate because normally an individual who commits a serious and dangerous crime is likely to commit a similar crime again, making them also a dangerous individual. Hence, assessment takes into consideration the risk of reoffending. Whether a dangerous individual is likely to reoffend is difficult to know, as prediction is not a pure science. This has been shown in cases where clinicians have made false positive (FP) and false negative (FN) errors which have led to the unnecessary incarceration of some offenders and the release of others who have later reoffended. Using statistical or actuarial approaches appears to be more successful than mere clinical assessment. This is because they rely on factors which group offenders according to similarities such as age, gender, criminal history and current offence. These factors are static factors which cannot be changed by treatment or rehabilitation interventions, but dynamic factors can. This might come about through changing offender life situations such as criminal friends, employment and social/cognitive skills. Assessing for dangerousness can be problematic in cases where the individual comes across as clear thinking and cognitively competent, which is certainly true of terrorists and suicide bombers. Also in this group are some criminal psychopaths who at a superficial level can appear socially, cognitively and emotionally stable, such as Mick Philpott, who set fire to his house, killing his children. Forensic assessment has to be done carefully to separate those who are dangerous as a result of a mental disorder, a mental impairment or a psychopathic disorder. We also have to consider individuals who do not fit into these categories but whose dangerous behaviour is the result of indoctrination into extreme political ideology (i.e. terrorists and suicide bombers).

RECOMMENDATIONS FOR FURTHER READING

Dolan, M. and Doyle, M. (2000). Violence Risk Prediction: Clinical and Actuarial Measures and the Role of the Psychopathy Checklist. *The British Journal of Psychiatry*, 177, 303–11.

Pinard, G.-F. and Pagani, L. (2001). *Clinical Assessment of Dangerousness: Empirical Contributions*. Cambridge: Cambridge University Press.

PSYCHOLOGICAL ASSESSMENTS AND INTERVENTION

Assessment is not a new phenomenon – there are Chinese records dating back to 1000 BC in which individuals were assessed for their suitability to hold a position in what was the equivalent of the Chinese Civil Service. Progressing forwards in time to the 1800s, the Chinese were further responsible for the development of psychological evaluation techniques. Although these tests were not directly related to clinical issues, they did focus on an individual's aptitude for positions of public office. Such tests were very different in design, structure and objective from modern equivalents, but nevertheless provided a good indicator of potential ability. For example, applicants were locked in a room and set the task of writing poems and essays about civil law, revenue and military affairs (Gregory 2011). If the written work passed, applicants would progress to the next stage, until they were whittled down to three potential applicants, from which one would be appointed. At about the same time, in 1885, German-born Hubert von Grashey introduced a battery of tests that were used to examine the abilities of patients with brain damage. Psychological testing continued to be developed thereafter by various researchers, such as:

- Wilhelm Wundt – beginning in 1879, developed tests to measure mental processes such as thought

- Alfred Binet – developed a test in the early 1900s to measure intelligence as a way of identifying children with special needs
- Robert Yerkes – in 1917, developed Army Alpha and Army Beta tests, used to distinguish the mentally incompetent from the mentally exceptional among potential army recruits.

(Gregory 2011)

There have been many types of psychological assessment developed since the early and mid-twentieth century, some of which are still used by forensic psychologists today. Many of these tests are derived from mainstream and clinical psychology; however, there are specialised assessments that are used only by forensic psychologists. These assessments are tailored towards testing aspects of an individual's behaviour and cognition that have legal implications. For example, testing an offender's intelligence has important implications concerning their moral understanding, and their understanding of the outcomes of their behaviour. Furthermore, testing for personality disorders can be informative in the identification of personality traits that can perhaps be modified. Forensic assessment, however, is often concerned with identifying aspects of an offender's behaviour that can be rehabilitated or improved by appropriate treatment intervention. This does not mean that forensic assessment is limited to the offender, for it can equally be used to examine the state of mind of the victim and witnesses who are likely to be interviewed by the police and to provide evidence in court. Forensic psychologists might also be involved in child custodial cases where there is a question over the suitability of one or both parents to provide care for their children. If the assessment reveals that the mental state of one of the parents puts the child at risk then the other parent is given full custody. If, however, both parents are held irresponsible and will put their child at risk through neglect and rejection, or physical and sexual abuse, then social services intervene by finding temporary or permanent parental replacements such as foster care.

Hence there are numerous ways in which forensic assessment can help forensic psychologists to make informed decisions. These informed decisions might involve offenders, individuals awaiting trial (i.e. those on **remand**), victims or witnesses, and can occur in a prison setting, probation office, police station, psychiatric establishment, prison hospital, solicitor's office or the client's home. In the next section, forensic psychological assessment of offenders who have been found guilty of a crime and are serving a custodial sentence in prison, or a non-custodial sentence like a community-based sentence, will be considered. In the case of a custodial sentence the offender's freedom is taken away. The offender who is given a non-custodial sentence, however, might be expected to pay a fine or serve the community by cleaning graffiti off the walls of public buildings or cleaning the streets while reporting regularly to a probation officer. There have been a few cases where celebrities have been given community service, such as the singer Boy George, who in 2005–6 was fined $1,000, had to agree to drug treatment in London and served New York by sweeping its streets.

ASSESSMENT AND INTERVENTION FOR SENTENCED OFFENDERS

Forensic psychologists use different assessments to ascertain an offender's mental state and cognitive functioning. When an individual is found guilty of committing a crime, one of the first assessment procedures is to ascertain the seriousness and dangerousness of the criminal act so that an appropriate sentence can be given. A second assessment is conducted to calculate the risk of the offender reoffending. Assessments can be general, designed in such a way as to highlight problem areas which might influence offender criminality. Tests can, for instance, identify social behavioural deficits that might contribute towards the offender behaving aggressively and violently when in direct contact with other people. These social behavioural deficits can then be followed up through more specific forms of assessment. When assessing offenders in this way, forensic psychologists have to consider two important legal factors: punishment and rehabilitation. It is important that the offender receives the appropriate level of punishment, but at the same time has opportunities for rehabilitation while still serving a sentence. Forensic psychologists, therefore, are required not only to identify areas of concern but also to advise on how changes to these identified areas can be put into practice using appropriate interventions. It might be the case that specialised treatment intervention can modify behaviour and, in so doing, help to rehabilitate the offender. An example of this is when uncontrolled anger can be managed through treatment interventions that teach offenders how to respond in a socially appropriate way – a way which deters them from acting aggressively towards another person. If an appropriate social response can be elicited at all times, then the offender is more likely to respond positively to their rehabilitation.

This 'What Works' philosophy is an important one that drives the development of effective assessment used by forensic psychologists to detect any risk of reoffending. It is assumed that by introducing effective interventions, designed to equip an offender with the appropriate skills to curb their criminal behaviour, reoffending should be reduced. According to Farrow et al. (2007), 'The emphasis on face-to-face work now had to shift to the type of interventions that would follow upon assessments and to the element of control, both of the offender, and what they might do in the future' (p. 12). They further state that 'Careful attention to the principles of risk, responsivity and diversity supports the potential to provide relevant and effective interventions for offenders' (p. 14). What this amounts to is that risk assessments should be effective at identifying those needs of offenders that can be tackled using reliable interventions. These reliable interventions should prove effective in reducing the likelihood of an offender reoffending. However, forensic psychologists first need to perform risk assessments and then design risk management programmes geared towards all types of offender, including those who might take their own life once incarcerated (see Box, pp. 95–6).

FORENSIC PSYCHOLOGISTS IN THE BUSINESS OF ASSESSING RISK

Forensic psychologists perform risk assessment and organise risk management programmes for the Prison Service and the Probation Service. Risk assessments performed are usually related to violent offenders, where prediction of future violent reoffending is paramount in decisions about implementing effective intervention. In the case of risk management, forensic psychologists analyse the factors that could potentially decrease or increase the risk of reoffending. Once the level of risk of reoffending is established, a programme devised to manage and supervise the offender is enforced. It is also important to identify offenders (violent or not) who might feel suicidal and are at risk of taking their own life.

Crighton (2000) has studied the figures for suicide in British prisons, where it has been estimated that 10 per cent of offenders who take their life do so within 24 hours of initial lock-up. Towl (2002) found that local prisons have a higher rate of suicide than national prisons, and was surprised that this should be the case given the transient nature of the population of these prisons. Why this should be the case is uncertain; however, it is possible that it has something to do with the type of prison population held in local prisons. Local prisons hold both those on remand and sentenced offenders who are likely to be moved elsewhere. As those on remand are awaiting their trial date, and so are innocent until proven guilty, it is likely that those who are innocent find it hard to come to terms with being incarcerated for a crime they did not commit. It is therefore important that forensic psychologists can also identify those who are at risk of committing suicide. Equally, offenders who are on probation can be at risk of committing suicide and need to be assessed so that effective preventative measures can be implemented.

Offenders who are serving a life sentence in prison, known as 'lifers', also undergo risk assessments. Morrissey and Towl (1991) suggest that the prison environment has a self-contained structure that takes lifers time to adapt to. The focus of intervention under these circumstances is to enable lifers to adapt to the prison system and the lifer system therein (Needs and Towl 1997). At the beginning of their life sentence, these prisoners are often at a high risk of suicide and need to be assessed for this (Crighton and Towl 1997).

Given that the prison population is diverse, there will be prisoners who have committed different types of crime, some of which will be very serious and others less so, and the nature of their identified problems and deficits will be varied. This will be explored in more detail in the next section.

PRISONER ASSESSMENT AND INTERVENTION

It is common under the prison system in Britain for prisoners to undergo interventions involving 'group-work' (Towl 2002). The objective of group-work interventions is to reduce the risk of prisoners reoffending, not only while in prison but once released into the community. Towl refers to such interventions as "offender behaviour programmes" that essentially have a cognitive-behavioural under-pinning. There are a variety of these offender behaviour programmes that are specifically tailored to address the nature of the prisoner concerned, such as treatment designed for sex offenders or appropriate programmes for the violent and dangerous offender. These offender behaviour programmes commonly tackle the cognitive and social deficits that offenders have, through tailor-made cognitive skills programmes. It is important to implement interventions that will help to rehabilitate the offender – hence, each offender's responsivity to the treatment programme is paramount in ensuring its effectiveness. It is for this reason that Blanchette and Brown (2006) argue that the identification of responsivity factors specific to each offender should be considered as part of their risk assessment (see Box, Responsivity and Diversity, pp. 97–8).

RESPONSIVITY AND DIVERSITY

Responsivity refers to an offender's response to treatment. How successfully an offender responds to treatment depends largely on a number of personal factors, such as having:

- Good emotional health
- Good mental health
- A balanced personality

- An even temperament
- Average cognitive abilities
- Average intelligence
- Good social interactive abilities
- Normal motivations
- Realistic aspirations
- Positive aspects pertaining to the individual's life.

Diversity is used to refer to the different types of offender that exist, in terms of not only their crimes but also demographical factors such as age, gender, ethnicity, culture and education.

In terms of responsivity, the success and effectiveness of planned and delivered interventions depends on the identification of responsivity factors through assessment. The identification of risk and the notion of responsivity have had their critics: not everyone agrees that focusing on risk assessment is a good thing. Ward and Brown (2004), for instance, advocate the view that risk assessment encourages a corrective attitude, where deficits are identified which must be put right. In other words, Ward and Brown argue that the assessment of risk encourages a focus on offender deficits at the expense of any strengths an offender has which could be drawn upon to encourage desistance from criminal pursuit. They also stress the importance of an offender's readiness to change their criminal lifestyle to a crime-free one. The responsivity idea can be made to work as long as practitioners are also aware of the offender's strengths and motivations, and consider these when implementing their rehabilitation programmes. Another element that practitioners should be aware of when drawing conclusions from their assessments of offenders is the extent to which offenders differ from one another, despite, for example, a shared assessment as being high risk.

There is diversity among offenders. Diversity will impact on the needs of the offender – young female offenders, for instance, will have different reasons for offending to young male offenders, who in turn will be different from adult males. Often, risk assessments create the impression that there is one correct solution, thereby ignoring the diversity factor.

A good example of putting risk assessment and notions of responsivity and diversity into practice can be found when considering the different types of crime committed and who the offender is (e.g. male/female, young/old, level of mental wellness). If we take the example of violent offenders, it is important to establish the nature of violence committed (i.e. the type of crime), for there is diversity within this group of offenders. The task of the forensic psychologist is to isolate the type of violence committed and consider why the offender committed a violent crime. Violence can be caused by a trigger such as extreme alcohol consumption or a domestic situation. In 1986, Henderson analysed male violence, finding that it can be contextualised within different types of situation:

- In conjunction with another offence (e.g. a theft that goes wrong)
- A family environment (e.g. an argument with a spouse that escalates to battering)
- Within a public space (e.g. a verbal insult that triggers a fight)
- Inside an institution (e.g. a psychiatric patient triggers violence)
- A combination of any of the above.

Moreover, violence can be used to achieve goals known to the individual, or can be incited through emotional arousal. The latter can be further divided into angry violence and expressive violence. While angry violence normally occurs due to negativity experienced towards a victim, expressive violence is a response to being frustrated, and any damage resulting from the violent behaviour is incidental. Understanding the offender is crucial in determining how best to assess and implement an effective intervention. Farrington (1995) claimed that the violent offender is likely to have demonstrated hyperactive and impulsive behaviour during childhood. Other antecedent behaviours of later violence are likely to include problem behaviours at school, low school achievement, criminal attitudes that often come from parents, and peer friendships supporting delinquent activity. These offenders are likely to find their violence rewarding, which reinforces the cycle of violence. McMurran (2002) summarises this relationship using a model that connects an event with the cognitions held by the offender, which then cause an emotional arousal response, resulting in violent behaviour. For example, violent offenders may have the following faulty cognitions:

- Seeing the behaviour of others as having hostile intent
- Having problem-solving deficits in social situations, making it difficult to see the outcomes of their behaviour
- Perceiving their behaviours as a consequence of their circumstances – hence, they are blameless
- Believing that everyone else shares their own perspective
- Believing their judgement to be faultless even when faced with evidence to the contrary
- Having a belief system endorsing violence.

In the case of emotional arousal, Zamble and Quinsey (1997) found that violent offenders often claimed to have lost control of their temper in situations of interpersonal conflict. This, in combination with social skill deficits such as interpreting the actions of others as hostile, makes violence an obvious behavioural option. Anger becomes the most common response to emotional arousal, which can trigger behaviours such as clenching the hand to form a fist and teeth gritting. These actions in turn reinforce the emotional arousal and support the individual's thoughts about other people, triggering an aggressive response. Given the interplay between event, cognition, emotional arousal and behaviour, it is important that all these aspects are considered in the assessment and intervention programme. Figure 4.1 provides an example of the questions that should be considered during assessment.

The questions asked during assessment help inform forensic psychologists of the best intervention programme for prisoners. In the case of violent offenders there will be a host of issues requiring different types of intervention. Some of these interventions will be aimed at controlling the offender's violent outbursts directly, while others will be indirect, through treatment aimed at substituting a lifetime of inappropriate responses with socially appropriate ones (see Box, pp. 101–3).

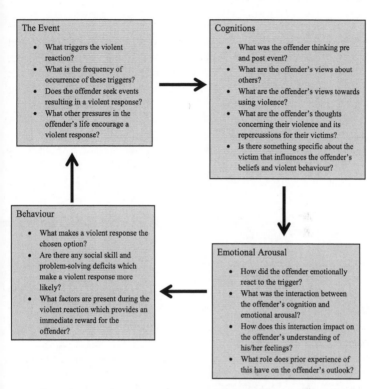

Figure 4.1 Examples of questions asked during assessment

INTERVENTIONS ADOPTED FOR VIOLENT OFFENDERS

Many of the treatment programmes for violent prisoners are based on cognitive-behavioural approaches with a strong anger management focus. In the U.K., for instance, the Prison Service has designed a National Anger Management Package directed at controlling anger exhibited by violent prisoners. The idea is to have a group of prisoners (no more than eight) who are made aware of the processes involved with becoming angry. The members of the group learn how to identify triggers that initiate their anger and to self-monitor their responses to these. They are taught how to control and manage their anger using techniques primarily focused on why they respond angrily, and to change the reasoning for responding this way (Keen 2000). The Prison Service provides a series of group-work sessions that help to achieve this aim. During the sessions, offenders are taught how to keep an anger diary with the aim of recording their thoughts and emotions and the consequences of their actions. They are taught to understand what anger is in physiological terms and the intricate interaction between cognition and action. By using soothing self-directed language and relaxation techniques they can try to avert an aggressive response. Other social skills, such as responding to social situations in a non-aggressive way and dealing politely with unwanted group pressure, are explored.

The problem with such prescribed anger management programmes is that they fail to consider individual differences across group members – who exhibit anger for a range of different reasons and have a variety of causes for their aggressive behaviours that might not be specifically addressed. Hence, for some prisoners anger management will be helpful but for others it will not.

The effectiveness of treatments for violent prisoners was reviewed by Gilbert and Daffern in 2010. They focused specifically on two approaches: Cognitive Self-Change Programmes and Multi-Faceted Interventions. The Prison Service in Britain has adopted the Cognitive Self-Change Programme – a cognitive-behavioural approach to altering the way an offender thinks about a situation or person. Instead of using a criminal mindset to solve a problem they are taught to use socially acceptable and appropriate values and attitudes for dealing with other inmates and prison staff. This programme educates offenders to resolve conflict situations using non-aggressive responses and to critically think about their aggressive reactions and what they really achieve. They learn how to thwart their aggressive impulses and to control and manage their behaviour appropriately. There are other skills taught which help them to interact in a socially friendly and acceptable way – this might involve learning language skills, being assertive in a non-aggressive way and interpreting other people's intentions and body language correctly. However, Gilbert and Daffern concluded that these programmes are too generic and therefore fail to alter a lifetime of aggressive behaviours.

In the case of Multi-Faceted Interventions, there are a number of components which are designed to help violent offenders to understand their aggressive behaviour and to monitor the thoughts and feelings associated with this behaviour. It is a package aimed at changing the way offenders behave both in general and more specifically towards their victims. The different areas that this intervention focuses on include the following training and education:

- Social and communication (language) skills
- Regulation of emotions
- Modification of cognition
- Moral understanding and reasoning
- Empathy training geared towards their victims
- Identification of triggers
- Life problem-solving skills that are socially appropriate
- Skills designed to prevent offenders from relapsing into a life of crime.

There appears to be empirical support for the effectiveness of the Multi-Faceted Intervention in terms of reconviction rates. After a two-year follow-up period, the number of reconvictions for violent crimes by offenders who had attended the programme was half that for those who had not.

HOW FORENSIC PSYCHOLOGISTS PROVIDE TREATMENT FOR SEX OFFENDERS

Although treatment interventions for violent offenders overlap to some extent with the approach used for sex offenders, it is important, when devising a programme for sex offenders, that the motivations underlying their sexual acts are considered. It is because of their essentially different motivational focus that there is a variety of treatment programmes used in British prisons. Assessing sex offenders is an important stage in the process of developing the right treatment intervention. This is because the sex offender profile can be divided into many types, including those who have:

- A preference for children
- A preference for children and adults
- A preference for females of any age
- A preference for males of any age
- A preference for teenagers and adults
- A preference for adults.

Furthermore, criminal sexual behaviours can be classified according to three main categories:

1. Rape
2. Child molestation, known as paedophilia
3. Paraphilias (deviant sexual attractions occurring towards objects or people).

These categories are by no means mutually exclusive, as shown by Abel et al. (1985), who found that 50.6 per cent of rapists had also molested children, 29.2 per cent had exposed themselves, 20.2 per cent had secretly watched people in their bedrooms (known as voyeurism) and 12.4 per cent deliberately rubbed their genitals against an unknowing victim (known as frotteurism). These classifications have been further categorised according to the underlying motivations for the sexual acts. In the case of rapists who force sexual intercourse with a non-consenting victim, the method of rape is determined by their underlying motives. Cohen et al. (1969) based their classifications on the extent of sexual and aggressive motives that influenced the offender's behaviour – hence deducing four subtypes:

1. Displaced aggression – sexual act comprises high aggression and low sexual arousal

2. Compensatory rape – sexual act comprises high sexual arousal and low aggression
3. Sex aggression diffusion – aggression is eroticised by sex with violence so that both aggression and sexual arousal are high
4. Impulsive rape – an opportunistic act where both aggression and sexual arousal are low.

Similarly, paedophiles have underlying motives that they satiate through their deviant sexual acts. Cohen et al. (1969) found three subtypes:

1. Fixated – feel safe and comfortable with children and so make friends with children
2. Regressed – show sexual interest in adults but when they feel their masculinity is compromised they regress towards preferring children
3. Aggressive – perform sadistic acts using force on children.

In the case of paraphilias, these are legally acceptable as long as both partners are consenting to the behaviour. In cases where a person is coerced to perform or participate in deviant sexual acts, then they become a victim. Non-consenting paraphilia is classified as a sexual offence and may include the following acts:

- Lust murder – the extreme form of sexual sadism
- Necrophilia – sexual acts with a corpse
- Zoophilia – sexual acts with animals, also known as bestiality
- Exhibitionism – indecent exposure
- Telephone scatologia – obscene phone calling
- Voyeurism – arousal by secretly looking at naked bodies
- Frotteurism – arousal by touching people in public, such as touching a woman's breast on a crowded train.

As can be seen from the diversity of sex offences committed, and the underlying motives for committing them, the task of devising an appropriate treatment programme is not an easy one for the forensic psychologist. It is not surprising, therefore, that a host of different interventions have been developed (see Box, pp. 106–7, for those commonly used).

INTERVENTIONS ADOPTED FOR SEX OFFENDERS

Often an integrated approach to sexual offending has been implemented in which attempts have been made to explain sexual offending by looking at historical factors that might have influenced the behaviour; personality; demographic factors such as gender and age; contextual triggers for violence; and clinical features like brain damage sustained through abuse. In the case of the latter, neuro-scientific accounts of the behaviour which look at brain and neuropsychological factors are often explored, as well as the biology (i.e. genetics) and ecology (i.e. social learning via the social and physical environment) associated with the individual. Ward and Beech (2006) claim that by taking an integrated approach to understanding sex offenders, forensic psychologists are better informed about ways forward in treating such individuals.

Sex offenders have obvious social and emotional deficits which make it difficult for them to control their emotions, deviant sexual arousal and impulsive actions. Moreover, they have distorted cognitions about their victims, such as 'all women say no when they mean yes' or 'children need a sex education and the best way to learn is by experience'. Given these problems, forensic psychologists need to devise a treatment programme which addresses all these facets of problem behaviour.

Target areas for treatment and appropriate intervention can be divided into the following:

- Lacking empathy – expressive therapy (arts, music, dance and drama); victim empathy training
- Anger – anger management; stress management; relaxation techniques
- Difficulty forming relationships – social skills training; assertiveness training; self-esteem training
- Cognitive distortions – cognitive restructuring using cognitive-behavioural programmes such as Sex

Offender Treatment Programme (SOTP) and Sex Offender Treatment Evaluation Project (STEP)

- Deviant sexual arousal – drug treatment; cognitive-behavioural techniques; behavioural therapy
- Impulsivity – self-control training; stress management; drug treatment.

Offenders can be assessed and treated outside of a prison environment by forensic psychologists and the Probation Service. Offenders who are supervised by a probation officer have often committed crimes that are not perceived by the judiciary as dangerous or serious enough to pose a risk to society – hence, they do not need to be imprisoned. This group of offenders, however, can also include prisoners who are released from prison on a licence of parole. These ex-offenders are considered to be of moderate risk such that they need to report to their probation officer on a regular basis – hence, their needs are likely to be different from other probationers. Treatments available to probationers will be considered next.

PROBATIONER ASSESSMENT AND INTERVENTION

In England, Wales and Northern Ireland (there is no Probation Service in Scotland; equivalent roles are carried out by Criminal Justice Social Workers, CJSWs) the National Probation Service has introduced initiatives such as the Aggression Replacement Training (ART) programme, designed to deal with a multitude of problems that offenders might have. It is a multi-skill training approach offering personal, interpersonal and socio-cognitive skills to offenders. These newly acquired skills can be practised in a safe environment, normally as part of a group. Developed by Goldstein in 2004, the underlying assumption is that aggression is a consequence of combined internal and external causes. In the case of internal causes, Goldstein grouped factors as follows:

1. General deficits of personal, interpersonal and socio-cognitive skill – this refers to social and communication difficulties that offenders often encounter. A good example of this is a case study provided in a report commissioned by the National Offender

Management Service (NOMS) in 2009 (Billiald 2009). This case example highlights the problems experienced by some offenders with communication and other learning difficulties (see Box below). The ART programme aims to enhance offender personal, interpersonal and socio-cognitive skills by enabling them to identify their areas of difficulty and to develop skills they are taught. They are taught pro-social skills which help them to interact with other people, and to understand and be able to interpret the body language of others and its intent.

CASE STUDY

A man was sentenced to supervision and unpaid work for an offence of common assault. He was suspended from the unpaid work due to his behaviour: he would not follow instructions and swore at the supervisors. His offender manager undertook some research and discovered that the man had been identified as having learning difficulties at school and displayed this behaviour even back then. It was also recorded that he had difficulty in understanding what others said to him. The offender manager thought that the man might have been falling foul of the rules because he did not fully understand the instructions being given to him. The individual in question would have been an ideal candidate for the ART programme and would have learned to improve his understanding of other people and his interpersonal skills.

2. Offenders commonly experience an inability to control their anger. Probationers are offered anger management training designed to encourage self-control, curb aggressive behaviour and reduce feelings of anger. Identification of triggers is the first step towards understanding the repercussions of being angry and the effects it has on others. The ART programme helps offenders to be aware of these triggers and to counteract their feelings of anger and aggressive response by providing alternative ways of coping. They are also taught different socially acceptable strategies (e.g. negotiation skills) that can be used instead of aggression.

3. As part of the ART programme, offenders are taught moral reasoning and empathy skills, which are at the crux of offenders' aggressive behaviour towards their victims. Their moral reasoning skills are very basic, levelling with those of a young child. This means that their view of the world is self-centred, contributing towards their failure to understand anyone else's point of view. Unfortunately, when viewpoints do clash this acts as a trigger for aggression. Palmer described five stages of moral reasoning that offenders use: 'offending is justified if punishment can be avoided ... ; offending is justified if the rewards are judged to outweigh the risks ... ; offending is justified if it maintains relationships ... ; offending is justified if it is in the interests of society or is sanctioned by a social institution (i.e. religion) ... ; offending is justified if it maintains basic human rights or further social justice (e.g. human rights protester who is arrested for a public order offence ...)' (Palmer 2003, p. 100). It is such morals as these that practitioners and probation officers are seeking to counteract.

Palmer claimed that the different skills that the ART programme aims to achieve are integrated by considering 'what to do ... how to do it ... and why to do it' (Palmer 2003, p. 170). Thus 'what to do' translates to social and interpersonal skills, 'how to do it' to anger management and 'why to do it' to moral reasoning. In 2000, Sugg found the reconviction rate for offenders who successfully completed the ART programme was 20.4 per cent, in contrast with 60 per cent for the control group.

While the ART approach is popular in England, Wales and Northern Ireland, in Scotland the CJSWs use the Constructs: Positive Steps to Stop Offending Programme. This programme is aimed at medium- to high-risk offenders who have social skill, problem-solving and pro-social behavioural deficits. In a similar vain to the ART programme, attitudes are changed in such a way as to reduce reoffending behaviour and to lead offenders to adopt a pro-social lifestyle.

In the 1990s, a programme piloted in Wales called Straight Thinking on Probation (STOP) was designed to enhance cognitive deficits found in many offenders. These cognitive skills focused on enhancing moral reasoning, controlling anger, regulating emotions, enhancing empathy, improving problem-solving and interpersonal skills, challenging cognitive distortions and enhancing self-control. There was some success, in that reconviction rates saw a 35 per cent drop. The Think First programme initiated by the Probation Service relies on a battery of tests to identify specific cognitive deficits, which are then challenged by reducing crime-centred attitudes and increasing self-esteem (McGuire and Hatcher 2001). The Probation Service in Britain also provides Education Programmes for those convicted of alcohol- and drug-related offences – in particular those linked with driving offences. Such offenders are often given a probation order with the condition that they attend an Education Programme run by the Probation Service (see Box, South Glamorgan Probation Service Experience, pp. 110–11).

THE SOUTH GLAMORGAN PROBATION SERVICE EXPERIENCE OF EDUCATING OFFENDERS

During the 1990s, the Addictions Unit, part of the South Glamorgan Probation Service in Wales, U.K., ran Alcohol Education Groups (AEGs) for drink drivers. These offenders were given a probation order with the condition attached that they attend an AEG. The AEG usually ran for eight weeks; offenders had to attend alcohol free and were breathalysed to check the content of alcohol in their breath. If their breathalysed results indicated alcohol in the breath on three separate occasions, they were given a custodial sentence. During the eight weeks, offenders attended a structured group and were informed about the effects of drugs or alcohol on their body. The thoughts and feelings that typically perpetuate a cycle of abusing substances and offending were challenged by the group leader and discussed by all group members. Assessments such as Readiness to Change and Attitudes towards Alcohol were made both before the group began and after it had finished. This was to ascertain whether a shift of attitude had occurred in terms of wanting to change their abuse of alcohol, offending behaviour and lifestyle. The Offender Group Reconviction Scale Version 2 (OGRS2) was also used to measure the risk factor of offenders reoffending once their probation order was completed. In terms of offenders wanting to change (as measured by the scores of the three assessments at the end of the group), AEG proved to be relatively successful, as reconviction rates for drink driving decreased (Taylor and Maguire 1992).

While assessments and treatment interventions have been used widely by the Prison and Probation Services, the development of these are based on clinical effectiveness research by forensic psychologists. Moreover, these are founded on psychological principles and theory. Forensic psychologists are also involved in cases where there is no established offender (i.e. where no one has yet been found guilty and sentenced). These cases take on a variety of forms, including child custody, guardianship, informed consent, civil commitment, trial consulting, **tort** claims and victim assessments in tort cases. A selection of these assessment responsibilities will be discussed next.

ASSESSMENT OF CASES WHERE AN OFFENDER HAS YET TO BE PROVEN

Forensic psychologists not only assess and treat the guilty but are also involved in cases where an individual may have been a victim (known as the plaintiff) of a **tortious** act committed by the defendant (known as the tortfeasor). In such cases both the defendant and plaintiff may undergo assessment as part of the evidence-gathering process, to establish and contextualise the facts of the case.

WHAT IS A TORTIOUS ACT?

A tortious act can be defined as a wrongful act or an infringement of another person's right that contravenes **Tort Law**. A tort, therefore, is a civil wrong causing harm or loss to the plaintiff, who can take the defendant to court to make a claim for damages caused.

Tort Law (called Delict Law in Scotland) contains legislation listing the rights, obligations and remedies that guide the courts in cases of tortious acts. This can be divided as follows:

1. Negligence torts – pertain to wrongful acts resulting from behaviour that is negligent, such as riding a bicycle into a neighbour's garden and destroying their hedge. It can also refer to malpractice caused by a failure to be diligent.
2. Intentional torts – acts of this nature involve a deliberate attempt to cause harm to someone or an institution. Examples of such deliberate acts include fraud, defamation and battery.
3. Strict liability torts – this can involve product liability, where a purchased item inflicts harm on the user. For instance, a pizza-cutter cuts a finger off even though it was used as instructed by the manufacturer. The manufacturer can be taken to court as they are liable for the harm caused.
4. Nuisance torts – these can be a direct consequence of a person's actions, or indirect, such as noise pollution in the street. These cases can be more difficult to prove, especially when a neighbour is making noise, thereby being a nuisance. Under these circumstances, assessment of the plaintiff's health by a forensic psychologist might be helpful to the courts as it provides evidence of suffering or harm. As the response to noise pollution varies greatly from individual to individual, an assessment would be necessary for clarification. It is important that people are able to enjoy living at their property without others causing noise and pollution, which is why they can claim a tort action privately by taking the defendant to court and holding them liable.

The remedies to different tort claims usually involve compensation for damages caused (more often than not a pay-off sum) awarded by the court. If, however, there is potential for future harm to the plaintiff, the court can grant an injunction on the defendant. This can be seen in cases of a husband threatening physical harm to his wife or children, for instance. Again an assessment by a forensic psychologist is useful in ascertaining the extent of possible future danger to the plaintiffs. Assessing the defendant's state of mind is an important feature here as it helps clarify the plaintiff's situation and possible options. There have been a number of famous celebrity cases where restraining orders have been issued by the courts for the protection of the wife or girlfriend: Charlie Sheen's case particularly stands out (see Box below).

THE CASE OF CHARLIE SHEEN'S RESTRAINING ORDERS

Actor Charlie Sheen has a string of arrests to his record. In 1990 he shot his fiancée, Kelly Preston, in the arm. She called off the engagement despite the incident being considered an accident. Sheen married his first wife, Donna Peele, in 1995 but they divorced in 1996. Sheen was then arrested for physically abusing his girlfriend in 1996. He received a one-year suspended prison sentence and two years of probation. In 2002 he married his second wife, Denise Richards, but they divorced in 2006 on the grounds that he abused alcohol and drugs and on numerous occasions had acted violently towards her. He was issued a restraining order for violence against Richards which stipulated that he was not allowed to be within 300 yards of her and their children. She claimed in court that he had physically abused her and threatened to kill her. He married wife number three, Brooke Mueller, in 2008, but in 2009 she complained of assault and by 2011 they were divorced. Mueller obtained a restraining order against Sheen for violence and harassment. She also tried to get a restraining order to prevent him from seeing his children but she lost custody of the children due to her addiction problems and was forced to attend the Betty Ford Center. The children were placed in the custody of his second wife, Denise Richards. Sheen was also charged with misdemeanour and sentenced to 30 days of rehabilitation, 30 days of probation and 36 hours of anger management.

THE ROLE OF FORENSIC PSYCHOLOGISTS IN FAMILY LAW

Forensic psychologists are often referred cases of divorce and child custody by a solicitor acting on behalf of the client. These cases are assessed under the Family Law Act of 1996 and in England, Wales and

Northern Ireland are conducted by the Family Division of the High Court, the County Courts or Family Proceedings Courts (overseen by a trained Magistrate). In Scotland such cases are conducted by Sheriff Courts, or the High Court for the more serious offences like murder and sexual offences involving children. With the introduction of the Children Act in 2004, in custodial cases, the welfare of the child is of paramount importance. Hence, if there is any suggestion that the child might be suffering from neglect, rejection or other types of mental and physical abuse, the Family Proceedings Court has the authorisation to separate those being abused from the abuser and to ensure their safety. In these circumstances a solicitor acting on behalf of the aggrieved parent might consider the assessment of a forensic psychologist, not only of the children for signs of trauma and stress, but also of the parent who is a victim and the parent who is the abuser. Taylor (1979) gives an example of a case where the father's sexual orientation was the central psychological issue. The mother did not want her homosexual husband to see his children, on the grounds that this might cause harm to the children. The forensic psychologist had to acquire extensive evidence concerning the specific details of the father's homosexual behaviour and the potential impact this might have on his children. In order to assess child custody cases, forensic psychologists use a checklist provided by the Family Proceedings Court (see Box below).

CHILD PROTECTION CHECKLIST USED IN BRITAIN

- The expressed wishes and emotions of the child, contextualised by age and ability to understand the situation
- The child's needs, which can be condensed to physical, emotional and educational
- The impact of change resulting from parental separation or social service intervention on the child
- Demographical information such as age, sex, culture and parental nurturance that are relevant to the child
- The extent of harm already suffered
- The risk of future harm
- The extent that the child's immediate needs can be sufficed by the parents, relatives or social services

While the Child Protection Checklist provides a good under-standing of the child's predicament, it is important to assess all involved – both parents and other family members. The Home Inventory has commonly been used by forensic psychologists to assess the dynamics of family structure and function, and the impact this has on the child in question.

With the introduction of the Tender Years Doctrine in Britain during the late nineteenth century, the custody of children was automatically entrusted to the mother. This doctrine had spread to the U.S. and Europe by way of the British Empire but by the end of the twentieth century it was abolished. The reasons for abolish-ing it in the U.S. rest on the notions of equity and contravention of the Fourteenth Amendment. This Amendment states that all citi-zens of the U.S. are to be given "full and equal benefit of all laws" (Civil Rights Act of 1866). The implication of this in relation to child custody cases is that fathers should have equal rights to nurture their children. In the U.K., however, the judiciary still follow tenets of the Tender Years Doctrine. Lord Donaldson, in 1992, pointed out that a preference for the mother (given all is equal) over the custody of a baby is usually followed, although in the case of a child different considerations might apply. This view still tends to apply today, although there is support for shared custody where the lion's share belongs to the mother. Despite recent research suggesting that both father and mother are needed to ensure a child's optimum psycho-logical development (Kelly and Lamb 2000), the courts still favour the mother over the father. That is not to say that there are not cases where the court acknowledges the father, a relative or social services as preferable to the mother.

In the U.S. in 2007, a celebrity had a very public mental breakdown – Britney Spears. Being a famous pop star, her 'odd' behaviour was reported and captured by the media, including scenes where she shaved her head to outwit a drugs test and spoke in an English accent. At the time it was reported by her ex-manager that she was taking up to 30 drugs per day. Britney Spears' abuse of drugs led to a breach of her contract, resulting in her ex-manager suing her and taking her to court. She was eventually hospitalised and lost custody of her sons to ex-husband Kevin Federline. Assessment of her mental health and drug addiction led to her being considered a danger to her children at the time.

The cases of Charlie Sheen and Britney Spears were highly publicised by the media, making the headlines almost on a daily basis. It is difficult for celebrities to control what is written about them by the media, but any assessments undertaken by forensic psychologists would be subject to confidentiality rules as specified by the representing professional body (i.e. the British Psychological Society or the American Psychological Association). Ethical issues concerning assessment and treatment determine the conduct of the practitioner and are there for the purpose of fair-play and equity.

ETHICS UNDERLYING ASSESSMENT AND TREATMENT

Forensic psychologists practising in Britain follow the Code of Conduct set out in the Royal Charter of the British Psychological Society (BPS) (British Psychological Society 2009). In the U.S., the American Psychological Association (APA) stipulates the equivalent Ethics Code (American Psychological Association 2002). Of relevance to this discussion are the codes of 'obtaining consent', 'confidentiality' and 'personal conduct'. It is important that all practising forensic psychologists should know the professional ethics code, as well as the relevant laws and regulations of the jurisdiction in which they practise. In the U.K., for instance, this will amount to understanding mental health legislation entailed in the Mental Health Act of 2007 and the 1984 Police and Criminal Evidence Act (PACE), which have their own Codes of Practice.

ASSESSMENT

Informed consent is necessary in order for forensic psychologists to perform an assessment, whether this is a clinical interview or psychometric testing. In the case of psychometric testing, many tests have been evaluated for their accuracy of prediction based on a series of scores obtained from different population samples. The Psychopathy Checklist-Revised (PCL-R), for instance, has an exceptional 'hit-rate' at identifying violence and sexual violence, particularly that exhibited by psychopaths among prison populations. This was corroborated by the MacArthur Violence Risk Assessment Study, which also identified a strong connection between violence and psychopathy (Monahan et al. 2000). Despite the successes of the PCL-R, it has been criticised by Freedman as creating a high number of false-positives (test indicates psychopathy without evidence of it), leaving it unreliable (Freedman 2001). Using statistical prediction also has its problems. As statistical prediction gives an indication of how a group of individuals are likely to behave, it cannot precisely determine the behaviour of a given individual (Copas 1983). Statistical predictions offer information about an attribute or many attributes that an individual shares with a particular group (e.g. violent offenders). This fails, however, to predict future violent acts for all individuals belonging to this group. As Prins (1996) points out, the practitioner still has to interpret what it means to be a member of the violent offender group. The emphasis of some statistical tests on historical variables, Maden (1998) argues, produces unchanging or static evaluations of risk when in fact changes of circumstance can alter the individual's level of risk. It is for this reason that risk assessment should be based on dynamic factors which are in constant flux and need to be examined on a regular basis to ensure the appropriate interventions are in situ. Therefore, while psychometric tests provide information about the violent offender, for example, it is still the task of the forensic psychologist to interpret what the results of these tests signify. There have been misdiagnosed cases not just in the U.K. and U.S. but throughout the world. A case in point is the abuse of psychological assessment, diagnosis and reporting in South Africa during the years of Apartheid (see Box, pp. 117–8).

ASSESSMENT OF EUGENE DE KOCK

During the Apartheid years, White and Black citizens of South Africa were treated differently; the law favoured White people and actively disadvantaged Black people. The daily lives of White and Black people were kept segregated, to the extent that they were legally required to use separate buses. This caused many social problems and unrest, resulting in violence and rebellion throughout the country. The police controlled violence using violence to subdue any Black uprisings. One approach by the South African government was to employ Eugene de Kock as an assassin.

He commanded the Counter-Insurgency Unit of the South African Police to stop Black anti-apartheid activists through kidnap, torture and murder, earning the nickname of 'Prime Evil'. In 1994, his record of tyranny became apparent, and in 1996 he was charged for 89 offences. In his defence, an expert psychologist's report documented that he suffered from Post-Traumatic Stress Disorder (PTSD). This was later examined by Foster and Nicholas (2000), who concluded that he failed to meet the diagnostic criteria. They accused his defence of presenting misleading evidence as a means of commuting his sentence. He was nevertheless eventually sentenced to 212 years in prison. Eugene de Kock is a good example of the difficulty involved in assessing potentially dangerous individuals. While there have been accusations that his PTSD assessment was false, other psychologists claimed he suffered from 'cognitive dissonance', which refers to a combination of inconsistent attitudes, thoughts and beliefs that influence decision-making outcomes – in his case it was said to explain his continued violent behaviour. Nicholas (2000), however, concluded that this type of poor quality assessment and reporting only reflects badly on psychology as a profession.

Closer to home in Britain, Slack (2009) reported in the *Daily Mail* that 65 killers released from prison reoffended within five years of their release during the new millennium. In many of these cases the reoffending involved extreme violence, paedophilia, sex attacks and murder. Named cases include:

- Glyn Dix, who was imprisoned in the 1970s for murder and, when released in 2001, murdered his wife, using a knife and hacksaw to cut her into 16 pieces
- Douglas Vinter, who stabbed his victim to death in 1996 and, when released in 2008, strangled and stabbed another victim to death.

Edward Garnier, a Conservative justice spokesman, said 'Life-sentenced prisoners should not be released where there is a danger of further serious offending, and those who are judged suitable for release should be subject to the utmost supervision for the rest of their lives' (quoted in Slack 2009). This implies that practitioners (such as forensic psychologists) responsible for assessing these 65 cases were making the wrong decisions for whatever reason. Their assessments of these lifers are contributing to making false-negative errors, in which the lifer is deemed harmless and unlikely to reoffend when in fact they are a time-bomb waiting to explode. Ministry of Justice figures show that during the first three months of 2009, 501 serious offences were committed by offenders released from prison or who had just completed a community order (Whitehead 2011). The importance of accurate assessment in the evaluation of whether dangerous prisoners have been sufficiently rehabilitated is again a hotly debated issue.

TREATMENT

Both the BPS and APA state that any treatment intervention individuals receive (whether offender, victim or witness) should respect their dignity, be effective and humane, be based on accurate assessment, and be diagnosed and administered with informed consent. Furthermore, there should be an air of empathy during the administration of treatment. There have been a few cases of children labelled as sex offenders who had received a form of therapy called cognitive restructuring which failed to respect their dignity. Cognitive restructuring involves the use of a penile plethysmograph to record any penile erection while being forced to listen to or view sexually stimulating material. In the case of shame aversion therapy, the individual has to make their sexual thoughts, feelings and fantasies public to the researchers. This can be very humiliating and leaves nothing to the imagination. Cognitive restructuring that involves the use of arousal reconditioning means that the sexual feelings of children and adolescents become public and can be subjected to manipulation. The problem is the lack of understanding regarding the normal course of sexual development during adolescence, and the impact these therapies have on the developing mind. These therapies appear to control the emotions and behaviour rather than promote healing.

It is important that any treatment intervention is based on sound clinical effectiveness research and should be used only if:

- An accurate diagnosis has been established via appropriate and reliable means of assessment
- It is effective, safe and humane
- It is ethical and morally sound
- It does not stigmatise
- There is informed consent
- Any drug use is prescribed
- A choice to decline treatment is apparent
- The potential dangers of therapy are pointed out.

Informed consent is required before the commencement of any treatment and this is highlighted in the ethics of the BPS and APA. In the U.S., however, juvenile sex offender treatment is often involuntary, with 68 per cent of programmes being run on an outpatient basis, violating the stipulation of requiring informed consent (Burton and Smith-Darden 2001). Under the Code of Ethics of the Association for the Treatment of Sexual Abusers (ATSA) in the U.S., involuntary treatment is condoned only for use with individuals with severe mental illness who pose an immediate risk of danger to themselves and to others (ATSA 2001). Such cases, Burton and Smith-Darden argue, are in the minority. They believe that treatment works best when the individual consents and embraces the underlying philosophy of the therapeutic intervention (National Mental Health Association 2004). This does not appear to be happening in every case, as the case against the Sexual Behavior Clinic in New York demonstrates (see Box, pp. 120–1).

JUVENILE OFFENDER'S NIGHTMARE TREATMENT

Elaine Rivera, in a report to *Newsday* (an American daily newspaper serving the New York City borough) in 1993, described the case of a 15-year-old boy who was treated at a Sexual Behavior Clinic in New York after being charged with sexually abusing his sister. He was given little choice regarding his treatment – it was either undergo therapy or go to jail. The boy, then 18, said that his pants were lowered around his ankles and he was forced to place a round, mercury-filled plastic device around his penis, and further forced to wear earphones and listen to pornographic tapes, including descriptions of sex between adults and children, and between children and children, violent rape, forced sex and other abnormal sexual acts. He was also encouraged to masturbate. In defence of the treatment programme, an administrator representing the Community Service of the New York State Office of Mental Health reported it to be ethical and effective. He claimed that continually subjecting the sex offender to his own deviant sexual fantasies would eventually cause the arousal experienced to decrease and the fantasies to become boring. It was further stated that 'They've all admitted to sexual offenses. These kids can either go through the program or go to jail' (Richard Herman, cited in Rivera 1993).

The juvenile's experience of this type of therapy is common, as a review of the Phoenix Memorial Hospital in Arizona demonstrated. Yankowski (1992) described the treatment of child sex offenders as part of the Phoenix Memorial Program based at the hospital. There was extreme use of a penile plethysmograph at the hospital, which, although used in many sex offender programmes, is not without criticism from both legal and scientific quarters over its efficacy. Yankowski believes that it labels the child as sexually deviant, leading to unnecessary treatment causing humiliation and harm. Furthermore, the treatment of child victims and offenders was the same. Yankowski reported that one child was forced to admit to being an offender even though he/she was a victim of sexual abuse – this could have caused some psychological damage. Yankowski's review also documented the circumstances surrounding the use of the penile plethysmograph, such as viewing naked men, women and children in compromising positions. These children (especially child victims) may have been subjected to such explicit sexual images for the first time, potentially leading to future deviant sexual behaviour. Even child sex offenders with learning disabilities or on prescribed medications experienced the same treatment, adding to any self-esteem issues they may already have had. Finally, informed consent from the parents was believed to have been coerced. The parents were told that if they signed the consent form then their child would be allowed to come home once they had successfully completed the programme. Also, there was no 'drop-out' clause for the parents to sign allowing their child to disengage from therapy once it began.

These cases, although unfortunate, are rare. Treatment interventions are subject to years of clinical research designed to test their effectiveness in rehabilitating offenders. Forensic psychologists, as part of their professional role, are actively engaged in this type of research to promote the professionalism of their discipline.

SUMMARY

Different types of assessment have been developed over the years, but those most commonly used by forensic psychologists involve the evaluation of cognitive, emotional and social aspects of development. There are, however, specialised tests that forensic psychologists use to assess particular behaviours of offenders. These are used to evaluate whether the offender has changed and become a reformed person. The purpose of these assessments is to shed light on the nature of thoughts and feelings held by offenders and whether they have been rehabilitated and are therefore safe to be released into the community. Forensic psychologists also use assessments (tests and clinical interviews) to help devise treatment programmes for offenders. Accurate assessments are important in the development of relevant and suitably tailored therapies for offenders with different histories of criminal activity and cognitive/emotional/social skills deficits. In prison, there are different intervention programmes which have been shown to be effective and successful in treating violent offenders, such as the National Anger Management Package, Cognitive Self-Change Programmes and Multi-Faceted Interventions. In the case of sex offenders, both the Sex Offender Treatment Programme and the Sex Offender Treatment Evaluation Project have proven to be effective interventions. The Aggression Replacement Training programme has proven successful at reducing reoffending for offenders on probation by addressing deficits that offenders commonly face, such as anger control, moral reasoning and empathy, and interpersonal and problem-solving skills. The Probation Service runs different types of group interventions. In order to ensure that offenders are suited to these group interventions, probation officers perform assessments supplemented by tests often devised by forensic psychologists (e.g. Readiness to Change and the Offender Group Reoffending Scale Version 2). Forensic psychologists also provide reports through assessment for cases where guilt or innocence has yet to be established. Often these cases are referred by a solicitor and are treated under Tort Law. There are many types of tortious act, categorised as negligence, intentional, strict liability and nuisance torts. Forensic psychologists are commonly involved in the assessment of divorce and child custody cases. In Britain these are assessed under the Family Law Act but may also involve the Children Act. There are guidelines for assessing these cases which are followed rigorously. The ethics underlying assessment and treatment of offenders and victims, as outlined by professional bodies representing forensic psychologists such as the BPS and APA, are strongly adhered to. This does not, however, always protect offenders and victims from errors of judgement based on inaccurate assessment and from the damaging effects of unregulated treatment interventions.

RECOMMENDATIONS FOR FURTHER READING

Crassati, J. (2004). *Managing High Risk Sex Offenders in the Community: A Psychological Approach.* Hove, UK: Brunner-Routledge.

Rich, P. (2003). *Understanding, Assessing, and Rehabilitating Juvenile Sexual Offenders.* Hoboken, NJ: John Wiley and Sons.

5

PSYCHOLOGICAL VULNERABILITY

Psychological vulnerability appears in many different forms and is caused by a multitude of factors. Despite, however, the many guises of psychological vulnerability, its various impacts on an individual's life and future behaviour have one thing in common – they can be devastating. The concept of vulnerability is of significant importance to individuals caught up in crime, whether as a victim of crime, a witness to a crime, a defendant charged with a crime or a prisoner serving a sentence for committing a crime. All will be considered in this chapter.

Vulnerability, in general terms, refers to an individual's propensity to succumb to factors that have a negative outcome. A concept related to vulnerability which might be considered its polar opposite is resilience. Unlike vulnerability, resilience implies a positive outcome. In the case of resilience, the individual has developed an inner strength to combat the negative impact of adversity. Hence, an individual's resilience can be understood as a consequence of protective factors (e.g. a secure attachment during childhood) enabling them to survive adverse life events. Those who are vulnerable have generally had a different life experience – they are more likely to have been exposed to numerous risk factors (e.g. experiencing rejection or neglect during childhood). This implies that they are less likely to cope effectively with and escape the negative consequences of adverse life events in adulthood. Risk, vulnerability and protective factors can be defined in the following way:

- A risk factor can be considered a predictor of a poor outcome and causes damage to a person
- A vulnerability factor forms a part of the individual that enables a risk factor to have a damaging effect
- A protective factor is helpful to the individual and can contribute towards combating the detrimental effects of a risk factor.

There has been much research investigating the risk factors for vulnerability and the protective factors for resilience. Rutter and Giller (1983) outlined five contributory high-risk adverse factors for delinquency and factors which protect children from leading a criminal lifestyle:

- Parental criminality (i.e. parents who commit crime and have criminal ideals)
- Intra-familial discord (i.e. disputes between family members, especially the parents)
- Inconsistencies in response to unacceptable behaviour (e.g. inconsistent punishment by the parents)
- Family size and number of siblings (e.g. large families may have less time and resources to allocate to each child)
- Socio-economic status (e.g. the amount of disposable income available for the family) (See Box, pp. 125–8).

THE FIVE RISK FACTORS THAT ARE LIKELY TO INCREASE VULNERABILITY

1. Parental criminality – West and Farrington (1973) found that 37.9 per cent of boys who became delinquent had a parent with a criminal record before the boy reached the age of ten. Many other studies, such as McCord (1986) and Thornberry et al. (2003), corroborated these findings, so much so that for some psychologists the view held was that an 'intergenerational transmission' of aggression and delinquency was occurring. This means that from

one generation to the next an essentially criminal mindset was being instilled in children by their criminal parents through the process of **socialisation**. Socialisation is the process by which children are taught socially appropriate attitudes, values and mores of society, the idea being that when children are most impressionable their behaviour is guided to follow the rules set by society, helping them to become law-abiding citizens. In the case of children with criminal parents, they are instead socialised to accept criminal or deviant ideals, resulting in their likely future delinquent behaviour.

2. Intra-familial discord – this refers to the extent of parental conflict that causes family disruption. Many studies have shown that separation due to parents leaving or divorcing has consequences for the child's future behaviour. A constant finding is that separation from one or both parents during the first ten years of a child's life can cause behavioural problems (Farrington 1992). Separations due to illness or death, however, had little impact on later delinquent behaviour. The problems arose from acrimonious separations due to marital breakdown and divorce, which in some cases continued for many years. Unresolved parental issues within marriage could also result in disruption to the parents' relationships with their children. This could be demonstrated in a lack of interest in their children's leisure pursuits or having low expectations of their children's career prospects. Glueck and Glueck (1950) found that the parents of 'delinquents' were less affectionate to their children and were more rejecting. Rejection and abusive childhood experiences as contributory factors for delinquency feature time and time again in research findings. Both feature as important factors for the development of the affectionless psychopath in Bowlby's Theory of Attachment (Bowlby 1958). Here, Bowlby outlines the importance of a secure bond between mother and child (although the mother could be substituted by a carer). A good secure attachment bond helps the child develop into an adult capable of forming strong relationships with other people. In his

study of 44 juvenile thieves in 1944, Bowlby showed that those who experienced prolonged separation within the first two years of life tended to exhibit affectionless psychopathy. The juveniles who exhibited affectionless psychopathy found it difficult in later years to form relationships with other people or experience positive emotions like empathy and warmth for others.

3. Inconsistencies in response to unacceptable behaviour – discipline guides the child's behaviour and offers an understanding of society's boundaries regarding forbidden or permissible behaviour. If the discipline is inconsistent then the rules governing these boundaries become confused. Likewise, if discipline is ineffective then the message about why certain behaviour is wrong becomes lost. Maccoby and Martin (1983) described two types of interaction: affection versus rejection/hostility and control versus undemanding/permissive. These two dimensions combine in different ways to produce four distinct parenting styles. The first is authoritative, consisting of acceptance and demanding. This is a good parenting style, as it encourages the child to develop self-control and self-confidence. The second is authoritarian, which has negative consequences for the child as it relies on a rejecting and demanding approach. This promotes low self-esteem and poor moral development. The third is known as indulgent, because the parents simply accept the child without providing any boundaries (they are undemanding). This leads to a spoilt child with poor socialisation skills. The fourth is neglect, which also leads to poor socialisation, only here the child is angry as a result of rejecting and undemanding parenting.

4. Family size and number of siblings – West (1982) showed that delinquents tend to come from large families (i.e. four or more children). There are a variety of reasons for this but the main causes tend to stem from poor supervision, discipline and parental attention – all a consequence of having many children. Another factor is that younger siblings might be more inclined to model their behaviour on older delinquent siblings.

5. Socio-economic status – Rutter and Giller (1983) argued that relative poverty in families is linked to delinquency. This more tentative point is likely to be linked with large family size. Given that larger families are more likely to experience relative poverty, the reasons explored above are more likely to cause delinquency than low socio-economic status per se.

While the above risk factors can change the life course of an individual from being law abiding to being criminal, protective factors tend to negate risk factors, thereby promoting conformity to society's rules and norms. There are many protective factors, some of which are considered in the Box below.

PROTECTIVE FACTORS THAT ARE LIKELY TO DECREASE VULNERABILITY

- Maternal affection
- Supportive relationships
- Significant adult in a child's life
- Non-delinquent siblings
- Non-delinquent peers
- Family, school and/or hobby involvement
- Authoritative parenting styles
- Religion
- First-born
- Female
- Even temperament
- Good self-esteem
- Good coping skills
- Positive life outlook
- Social competence
- Intellectual abilities – able to problem solve, understand social situations
- Achievement-motivated
- Good life opportunities – moving away from adversity

When we think of the role of the forensic psychologist in the assessment and treatment of the psychologically vulnerable, the image is of a professional who works with an offender with mental health issues. As demonstrated, being vulnerable does not necessarily involve mental illness. Furthermore, within a legal context, psychological vulnerability generally pertains to individuals who are easily confused and susceptible to accepting information or evidence presented against them. Individuals of this disposition include the mentally disordered, but also young children and senior citizens. A good example of this in action is the case of Michael Crowe, who was falsely accused of murdering his 12-year-old sister Stephanie in 1998 (see Box, pp. 129–30).

THE 14-YEAR-OLD FALSELY ACCUSED OF MURDER

Stephanie Crowe was found dead in her bedroom in Escondido, California, with nine stab wounds. Her brother was immediately suspected of murdering her because he had said that in the night he woke up with a headache and so went to the kitchen to get some milk. The police assumed that he would have seen his sister's body blocking the doorway to her room as he went to the kitchen. From this, police concluded that he failed to alarm his parents of what had happened because he was the murderer. Their first error, however, was the assumption that Michael Crowe's bedroom was opposite his sister's room. The second was the over-interpretation of Crowe's behaviour when the police first arrived – he was playing a game and appeared distant while the remaining members of the family were grieving. Yet Crowe and two of his friends confessed to the murder – why, if they did not do it?

Crowe was questioned for 27 hours over a three-day period. Confessions were obtained after the police had falsely told Crowe that they had physical evidence implicating him, and also that his parents believed he was the murderer (Wilkens and Sauer 1999). Edward Humes worked for the Knight Ridder/Tribune Service at the time and reported that the police coerced all three boys into confessing to a crime they did not commit (Humes 2004). After the videotapes of the interrogations were analysed, it was concluded that the police had subjected the boys to psychological torture, responsible, it is believed, for the fabricated version of events and description of the planning of the murder. All three boys were young and vulnerable to the questioning style of the police. Had an appropriate adult been present during the interrogation, a requirement introduced in the U.K. under the Police and Criminal Evidence Act of 1984 (discussed later), the boys would not have been pressured to confess in the way that they were. In the U.S., the 'Miranda warning' (discussed later) provides suspects with protection from self-incrimination. In this case, however, the Miranda warning was not sufficiently explained. This case demonstrates that some individuals are more psychologically vulnerable than others and are less able to cope with the pressures of police interrogation.

Thus far, our focus has been on the vulnerability of those accused of committing crimes, but what of victims or witnesses – might they not also be vulnerable?

VULNERABLE VICTIMS AND WITNESSES OF CRIME

In a study by DeValve (2005) it was shown that 67 per cent of victims of personal crime had suffered from some kind of psychological trauma such as anxiety or panic attacks. The study also found that 53 per cent felt unsafe in their home and isolated or alone. The psychological condition known as Post-Traumatic Stress Disorder (PTSD) is a common consequence of victimisation, especially in personal crimes such as violence and rape. These types of crime can be very traumatic for the victim, often making a full recovery a challenge. There are some victims who feel especially psychologically compromised, while others seem to recover from their ordeal relatively unscathed. This suggests that there are individual differences in terms of psychological vulnerability and resilience to traumatic experiences such as being a victim of a violent crime. There are many reasons why people vary in their resilience to traumatic events such as those outlined earlier.

Of course, there must be an interaction between personal dispositions towards vulnerability or resilience, and the nature of the crime experienced by the victim. It is important to remember, however, that psychological vulnerability might not only lead a person to criminality but can also occur as a consequence of a traumatic experience such as a mental breakdown. As DeValve's study shows, many victims of crime can feel psychologically vulnerable. It is important that victims are assessed and treated by a practitioner such as a forensic psychologist, and that the law provides recourse to justice for the victim, for example in the form of a prison sentence for the offender and/or compensation for the victim. Victims often feel a sense of helplessness and fear during their ordeal which can lead to PTSD after the event. Furthermore, PTSD can develop because of the victim's negative cognitive appraisal of themselves in light of such an event. For instance, a child victim of molestation might feel defaced or devalued in some way and might see the acceptance of compensation as 'dirty money'.

In Canada, a report showed that victims often failed to report a violent incident to the police. The reasons given varied: of those who did not report a violent incident, 60 per cent wanted to deal with it in another way, 29 per cent felt the police were unable to do anything and 11 per cent feared reprisals from their persecutor. Furthermore, Gannon and Mihorean's (2005) statistical findings suggest that violent victimisation impacts on the emotions of victims by evoking anger (32 per cent) followed by feeling upset, confused or frustrated (20 per cent) and fear (18 per cent). The majority of victims approached friends and the family for support (90 per cent), but 9 per cent sought the help of a psychologist and 10 per cent a medical practitioner (Ministry of Public Safety and Solicitor General 2009).

Victims with intellectual disabilities are less likely to report their ordeal to police than non-impaired victims. Non-reporting among this population can be as high as 97 per cent and even when they do report to the police, the criminal justice system often excludes them from any court proceedings on the grounds that they will make unreliable witnesses. Willner (2011) claims that despite the use of closed-circuit video systems and guidelines concerning the reporting and investigation of abuse allegations, victims with intellectual disabilities are still disadvantaged. It is possible, however, for victims who are compromised by their intellectual impairments to have their abusers tried in court and found guilty. One such case was reported by Gudjonsson et al. (2000), who were involved in the assessment of about 50 intellectually disabled male and female residents in two separate privately run residential homes. There were allegations of staff ill-treating the residents. Different measures were taken in order to suffice the stipulations by the judge that witnesses should be able to understand what an oath is and the implications it has, and that they had to be able to provide a reliable account of what they had witnessed. As many had communication problems and poor memory recall, it is not surprising that their performance on the Wechsler Adult Intelligence Scale (WAIS) was low. When they were asked what the standard oath used in court meant, about a fifth could provide a satisfactory answer and they tended to have an IQ over 60, as measured by the WAIS. Those who had an IQ over 50 (about a fifth) could explain what a lie meant. The Gudjonsson **Suggestibility** Scale (GSS; Gudjonsson 2003) was used as a measure to score how suggestible individuals were to the content of leading questions (i.e. questions that prompt a particular desired response). Those with intellectual impairments tend to succumb to leading questions more than other witnesses, but this might be more a consequence of having less memory capacity. Furthermore, they are less likely to be suggestible to leading questions when they are sure of events. When they are sure of events (especially those involving personal factual information) then they can provide reasonably accurate testimony (Kebbell and Hatton 1999) and are more resistant to suggestion (Milne et al. 1999). Hence, the criminal justice system should not automatically exclude those with intellectual disabilities from due process.

Forensic psychologists are also involved in assessing and treating witnesses who have been affected by the very nature of what they have just seen happen to a victim of a criminal event. An example of the psychological effects of a horrific crime on witnesses and surviving victims occurred in 2001: the incident now infamously known as 9/11. In New York, U.S., the twin towers of the World Trade Center, housing thousands of workers, came under terrorist attack when two aeroplanes (American Airlines Flight 11 and United Airlines Flight 175) were deliberately flown into both the North and South towers. The first plunged into the heart of the North Tower at 8.46am, causing fire and eventual structural collapse. Because of its proximity to 7 World Trade Center, debris from the tower damaged and set fire to that building, which also collapsed. The second plane plunged into the South Tower at 9.03am, also causing fire and the collapse of the building. Many witnessed the event at street level and worldwide as it was broadcast live. Some victims survived their ordeal by escaping from the lower levels before the buildings collapsed, but many died instantly on the impact of the planes, succumbed to smoke inhalation or were crushed by the collapsing buildings. There were other victims too – the fire-fighters and the families of those who died. The aftermath of the event left many people injured, grieving and with numerous psychological problems. Some of the victims of, and witnesses to, this event developed PTSD. This condition can be very debilitating, causing much distress to sufferers. PTSD sufferers describe night terrors and sweats, and strong memories of events constantly being replayed and acted out in their minds at any given moment by an unsuspecting trigger. Forensic psychologists were involved in assessing and treating witnesses and victims who experienced the debilitating psychological symptoms of PTSD caused by 9/11.

Also in common with victims, witnesses can experience fear of being recognised by the offender and the possibility of any reprisals. This fear can prevent them from giving evidence in court. The pervasiveness of witness intimidation is rife. In the U.K., a survey revealed that 53 per cent of witnesses appearing in a criminal court to give evidence had been directly threatened and 17 per cent feared intimidation (Hamlyn et al. 2004). A study of witness intimidation in the Bronx County of New York revealed that 36 per cent of witnesses who appeared in the criminal courts had been directly threatened, and, of the remaining non-threatened witnesses, 57 per cent feared reprisals (Davis et al. 1990).

Psychological trauma and fear of reprisals are more common among victims and witnesses than originally believed to be the case. Therefore it is important that there are counselling services and offers of treatment available for vulnerable victims and witnesses of crime.

VULNERABLE SUSPECTS OF CRIME

The case of Michael Crowe (see Box, pp. 129–30) is a prime example of the experiences of a vulnerable suspect, in this case a young boy who was subjected to police interrogation and confessed to a crime he did not commit. There are many examples of this happening in both the U.S. and U.K., and no doubt in many other parts of the world. In the U.K. during the 1970s, there was a spate of IRA bombings; one of these, a pub bombing in Guildford in 1974, resulted in the arrest of four men who became known as the Guildford Four. All four men had their cases overturned, but only after spending 15 years in prison. When they were released in 1989 they gave an account of how their confessions were forced due to serious police malpractice. In the year of their release, Sir Ludovic Kennedy reported on Gerrard ('Gerry') Conlon's (one of the Guildford Four) experience of police coercion:

> After relating how the police had spent some time calling him 'an effing, murdering Irish bastard', squeezing his testicles, hitting him in the kidneys and slapping his face, Conlon wrote: 'I was crying and frightened. Simmons [a senior police officer] said if I didn't make a statement, he would ring Belfast first thing in the morning and I would never see my mother or sister again. The last of my resistance shattered when he said this. I was crying and shaking uncontrollably. I said my family hadn't done anything. I fell apart. Simmons said what happened to my family was up to me. I said I would make a statement like they wanted, but it wouldn't be true as I really didn't do it.'

(Kennedy 1989)

Since such cases have come to light in the U.K., the introduction of the Police and Criminal Evidence Act 1984 (PACE) has ensured that police practice for the interrogation of vulnerable suspects must involve an 'appropriate adult' being present to monitor the individual's situation and explain it to them – in effect, they have a mediator's role. PACE (Northern Ireland) Order was introduced in 1989, and the equivalent, called the Criminal Procedure (Scotland) Act, to Scots law in 1995. In the U.S., a similar scheme, known as the Miranda rule (also known as Miranda rights or Miranda warning), provides suspects with rights to protect themselves from self-incrimination. The Miranda rule provides three guarantees:

- The right to remain silent
- The right to legal counsel during interrogation
- The right to legal counsel paid from public taxes.

Juvenile suspects considered to be vulnerable have an additional three Miranda rights:

- Police must provide a written notice defining the specifics of the charge before any hearing
- Police must inform the accused of a state-funded attorney
- What self-incrimination leads to is made clear, so that ignorance cannot be used as a later excuse.

Given that there is much emphasis on obtaining a confession it is important for the rights of suspects to be protected from coercive interrogation. There is, however, a different problem concerning a suspect's vulnerability which has nothing to do with police inter-rogation. This has been labelled as **interrogative suggestibility**, first introduced by Gudjonsson and Clark (1986) as 'the extent to which, within a closed social interaction, people come to accept messages communicated during formal questioning, as a result of which their subsequent behavioural response is affected' (p. 84). The Gudjonsson Suggestibility Scale (GSS) was designed to detect an individual's level of susceptibility to interrogative pressure and their acceptance of misinformation. It is a simple procedure requiring an interviewee's attention to a spoken narrative, the content of which they are asked to recall, first immediately and then 50 minutes later. A total of 20 questions are asked about the narrative, of which 15 are leading questions. From these questions four scores can be derived. The first score is Yield 1, which represents the number of suggestions accepted from the leading questions. Negative feedback is then given to the interviewee by saying 'You have made a number of errors. It is necessary to go through the questions once again, and this time, try to be more accurate.' All 20 questions are repeated and Yield 2, Shift and Total Suggestibility scores can be calculated. Yield 2 is the number of suggestions accepted from the leading questions after the negative feedback was given and represents the extent to which interviewees give in to the leading questions. The Shift score represents the number of changed responses to the questions after the negative feedback. This provides an indication of the interviewee's ability to cope with interrogative pressure. The Total Suggestibility score is derived by adding the Yield 1 and Shift scores. In the case of interviewees rejecting the negative feedback there is no problem of susceptibility to suggestion, but for those who accept the negative feedback there is reason for concern.

The GSS has been helpful to police in the detection of suspects vulnerable to interrogative suggestibility, and has been of particular use when applied to children (Westcott et al. 2002), the elderly (Mueller-Johnson 2009) and those with learning disabilities (Gudjonsson et al. 2000). An adaption of the GSS called the Visual Suggestibility Scale for Children presents material visually and aurally to children. Children are asked about an event that occurred at school which also contains details that did not happen. The scores derived using this test show a linear relationship between level of suggestibility and score (Scullin et al. 2002). The GSS can be administered to witnesses and victims, although their testimonies are considered to be honest and less self-serving than those provided by suspects and, in particular, defendants. The problems of obtaining accurate accounts from witnesses and victims are generally associated with their inability to communicate memories of the criminal event when questioned (Kebbell and Hatton 1999). The GSS is a useful tool in detecting individuals who are vulnerable and therefore likely to agree with suggestions put forward to them by the police. It is important to detect suggestible victims and witnesses who might otherwise be influenced by information, in order to avert a possible miscarriage of justice. Detecting suggestible suspects is equally important as it helps prevent them from making false confessions which allow true perpetrators to escape justice.

VULNERABLE DEFENDANTS

The identification of vulnerable defendants has implications for their being able to stand trial. Questions arise concerning the defendant's ability to understand the complexities of a court procedure and to respond to cross-examination. It is important, therefore, to establish whether a defendant is competent to stand trial simply because this changes how they are legally processed. For example, the mental state of an individual will have an impact on the way they are treated during the police investigation process, how they make a plea of guilt, what happens during the trial and how a decision of sentence is presided (Gunn and Buchanan 2006). One reason why it is so important to establish whether a defendant is competent to stand trial rests on the stipulation by the criminal justice system that he or she should be in a position to contribute towards their own defence. There is a long history, dating as far back as the fourteenth century in Britain, of the view that those incapable of attending a law court (i.e. as a result of mental impairment) should not be tried. This notion relates to the image of a fair and dignified criminal justice system with strong, honest and moral principles (Zapf and Roesch 2001).

In the U.K. and U.S. there is more emphasis placed on the importance of establishing a defendant's competency to stand trial than in Continental Europe. There is a good reason for this which can be traced back to differences in legal systems. The legal system operating in the U.K. and U.S. is based on adversarial law, which relies on a judge and jury and two opposing sides – the prosecution and the defence. Information is presented to the judge and jury via the prosecution and defence lawyers, who call upon witnesses, the victim and defendant to present their evidence. Not so for many European courts, which operate instead under the inquisitorial system. In this case the truth is attained via the inquiring judge, therefore there is no need for an assessment of fitness to stand trial. In some countries, such as Austria, there is no legal stipulation concerning fitness to stand trial. If there is some question over the mental state of the accused then the judge will request a psychiatric report. In the U.K., there are typically around 20 cases annually where the defendant is judged unfit to stand trial. In contrast, in the U.S., this can be as many as 60,000 a year (Bonnie and Grisso 2000). What happens in the case of child defendants? Can they be tried? (See Box, pp. 137–8.)

CAN WE TRY CHILDREN?

Doli incapax is a Latin term concerning whether we should be allowed to try children who have committed crime. This term was introduced to English law in the fourteenth century and is used to question whether a child is fit to stand trial. It rests on the assumption that children below a particular age will be incapable of understanding the difference between right and wrong. Therefore, when they commit a criminal act, it is important to establish if they knew and understood that their behaviour was morally wrong. Different countries have different age cut-off points for criminal responsibility and therefore for the legal right to try a child. In England, Wales and Northern Ireland this is set at 10 years of age, whereas in Scotland, Canada, Greece, Turkey and the Netherlands it is 12. Japan has the highest set age of 20, while in Switzerland, Nigeria and South Africa it is as low as 7. Most American states are towards the higher end at 18.

Vulnerable defendants with mental problems can be identified through forensic psychological assessment resulting in the conclusion that they are incompetent to stand trial. Under such circumstances a different course of action is required that does not involve criminal courts. In the U.K., the McNaughton Rules were introduced in 1843 as a consequence of Daniel McNaughton murdering Edward Drummond, Prime Minister Robert Peel's private secretary (see Chapter 3). A special verdict of 'not guilty by reason of insanity' was a consequence of the McNaughton Rules that is still used today. The reasoning behind the special verdict is to prevent vulnerable offenders from having to experience court proceedings. They are effectively charged for their crime and punished but are averted from the criminal justice system because they are too incompetent to offer a defence. A forensic psychologist in Britain who clinically assesses a defendant and finds them unfit to stand trial could suggest they be transferred to a high security psychiatric hospital like Broadmoor, thereby bypassing any prosecution. Under these circumstances the defendant can plead insanity and is given a special verdict of 'not guilty by reason of insanity'.

Grubin (1996) describes the current system operating in the U.K. as offering vulnerable offenders the opportunity to be tested prior to any court proceedings. The test takes account of the defendant's ability to:

- Understand the evidence presented for and against them
- Instruct their lawyers regarding their case
- Monitor what happens in the courtroom
- Comprehend the court charges and the consequences of being found guilty.

If a defendant is unable to stand trial due to a mental issue (according to Grubin this is usually schizophrenia) then they are compulsorily detained for an indeterminate period in a psychiatric hospital. Furthermore, a hearing follows where the likelihood of the defendant having committed the crime is considered. If the panel decide that the accused is innocent then a discharge follows and the individual can walk free. In the U.S., the system is slightly different (see Box below).

THE U.S. EXPERIENCE

The following, arising from the Supreme Court Ruling in the case of *Dusky* v. *United States* in 1960, is used as a measure to establish whether the defendant is fit to stand trial:

> ... sufficient present ability to consult with his lawyer with a reasonable degree of rational understanding ... rational as well as factual understanding of the proceedings.
>
> (Heilbrun et al. 1996)

In the U.S., the MacArthur Competence Assessment Tool for Criminal Adjudication is used to ascertain whether the defendant has the cognitive capacity to play an active role in the courtroom. This test is implemented by providing the defendant with a brief description of a criminal event and the chain of consequential actions that follow. The defendant is then asked questions referring to court procedure and the roles of the legal team. To ensure that they understand and can follow the courtroom proceedings, they are asked questions about the reasoning behind the decisions made.

VULNERABLE OFFENDERS AND PRISONERS

It is interesting that, despite the safeguards in place during the investigative process, vulnerable offenders are incarcerated in a prison environment. This has become a major problem for prisons in the U.K. and in other countries also. Smith and Borland (1999) assessed a sample of British female prisoners using the General Health Questionnaire (GHQ). They found that more than half of the sample scored high on the GHQ, suggesting that they had psychiatric issues. Research findings by Parsons et al. (2001) indicated that as many as 59.4 per cent of females on **remand** across British prisons had some kind of mental disorder. The disorders in order of prevalence were: psychosis, anxiety, mood and personality. In the U.S., Martin and Hasselbrock (2001) also found a high representation of psychiatric disorders among female prisoners, especially depression. In 2006, Fellner found that 16 per cent of adults in prisons have a mental illness, which is between two and four times higher than in the general population. Furthermore, prisoners with mental illnesses are more prone to violating prison rules, leading to their confinement and segregation – both providing opportunities for self-harming and suicidal behaviour.

It is important to note, however, that female offenders are increasingly given a psychiatric diagnosis (Kendall 2004), and when appearing in court they are more likely to receive detention in a psychiatric unit, usually a special hospital. Given that 40 per cent of female prisoners sought psychiatric treatment before they were imprisoned, it is not surprising that the prevalence of female prisoners with mental disorders is so high (Kesteven 2002). The nature of psychiatric problems of 64 female offenders admitted for treatment under the Mental Health Act was calculated by Xenitidis et al. (1999) as:

- 48.4 per cent – psychotic illness
- 18.8 per cent – non-psychotic mental illness
- 17.2 per cent – autism
- 25 per cent – epilepsy.

Psychiatric disorders in prisoners are often implicated in self-harming and suicidal behaviour. Coid et al. (1992) found that many female prisoners had been sexually or physically abused in child-hood. According to Andrews et al. (2000), abusive childhoods can have a lasting effect on an individual's psychological development such that they are susceptible to psychopathology in adulthood. Furthermore, studies have shown that there is a link between feeling shame from early abuse and suicide in female prisoners (Milligan and Andrews 2005). In some British prisons, such as HMP Holloway and HMP Liverpool, prisoners who have self-harmed are assessed by a forensic psychologist for their suitability to have group support or a counsellor. Suicide is a problem not only for female prisoners but for males also, especially young males with mental health issues. The Safer Custody Group (2005) reported that the rate of suicide in U.K. prisons is 12 times higher than is found in the general popu-lation, and it is greatest among prisoners with mental health issues (Towl and Crighton 2000). However, the system used by many forensic psychologists of classifying prisoners as suicidal or non-sui-cidal lends itself to problems of false negatives. Under these cir-cumstances, the prisoner would be considered as a non-risk of suicide when he or she is in fact a risk – this means prison staff are less inclined to perform suicide checks.

According to James (1996) there are points in time when prisoners are at a high risk of suicide:

- Soon after admission to prison
- When the individual shows signs of psychological improvement
- Times when offenders with psychological problems have leave from medium-secure units.

One of the most vulnerable groups of prisoners is young offenders. The Hospital Anxiety and Depression Scale (HADS), devised by Zigmond and Snaith in 1983, has been widely used as a measure for anxiety and depression. HADS was used to assess young Scottish prisoners who were considered a high risk of suicide and were therefore on Strict Suicidal Supervision (SSS). They were found to have higher depression scores than those not on SSS, and higher still when they had a history of suicidal tendencies (Biggam and Power 1999). The score from HADS is a good predictor of future suicidal behaviour and, according to Nieland et al. (2001), should be taken seriously. The notion of hopelessness, where the individual feels that there is no future and has abandoned all hope, is considered to be the link between depression and suicidal behaviour. Both depression and hopelessness are considered to be personal variables that determine an individual's level of psychological distress (Biggam and Power 1999). Prisoners on SSS are those who regularly report psychological distress in the form of depression and anxiety.

There is much research to show that having poor social and problem-solving skills can lead to feelings of depression and hopelessness which, in turn, increases the risk of suicide. Zamble hence Porporino (1988) identified many prisoners as having poor problem-solving abilities, meaning that they are easily overwhelmed, hence preventing them from coping with imprisonment and from participating in rehabilitation programmes. Furthermore, their coping abilities can become easily compromised when they are stressed by their prison environment. This means, for example, that those who prefer solitude and limited interpersonal interaction might, in withdrawing from prison life, focus their attention on their psychological problems and become increasingly suicidal (Eidin et al. 2002). Hence, poor social and problem-solving skills can make an individual vulnerable to suicidal behaviours. One extension of social and problem-solving skills is that of having a learning disability. There are a variety of learning disabilities that incarcerated offenders might experience which go undiagnosed and untreated, such as Attention Deficit Hyperactivity Disorder (ADHD). This is best highlighted by the case example of Billy Joe Friend (see Box, pp. 142–3).

15-YEAR-OLD BILLY'S WRONGFUL CONVICTION

Billy Joe Friend was unable to give evidence in his own trial because of his learning disability and the new laws stipulated by Strasbourg that children and young people should not be put on the stand. Despite this, he was convicted of murder in 1996. He was interviewed three times by the police but remained silent during the first two interviews on the advice given by his solicitor, who thought it was best he said nothing given his low IQ. He did, however, give an account during his last police interview of what happened and the role he had played. He lied about what had happened, but it was this account that was used at his trial and served against him. Despite Gudjonsson, a forensic psychologist commissioned to compile a report, raising the fact that the 15-year-old had a below-average IQ of 63 and was easily distracted and had a poor concentration level, he went to court. Given that he was unable to defend himself in the courtroom and therefore remained silent in court, the jurors were instructed by the judge to make adverse inferences about his failure to give evidence – in other words, it did not look good for him. There were three factors that the jury took into consideration:

- Billy Joe Friend did not take the witness box
- He did not answer police questions during his first two interviews
- He lied to the police during his third interview.

His case was reopened in 2003 by the Court of Appeal and a comprehensive neuropsychological and ADHD assessment of Billy Joe Friend, now 23 years old, was performed. The assessments demonstrated cognitive and behavioural impairments consistent with having childhood ADHD. Thus, despite having been considered fit to plead, his learning disability would have impaired his ability to participate in the court proceedings. It was concluded that he had not committed the murder he was convicted for and his conviction was quashed. Clearly, ADHD is a vulnerability that has long been overlooked (Gudjonsson and Young 2006).

SUMMARY

Psychological vulnerability can have a devastating effect on individuals accused of committing a crime they did not commit, simply because they are susceptible to believing their accusers. Vulnerability, however, can be considered in other ways also, such as in those who are at risk of becoming delinquents, as was pointed out by Rutter and Giller (1983) in their five high-risk adverse factors for delinquency.

An important variable which can help negate the impact of risk factors is the presence of protective factors such as maternal affection, non-delinquent siblings and peers, and religion. Psychological vulnerability is often perceived as something displayed by a person who has a mental illness. This, however, is not always the case, as demonstrated by Michael Crowe, the 14-year-old falsely accused of murdering his sister. Michael Crowe's vulnerability was his young age, which put him at high risk of interrogative suggestibility. Children, and people with a learning disability or a mental disorder, are particularly at risk of accepting information from the police during interrogation. It is because they are vulnerable that they succumb to interrogative suggestibility.

In the case of suspects undergoing police interrogation, it is important to establish if they are vulnerable to interrogative suggestibility. In the U.K., police legislation introduced as PACE in 1984 ensures that an appropriate adult should be present during interview who can mediate for an individual considered vulnerable. The Gudjonsson Suggestibility Scale is also used to detect an individual's level of susceptibility to interrogative pressure.

Defendants can be vulnerable too, and important decisions have to be made concerning their fitness to attend court. Defendants are legally expected to be competent enough to follow the court proceedings and to be actively engaged in their own defence. If it is suspected that they are unable to do this, then in the U.K. it is up to the forensic psychologist to clinically assess the defendant as unfit to stand trial.

It is not only those who are accused of committing a crime that we might consider to be vulnerable – victims and witnesses can be also. Victims who have suffered from psychological trauma, as a consequence of experiencing violence or rape for example, can develop PTSD, where flashbacks of the event interfere with their daily life. Not all victims, however, develop this, and in fact many overcome their ordeal, which suggests that there are individual differences concerning who will be vulnerable or resistant. Witnesses can also experience similar reactions to victims of crime.

Vulnerable prisoners can be problematic within a prison setting as they can become suicidal. Often, prisoners with a mental disorder, learning disability or poor social and problem-solving skills can become depressed and agitated by prison life. When this happens they find it difficult to cope with the prison regime and present suicidal behaviours. Young prisoners and female prisoners are especially vulnerable to suicidal behaviours.

RECOMMENDATIONS FOR FURTHER READING

Gudjonsson, G.H. (2003). *The Psychology of Interrogations and Confessions: A Handbook*. Chichester: John Wiley.

Smith, K. and Tilney, S. (2007). *Vulnerable Adult and Child Witnesses*. Oxford: Blackstone.

6

LEGAL PSYCHOLOGY

Offenders, victims and witnesses are dealt with differently both during police investigations and in the courtroom. This means that during police investigations, for example, victims and witnesses are interviewed differently from suspects. Police have a different focus when interviewing suspects as their aim is to find evidence implicating the individual in relation to a criminal event – this further extends to investigating other sources of information that corroborate the suspect's guilt. In the case of victims and witnesses, the emphasis is on obtaining details of the criminal event and the perpetrator's identity. It is not only the police who have a different focus for suspects, victims and witnesses; other areas of the criminal justice system do too. In the courtroom there is a different working ethos concerning the defendant from that concerning either the victim or the witness. This, in part, is a consequence of how cases are presented in court, and the intentions of the lawyers for the prosecution and the defence. As the defence lawyer presents evidence favouring the defendant (evidence that corroborates the defendant's innocence), the objective is to find flaws in the victim's and the prosecution's witnesses' testimony during cross-examination. The emphasis in the cross-examination by the prosecutor is to find flaws in the testimonies of the witnesses for the defence and that of the defendant (if he or she takes the stand). Most of the evidence presented for the prosecution is based on police investigation and the way that the resulting information is amassed in order to recreate the crime event. There are many stages in the process of solving crime and restoring justice where problems, such as false confessions that might be due to coercion during police interrogation, or unfair and biased representation in court, can occur. Problems arising during crime solving and in the courtroom can be avoided, however, by improving on the procedures currently in place. This is where the knowledge accrued by forensic psychologists, of human behaviour and in particular of the offender–victim–witness interaction, can be of considerable help to the different branches of the criminal justice system (i.e. police, probation, courtroom and prison).

Forensic psychologists have an abundance of information to refer to, including mainstream psychological research from the fields of cognitive and social psychology. Research from cognitive psychology has been particularly helpful in areas such as understanding how our memory performs under stressful conditions (e.g. during a criminal event), and the best ways of maximising memory retrieval. In the case of social psychology, understanding how social biases and attitudes interact to affect our perceptions of people has led to research findings about how the physical appearance of a defendant can influence the jury's verdict. Forensic psychologists are in the fortuitous position of being able to keep the criminal justice system informed of new findings from psychology – one example being the social science brief delivered to the judge via an *amicus curiae* (or 'friend of the court' brief). Another means of divulging information is through collaborative research. Collaborative research with police, probation and prison services has often been effective, and has led in many cases to changes in practice and ethos. For instance, it is through collaborative research between the police and forensic psychologists that an effective way of interviewing witnesses called the cognitive interview has been successfully implemented. Further research of this nature has also improved the way police interrogate suspects. The working ethos of having to obtain a confession no matter how the interrogation is carried out has been replaced by an equitable interview approach. Furthermore, the reliability of evidence presented in court, especially eyewitness testimony, is of paramount importance. As a consequence of psychological research on memory, the credibility of eyewitness evidence is questioned and scrutinised to ensure the description of events and of the perpetrator provided by witnesses is plausible. In the U.S., having an expert psychologist provide evidence concerning the reliability of eyewitness testimony is not uncommon. To understand how forensic psychologists can help improve practice in the criminal justice system, from its initial stage of police evidence-gathering to presenting a case in the courtroom, the legal process needs some explanation.

WHAT HAPPENS AFTER THE CRIMINAL EVENT?

Once a victim's or witness's account of a criminal event has been reported and recorded by the police as a crime, a process of criminal investigation occurs. Investigating a crime involves delegating police resources, under the supervision of the Chief Detective in charge of the case, to the task of interviewing the victim(s) and witness(es). If it is a homicide, then the forensic team gather physical evidence left at the crime scene and provide police with a plausible scenario of events during the murder. Forensic psychologists are rarely, if ever, involved in this process, although the information regarding the physical evidence can help inform any deductions made about the murderer's motivations and choice of victim. However, forensic psychologists do help police with their investigations, both indirectly (by providing optimum strategies for obtaining information from witnesses and suspects) and directly (by providing a probable profile of the offender).

In England and Wales, police have to present their case to the Crown Prosecution Service (CPS), which reviews the evidence and predicts the likelihood of the prosecutor successfully obtaining a guilty verdict. The equivalent to the CPS in Scotland is the Crown Office and Procurator Fiscal Service, and in Northern Ireland the Public Prosecution Service. Any cases where the CPS predicts a less than 50 per cent chance of conviction will not be presented in court. For those cases which do go to court, however, a process of preparing evidence for or against the suspect (currently on **remand** in prison) now takes place. In the U.K. the accused on remand has a series of interviews with the appointed solicitor acting as defence lawyer. In the U.S. these interviews are conducted by a lawyer who is referred to as an attorney-at-law. It is the responsibility of the defence lawyer to organise a team of lawyers who develop a case for the accused founded on evidence demonstrating his or her innocence (see Box, Solicitor or Lawyer, below).

SOLICITOR OR LAWYER: WHAT'S THE DIFFERENCE?

In the U.K. we generally use the term solicitor for someone who practises law and who represents the client in court. In the U.S. there is no use of the term solicitor; instead a lawyer is a person who both provides legal advice to the client and conducts their case in the courtroom. Generally in the U.S., however, the lawyer who represents a client in court (for either the defence or the prosecution) is known as the attorney-at-law, whereas the lawyer equivalent to a solicitor is known as the attorney. There are other interesting terms used: in the U.K. a barrister does not normally deal directly with the client (the solicitor tends to do this) but represents the client in the courtroom. In both the U.K. and U.S., the term 'counsel' pertains to a group of legal advisors working on the case behind the scenes.

Forensic teams working on behalf of either the prosecution or the defence endeavour to find flaws in the forensic evidence presented by the opposition (i.e. the defence attempt to discredit the evidence presented by witnesses for the prosecution and vice versa). By the time of the trial, both the prosecution and the defence should have their evidence ready for the court. In the courtroom, the interplay between expert witnesses, witnesses, the defendant and members of the judiciary is defined by courtroom etiquette (see Figure 6.1). In the U.K. this has been in existence since the introduction of common law courts based on an adversarial system of law during King Henry II's reign in the 1160s. This was cemented further by the Magna Carta drawn up by King John, as directed by his many barons, in 1215. From then on there have been modifications and additions in the form of new legislation.

Despite some common ground in the legal systems across the countries of the U.K., there are three legal systems in existence: English law, Scots law and Northern Ireland law. This means that

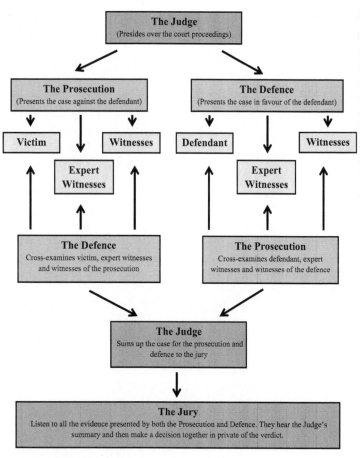

Figure 6.1 Outline of a typical courtroom procedure

there are variations in the way that courts are conducted and in the terminology used. Even though the adversarial system of law defines the courtroom structure and the role of the judge and jury, in the case of Scots law, for instance, there is an element of inquisitorial procedure. This comes in the form of the rule of special defences, where the accused (defendant) provides the prosecution with notice of the number of defences prior to trial; this is known as 'defence disclosure'. A failure to do so means he or she cannot argue the defence in court. This procedure is akin to the inquisitorial system, where evidence is brought forth to the inquiring judge and not a jury. Defence disclosure requires evidence to be presented to the prosecution, which then decides what can be presented to the jury in the courtroom. Before there was **geographical mobility**, the adversarial system relied heavily on witnesses saying what they had seen and knew about the offender. That is, since people largely remained in the same area for life they would be very familiar with others who lived in their locality. Even with geographical mobility today, there is much emphasis placed on the testimony of witnesses – too much, some may argue. This can lead to problems of mistaken identification and the incarceration of an innocent person, as demonstrated in the cases of Sam Hallam in the U.K. and Tony Ford in the U.S. (see Box below).

THE CASE OF SAM HALLAM

The eyewitness testimony of one person led to the arrest and conviction of Sam Hallam in 2005. He was accused of murdering 21-year-old Essayas Kassahun, a trainee chef working in London who was stabbed in the head in 2004. Hallam was 17 years old when he was arrested and 18 when given a life sentence for murder, but always maintained his innocence. There were two witnesses who claimed to have seen Hallam at the murder scene; however, one witness later withdrew her statement, commenting that she 'was just looking for someone to blame' (quoted in Evans 2012). There was no physical evidence from forensics to corroborate his presence at the crime scene. Nevertheless, he was convicted and spent seven years in prison before his conviction was quashed. QC Henry Blaxland said, 'It is our case that this appellant Sam Hallam – and I put it boldly – has been the victim of a serious miscarriage of justice brought about by a combination of manifestly unreliable identification evidence, the apparent failure of his own alibi, failure by police properly to investigate his alibi and non-disclosure by the prosecution of material that could have supported his case' (quoted in Evans 2012).

THE CASE OF TONY FORD

In El Paso, Texas, Tony Ford was convicted of murder in 1991 based on false eyewitness testimony. Ford gave two brothers, Van and Victor Belton, a lift to a house belonging to Armando Murillo. They went inside while Ford remained in his car waiting for them to return to the car so he could take them home. The next day he was arrested, as were the two brothers. Murillo had owed a debt to the brothers but had been unable to repay it, so they shot him dead and fired shots on a further three occupants of the household. Van Belton alleged that Ford had murdered Murillo, but in truth it was his brother who had fired the shots. During the investigation, witnesses (Murillo's sisters) were shown a photo spread which excluded Victor Belton but included Ford. One of the sisters selected a photo of a different man but the number of this photo was later attached to Ford's picture. The other sister selected Ford's photo after seeing pictures of him, named as the suspect, on the TV news and in newspapers. There was a major flaw in the way the photo spread was organised and the manner in which police obtained eyewitness evidence. There was no forensic evidence linking Ford to the crime scene, but despite this he was formally charged with murder. Further miscarriages of justice occurred when Ford was denied an expert witness to represent him. After Ford was found guilty, the Murillo sisters were asked if Ford resembled the man who killed their brother – their response was "maybe". After Ford had spent 16 years on death row, DNA linking Victor Belton to the murder was found in 2005, just eight days before Ford's execution date. The Innocence Project worked hard to ensure that Ford was acquitted of murder.

There have been many miscarriages of justice based on eyewitness testimony alone. Eyewitness testimony that is corroborated by other sources of evidence such as physical evidence from forensics can be powerful in ensuring the conviction of an offender, but without corroboration it can be a major cause of mistaken identification.

Miscarriages of justice, however, can also occur long before a case goes to court. The handling of an investigation can be hampered by inappropriate interrogation technique and the misinterpretation of evidence. Forensic psychologists have been involved in improving techniques of interrogation and the cross-connections of psychological with physical evidence. The collaborative research between police and forensic psychology will be considered next.

HOW FORENSIC PSYCHOLOGY HAS HELPED IMPROVE POLICE INVESTIGATION METHODS

To understand ways in which forensic psychology can help improve police performance we have to be familiar with the process of police investigation. Innes' (2002) review of homicide clear-up rates in England revealed that as many as 90 per cent of murders are solved. This, in part, could be due to cases that are easily solved. The ease of solving these crimes relies primarily on the suspect being known to the victim – usually a family member or friend. In such cases a suspect becomes apparent early on in the investigation. Police differentiate between 'self-solvers' and 'whodunits' according to whether there is an obvious suspect. In the case of self-solvers, there is an obvious suspect and physical evidence early on in the investigation; for whodunits, there is no clear suspect. The difference between self-solvers and whodunits determines the processes of investigation used (Innes 2002).

Approximately 70 per cent of murder cases are classified as self-solvers. Such cases normally follow a three-stage investigative approach:

1. Crime scene analysis, where information is collected and examined
2. Following lines of enquiry by interviewing the suspect and witnesses
3. Organising evidence to construct the occurrence of events that can be presented to the CPS.

It is less straightforward for whodunit cases, where an obvious suspect is less apparent. Innes (2002) highlighted five stages involved in whodunit investigations:

1. The initial response
2. Information burst
3. Suspect development
4. Suspect targeting
5. Case construction.

The initial response involves the collection of evidence at the crime scene and the gathering of information available from witnesses. This investigative procedure also occurs in self-solving murder cases. The information burst stage is when police gather more information by interviewing people associated with the victim and making more in-depth inquiries about the victim, such as any criminal connections. As the information and evidence increases in volume and changes in nature, the current suspect might be eliminated from further investigation and others implicated. Suspect development is all about narrowing the field of suspects down to one prime suspect, who then becomes the focal point of the investigation. This is done by targeting the prime suspect and providing evidence to show his or her involvement in the criminal event. Finally, the police piece together all the evidence in a logical sequence to provide a case construction that would hold up in court. During any one of these stages there is the potential for error, in both the way evidence is collected and the interpretation of evidence, which could lead to the apprehension of the wrong individual. Findings from forensic psychology can be particularly helpful in both the collection and interpretation of information.

There are many areas in which forensic psychology has helped improve methods and standards of police investigation:

1. Interviewing witnesses and victims and interrogating suspects
2. Recognition of deceit
3. Profiling offence details and linkage with offender profiling
4. Techniques of identification
5. Eyewitness testimony
6. Awareness of social biases in juror decision making (known as extra-legal defendant characteristics).

These improvements have derived from many years of mainstream memory and forensic psychological research. The first four points will be dealt with in detail here, and points five and six in Chapter 7.

Changes in interviewing strategy have led to more reliable and extensive information being gathered from witnesses and suspects. To understand the impact that psychology has had on interviewing strategy, it is first important to see what came before – the standard police interview, which will be considered in the next section.

INTERVIEWING WITNESSES AND VICTIMS AND INTERROGATING SUSPECTS

Research by Clifford and George (1996) showed that police officers across forces in Britain used a similar interview structure which has become known as the standard police interview. At many levels, this format of interviewing goes against the grain of how an interview should be conducted. According to Clifford and George, if a number of 'rules' are followed when an eyewitness to a criminal event is asked to describe what happened, this will enable them to recall a great deal more detail than the standard police interview allows for. Typical problems with the standard police interview include:

1. During a standard police interview, eyewitnesses are interrupted an average of 11 times. The first interruption typically occurs around 7.5 seconds into their response to the question posed. The implication of this is that witnesses have to constantly shift their attention back and forth in order to answer the initial question, which makes recall difficult. Also, constant interruption sets a precedent in terms of expectation – witnesses learn to be quick with their responses and keep them brief.

2. A closed question/answer format (e.g. 'what was the colour of the car?') tends to be used, instead of the much rarer open question format (e.g. 'what did the car look like?'). This means that questions are often out of sequence with the order of events. The implication of this is that witnesses repeatedly shift their focus of attention and, in doing so, reduce their retrieval of information by 19 per cent on average (Fisher and Price-Roush 1986). This further prevents them from elaborating on their responses, as the time between questions becomes limited.

3. The interviewer typically 'drives' the interview rather than the witness. As a result, the witness becomes passive and only

provides information that directly responds to the question posed. According to Bull (1992), if the witness drives the interview then this passivity can be avoided.

4. The interviewer also falls foul of leading and misleading a witness by unintentionally posing a question that includes information which a witness did not see during the criminal event. This could distort the original memory trace and mislead the witness into thinking that they had seen the details mentioned in the question. Elizabeth Loftus (2005) has conducted many experiments demonstrating the impact on memory recall of leading and misleading questions. In the standard police interview, negative phrasing (e.g. 'I don't suppose you can tell me ...') will demotivate a witness from trying to remember, as will the use of formal 'police speak'. Other problems include the failure to follow-up leads with a 'why' question, and the use of judgemental comments concerning the role of the witness in the investigation. This could prevent the formation of a rapport with the interviewing officer and therefore demotivate the witness from 'going the extra mile' to retrieve information.

The above problems are inherent in the standard police interview conducted across the country in all British police forces. This was a problem not only in the U.K. but in other countries such as the U.S., Canada and Australia. The standard police interview, however, has been slowly replaced by the cognitive interview, introduced by Fisher and Geiselman (1992).

COGNITIVE INTERVIEW

The success of the Cognitive Interview (CI) derives from four mnemonic principles underlying its structure.

- Principle 1 is the mental reinstatement of the context, which is an instruction given by the interviewer to encourage the witness to make a mental recreation of the context of the criminal event. This involves attention to how the witness felt at the time (internal) and their surroundings (external) during the whole event witnessed.

- Principle 2 is an instruction to report everything, which encourages the reporting of any and all details remembered.
- Principle 3 is an instruction to recall details of the event in a different order – this could be a reverse arrangement.
- Principle 4 involves changing the perspective, which is an instruction designed to encourage recalling details of the event from another witness' perspective.

The first two principles enable more cues that might have been encoded in association with memories of the event, and which hopefully encourage further information retrieval. The underlying theories behind the first two principles, multi-component theory of memory trace formation and encoding specificity theory, account for the success of CI. In multi-component theory, a memory trace is considered to have many different sensory associations, such as sound, smell and touch. Hence, questions that enable a witness to explore other aspects of a memory of an event could help activate further details concerning the event. Encoding specificity relates to the second principle; it suggests that the most effective retrieval probe is one which is consistent with how the event was originally encoded. Therefore, a retrieval probe (e.g., 'You said it was during the summer: was it a hot day?') reinstating the original encoding context will be more successful at inducing recall and recognition. Principles 3 and 4 relate to reconstruction theories of memory. Reconstruction theories of memory are concerned with how information stored can be put together again to obtain a new description of an event. It is assumed that during the reconstruction process, information encoded with the event that is less obvious or more implicit becomes highlighted and explicit. This means that witnesses can obtain access to more information.

The CI has endured structural changes which emphasise the first two principles more, and is known today as the Enhanced Cognitive Interview (ECI). The ECI has 13 basic skills which help improve the overall experience for the interviewee:

1. Building a rapport
2. Key listening skills
3. Encouraging spontaneous recall
4. Using open-ended question format

5. Pausing after responses to questions
6. No interrupting
7. Asking for detailed accounts
8. Enabling intense concentration
9. Encouraging the use of imagery
10. Enabling the recreation of the original context
11. Adopting the witness's perspective
12. Asking compatible questions
13. Referring to and following the sequence of the CI.

There are 11 phases of the ECI which help improve information retrieval by creating an effective rapport with the interviewer (see Box, pp. 158–9).

THE 11 PHASES OF THE ECI

Phase 1 – greetings, personalising the interview

Phase 2 – establishing a rapport with interviewee by asking neutral questions about the person

Phase 3 – purpose of interview is explained and interviewee's attention is directed towards describing everything about the event

Phase 4 – context reinstatement, where interviewee thinks about the context of the event (e.g. visualises layout of the shop)

Phase 5 – interviewee provides free-recall descriptions and details of the event

Phase 6 – questions are asked about what was described and there is further opportunity for interviewee to expand on their responses to the questions

Phase 7 – interviewer asks compatible questions which are consistent with interviewee's current focus of attention (they are encouraged to activate a mental picture of one part of the event and interviewer asks questions about it, then the next, and so on)

Phase 8 – interviewee recalls information from perspective of another witness, helping to facilitate further retrieval

Phase 9 – information is recalled in reverse order, encouraging further recall by dispensing with expectations of what should normally follow (we have organised sets of information about events, clouding our ability to recall the unexpected)

Phase 10 – interviewer summarises interviewee's account of the event and offers another opportunity to add further information

Phase 11 – closure is brought to the interview in order to reduce any tensions and to ensure interviewee leaves on a positive note

See Box, Dando and Milne's research, p. 159, for an example of a CI questioning format.

AN EXCERPT FROM DANDO AND MILNE'S RESEARCH SHOWING HOW CI SHOULD BE PERFORMED

I would like to try and help you to remember as much as you can. As I talk to you I want you to think about each of the things I say, as I say them. Closing your eyes or staring/looking at a blank wall may help you. To begin I would like you to try to think back to the day the event happened. Think about that day ... what had you been doing ... what was the weather like ... Think about the place that the event happened ... try and get a picture of it in your mind. Think about the layout of the place ... think of all the objects that were there ... think about the colours. Think about the smells. How did you feel at the time? Now think about the event and the people involved ... focus on what happened ... when you are ready I would like you to tell me everything that you can remember, in your own time and at your own pace.

(Dando and Milne 2009, pp. 5–6)

The second principle of 'reporting everything' reminds interviewees that all information is potentially useful, even if they think it to be irrelevant.

Some people hold back information because they are not quite sure that it is important or you may think that I already know this information. Please do not leave anything out. I am interested in absolutely everything that you remember, anything that pops into your head. Even partial memories and things you think may not be important. Please tell, just tell me it all.

(p. 7)

The third principle of 'changing the temporal order':

It is natural to go through the incident in your own order. However, I would like to try something which sometimes helps people to remember more. What I would like you to do is to tell me what happened backwards. I know it sounds hard but I am going to help you. To start, what is the very last thing that you remember happening ... what happened before that ... what happened just before that [this prompt can be repeated, if necessary, until the interviewee reaches the beginning of the to-be-remembered (TBR) event].

(p. 8)

The fourth principle of 'a change of perspective':

Try to recall the incident from the perspective of another person involved in the incident. Think about where he/she was and isolate everything that you can remember about them, as if they are in a spotlight. Describe what he/she would have seen.

(p. 9)

The amount of information recalled using the CI is considerably greater than the amount recalled during the standard police interview (see Figure 6.2), as demonstrated by Geiselman et al. (1985) in a study conducted in collaboration with the Los Angeles Police Department.

INTERVIEWING CHILD VICTIMS

Contrary to previous belief, a general recognition that child victims could provide reliable evidence was developed during the 1980s. In

	Standard Interview	Cognitive Interview
Correct information	29.4	41.5
Incorrect information	6.1	7.3
Confabulated information	0.4	0.7

Figure 6.2 The mean number of correct and incorrect responses and confabulated information obtained using the standard police interview and CI

the U.K., the Criminal Justice Act of 1991 allowed children to present their evidence via the medium of a videotaped interview with a specially trained police officer or social worker. This was considered by the Memorandum of Good Practice as an appropriate measure to take for children who might feel intimidated by court proceedings and by the presence of the defendant. This was part of a strategy for Achieving Best Evidence (ABE), a document first published in 2002 and updated in 2007 (Home Office 2002, 2007). ABE interviewing is based on Bull's (1992, 2010) research demonstrating the best strategy for interviewing vulnerable children. The ABE interview protocol has a four-phased approach consisting of:

1. Rapport
2. Free narrative
3. Questioning
4. Closure.

As part of planning and preparation for the interview, interviewers meet the child and consider a number of factors concerning the child such as family background, age, language, religion, gender, any special needs and the child's level of cognition and emotional stability. Interviewers are advised not to discuss the child's ordeal at this point, but should never prevent a child who willingly free-recalls significant events. The child's willingness to talk in an interview is assessed and steps are taken by the interviewer to prepare the child for a formal interview. Davies et al. (2000) highlighted a series of 'abuse trauma variables' that interviewers are to address before the interview. These include:

- Child's attachment to parents
- Age at onset of abuse

- Duration and frequency of abuse
- Type(s) of abuse
- Relationship to abuser(s)
- Extent of violence and aggression
- Existence of coerced sexual activity
- Any adult/peer support
- Any opportunity for child to disclose experience(s)
- Parental response to disclosure
- Existence of any previous intervention.

The ABE interview begins with rapport building. Here the child is allowed to talk freely about neutral topics unrelated to their ordeal. Towards the end of the rapport building the interviewer then establishes the 'ground rules' of the interview, such as telling the truth, and the purpose of the interview. The second phase of the interview allows the child to give an uninterrupted account of their ordeal, referred to as free narration. The interviewer can encourage further responses by using simple prompts like 'so tell me all about that' or 'then what happened?' During the third phase, the interviewer asks questions to clarify the child's account and relate it to the evidence – questions like 'what day did this happen?' Questions should be open-ended – beginning with when, who, what and where. Phase four is the summing up of evidence presented and brings a close to the interview. There is a return to discussion of neutral topics to allow the child to recover from the ordeal of recalling details of their abuse. The interview session is recorded on videotape which can be presented to the court at trial.

The National Institute of Child Health and Human Development (NICHD) developed a forensic interview protocol for interviewing the traumatised child which excludes the questioning and close phase. Developed by Lamb et al. (1996, 2007), it has been used as a protocol for obtaining information from children who have been abused. The protocol is based on mainstream psychological knowledge of how memory and the child's linguistic and cognitive abilities develop. The NICHD interview is similar to the ABE approach to interviewing but instead has three phases, known as introductory, rapport building and substantive or free recall. During the introductory phase, ground rules are set and expectations considered. A rapport is then established by encouraging children to talk about unrelated events such as hobbies they might have. After this children are encouraged to recall their ordeal and are allowed to do so by talking in a continuous stream of narration. Occasionally the interviewer will use open-ended prompts, which research shows are an effective method of obtaining more accurate information. The NICHD interview is considered to be an evidence-based scripted protocol. Even with children who have compromised cognitive or linguistic abilities, and therefore might find narration difficult, the interviewer will accommodate their needs. This is undertaken without downgrading the integrity of this 'best practice' approach. Research findings indicate that as a result of adoption of the NICHD interview protocol, more cases have been accepted for prosecution, more cases have gone to trial and there have been more guilty verdicts (Harris 2010). Both the ABE and the NICHD interview protocols enable children to give a narrative description of events and to recall a substantive amount of information to the level of detail required by the CPS.

THE PEACE MODEL OF INTERROGATING SUSPECTS

Forensic psychological research reveals the importance police place on obtaining a confession during the interrogation of suspects. For some police officers, the failure to obtain a confession is regarded as a poor outcome. Bull and Cherryman (1995) studied police interrogation techniques in detail and found that police regarded their interview as successful only when a confession was obtained. Given that the obtainment of a confession is considered of such importance by police officers, their interview style and structure is designed to encourage confessions. A study conducted by Holmberg and Christianson (2002) revealed that prisoners convicted of a serious crime were more likely to confess during interrogation as a consequence of the interviewing officer's attitude. Kebbell et al. (2006) identified six types of interview style that led to confessions: compassionate, understanding, non-aggressive, honest, non-judgemental and explanation of procedure. In the U.S., the Reid model contains documented advice on how to obtain confessions from suspects. This consists of two phases – phase one focuses on obtaining information and evidence whereas phase two is concerned with the interrogation itself and consists of nine steps. These nine steps provide an outline for how the interviewer should construct the interview – all step are designed to encourage the suspect to confess. In effect the police interview is structured to make the suspect believe that there is an abundance of evidence proclaiming the suspect's guilt. In the U K., Bull and Soukara (2010) found that the most common tactics used to induce a confession were:

- Disclosure of evidence
- Open, leading and repetitive questioning
- Attention to any contradictions made
- Challenging of the suspect's account
- Ability to manage the mood of the suspect.

In the U.K., since the introduction of the PEACE model, there has been an emphasis on using ethical measures in the interviewing of suspects. Griffiths has stated: 'any interview that probes a suspect's account, and explores possible motives and defences, should be viewed as being just as effective as one that gains a confession' (Griffiths 2008, p. 72). So what is meant by PEACE? PEACE is an acronym for:

- P – planning and preparation: this is the process of getting ready for interviewing and can be summed up as 'investigate then interview' rather than 'interview then investigate' (Ord et al. 2004, pp. 3–5).
- E – engage and explain: it is good practice not to have a stressed suspect, which is why it is important to first build a rapport. The interviewer has to use plain English and ensure the suspect understands the interview procedure and questions.
- A – account: a full account of the event is obtained from the suspect without any police interruption. Once details are obtained, the interviewer is allowed to challenge any inconsistencies.
- C – closure: the account is summarised and any points verified. The interviewer will inform the suspect of what will happen next in the criminal proceedings.
- E – evaluation: this is the end of the interview, and a time when the interviewer assesses and reflects on whether objectives were achieved.

The PEACE approach has had mixed results. There is great variation in the way the PEACE interview is conducted, with some elements of the approach being omitted or ineffectively conducted. One major problem is the limited time devoted to training police officers in the use of the PEACE interview. There is a tendency among British police forces to allocate only five days towards learning interviewing skills, which breaks down to two days spent on learning the CI and three on the PEACE approach. Given the intricate nature of acquiring interviewing skills, more time should be allocated, which is what the Investigative Interviewing Strategy (introduced in 2003 by the Association of Chief Police Officers, ACPO) aimed to do. Police training for interviewing and interrogation skills now lasts between one and three weeks and includes courses that can be residential, distance and workplace-based. The West Yorkshire police force now devotes three weeks of training to the PEACE approach.

Interviewing skills are useful for obtaining information about criminal events, but to what extent can the information acquired be considered as true, especially in the case of suspects? Can police be taught how to detect when a suspect is lying during interview?

POLICE RECOGNITION OF DECEIT

Psychological evidence suggests that we find it difficult to detect liars, and the police are no exception to this. In fact Garrido and Masip (1999) showed that experienced police officers were on a par with novice officers at separating suspects who were lying from those who were not. They further showed that police officers were no better at recognising liars than the general public – all performing at chance level. According to Ekman (1996), the psychology of lying is rather more complicated than the process of telling the truth because it relies on two assumptions: the protagonist intends to mislead someone and they do so without any notification to do so. Detecting liars is not easy. There are, however, observable non-verbal communications associated with specific emotions (especially when attempting to deceive) which are difficult to control consciously. Ekman (1992) identified a number of these non-verbal communications or behaviours that are indicative of lying:

- Increased sympathetic nervous activity, such as rapid breathing, blinking and sweating. When an emotion is experienced there is an increase in the activity of the sympathetic nervous system (SNS), part of our autonomic nervous system, which is beyond our conscious control. This nervous activity occurs when there is a **stimulus** signal to prepare for either fighting or running away, known as 'fight or flight'. When a suspect is lying, SNS activity occurs automatically and is revealed by the tell-tale signs of arousal. This arousal is interpreted by the suspect as, for instance, a fear of being caught out.
- Anger can often be detected, expressed, for example, through the raising of one's voice.
- Poorly prepared verbal communication is often littered with error, and continuous pausing provides evidence of a suspect experiencing the fear of being caught because of their lying. This might also be coupled with a high-pitched voice.
- Having a pale face indicates that blood is being redirected by the SNS to the muscles as a consequence of feeling anger or fear (i.e. in preparation for a fight or to flee).
- A suspect who is lying will try to fake the appropriate emotion. The suspect is likely to simulate facial expressions which he or she believes are appropriate. This is difficult to achieve and results in tell-tale signs of falsehood, such as having an asymmetrical facial expression or portraying an emotion too abruptly.
- If SNS activity is absent during the expression of negative emotions such as anger and fear then the emotional expression is likely to be faked.
- There is an assumption that certain features play a major role in the expression of an emotion. In the case of smiling, Ekman pointed out that it is not just the mouth that is important but also the muscles around the eyes (see Box, pp. 166–7).

THE IMPORTANCE OF CERTAIN FACIAL FEATURES IN THE EXPRESSION OF EMOTIONS

Without the activity of muscles around the eyes, the smile is false; this is known as the Duchenne smile. In the case of anger and fear, the forehead and eyebrows play a vital role in different ways. Anger is commonly faked unsuccessfully because of the complicated interaction of the muscles involved in its expression, which is why true anger is considered more likely to be an emotion of an innocent person. This was demonstrated in a study by Hatz and Bourgeois (2010) in which students were given the task of independently solving a mathematical problem. Students were then paired with another student (who was really a confederate working with the researcher) for a period of collective resolution. All students were told that they were not allowed to help the other student, even if they asked for help. There were two conditions, the first in which the student confederate remained anonymous and the second in which the student confederate broke anonymity, claiming it was okay to cheat. When students in the first condition were accused of cheating, they showed more anger, which was genuine, than those in the second condition. It was difficult, however, to separate those in the second condition who were innocent from those who were guilty, as they both expressed the same amount of anger.

Forensic psychologists have been helping police improve their skills at separating suspects who lie from those who tell the truth. In the Netherlands, police were trained to detect whether the relatives appealing to the public for the safe return of their loved one were telling the truth. They were presented with actual British police press conference recordings and had to decide whether the appeals were genuine and the emotions expressed truthful. Despite the use of strong cues such as diverted or focused eye gaze, the police officers performed at chance level; in other words, their hit rate was 50 per cent (Vrij and Mann 2001). These findings do not inspire confidence in the ability of police to detect liars.

Identifying effective behavioural measures can be useful in the detection of liars, but it is important to know what these behavioural measures are. In a study by Strömwall and Granhag (2003), police officers, prosecutors and judges were asked to provide the behavioural measures which they thought were effective in the detection of liars. These were then compared with forensic psychological findings. Interestingly, the police, the judiciary and forensic psychologists agree on some indicators of dishonesty but disagree on others. Strömwall and Granhag found the following:

1. Forensic psychology shows that liars make fewer body movements. Police believe they make more, whereas both prosecutors and judges do not think that body movements are a reliable predictor.
2. Police, prosecutors and judges agree with the forensic psychological literature that sparse detailing in statements tends to be a feature of false statements.
3. Forensic psychology findings suggest there is no reliable relationship between gaze aversions and lying. Prosecutors and judges believe there is no difference between guilty and innocent suspects. Police maintain that liars avoid eye contact.
4. Forensic psychology findings suggest that the pitch of the voice and lying are linked. Police, prosecutors and judges, however, did not entertain this as a feature of lying.
5. Police, prosecutors and judges agree with the forensic psychological literature that there is some evidence of statement inconsistency being a sign of lying.

Identifying behavioural measures indicative of lying is one way in which police competency at detecting liars can be improved. The following research findings by Bond (2008), however, could prove to be very useful in helping to improve police detection of lying suspects. Bond was able to identify police officers who were exceptionally good at detecting lies, labelling them as detection wizards. Bond identified these officers by giving them a series of four lie detection tests. Those who performed at an accuracy of 80 per cent or above were creamed off and given a further battery of lie detection tests the following day. The second series of lie detection tests were divided into four different conditions:

1. A mock crime interrogation (presentation of a fictitious case)
2. Work-relevant history for an employment interview
3. Discussion of people most influential in their lives
4. Description of videos they had seen.

The detection wizards were to interview authentic ex-prisoners under these four conditions, in the hope of providing four very different types of interview situation. The ex-prisoners either lied or told the truth in their four accounts. Police officers scored with an accuracy varying between 31 and 94 per cent. Those who scored 80 per cent or more were asked to continue assessing the different accounts offered by the ex-prisoners while wearing eye-tracking sensors. The eye-tracking sensors monitored the officers' eye gaze and showed them to be highly focused on non-verbal behaviours. This focused concentration on non-verbal behaviours helped them make quick and correct decisions about who was lying. These findings are very enlightening and suggest that officers could be taught the skill of identifying when a person is lying by homing in on non-verbal behavioural activity. If suspects can be forced to lower their guard during interrogation, the likelihood of them revealing their true emotions through their behaviour will be increased, making it easier for police to detect when they are lying. This is exactly what Vrij (2004) tried to induce by using **cognitive overloading**. When provided with too much information, the suspect will find it difficult to maintain the information in memory and to further process it. This creates a situation where the suspect finds the processing demands beyond their language processing limits, which makes it difficult to control their true emotions and non-verbal communication behaviours. Effectively, what happens is that they can no longer orchestrate their lies and manipulate their non-verbal behaviours to mask their true disposition. The art of cognitive overloading during interrogation is a simple interview strategy that could be introduced into police training.

PROFILING OFFENCE DETAILS AND LINKAGE WITH OFFENDER PROFILING

Profiling an offence and offender involves the task of classification – where linkages between elements of a crime and criminal are sought. This is not a novel idea; there is a long history of showing our tenacity for classifying the behaviours and actions of other people. This desire to classify people has not escaped the notice of those who have seen its potential for use by police in their criminal investigations. Being able to predict what type of person is likely to be culpable of committing a specific type of crime is very appealing to police and has become known as offender profiling. There are different focal points in profiling – some profilers adopt the approach of offence profiling, whereas others use offender profiling. The former concentrates on profiling details of the offence; the latter focuses on the offender. Whichever approach is adopted forensic psychology has offered the profiling method to help police make educated assumptions about the likely suspect and where the suspect can be located.

THE FBI APPROACH

The most widely known form of offender profiling began with the FBI Behavioural Science Unit based at Quantico, Virginia, in the U.S. under the authority of Robert Ressler (Ressler et al. 1986). The central focus of the FBI approach is on identifying and locating offenders who repeatedly commit the same crime, such as arsonists, serial rapists and serial killers. The original source of information used by FBI profilers was the many interviews undertaken by Ressler and his colleagues with incarcerated serial rapists and killers. The information from these interviews was stored on a computer database and cross-referenced with evidence from crime scene, forensics and victim reports, as well as recorded personal offender details. The combination of information enabled Ressler to examine the underlying gratification served by the crimes committed, and the motivations behind them. Based on this information, the FBI formulated two distinct classifications or typologies of serial killers: organised non-social and disorganised asocial (referred to as 'organised' and 'disorganised'). Each typology has a number of traits associated with it which are mutually exclusive (see Box, pp. 170–1).

SERIAL KILLERS CAN BE ORGANISED OR DISORGANISED

Hodge (2000) claimed that an offender's actions during the crime and their personality characteristics are connected. Hence, links between the offence, and the behaviour and personality characteristics of the offender can be forged by examining the crime scene. Personal characteristics of an organised serial killer, as defined by the FBI, include: socially adequate; sexually competent; charming; egotist; high IQ; controlled mood; lives with a partner; occupationally mobile; and has a masculine image. Crime scene characteristics include: planned offence; targets a stranger; selects a submissive victim; a controlled crime scene; performs aggressive acts; uses restraints; moves the body; takes the weapon; and leaves very little physical evidence. This criminal event is planned at all stages, including body disposal, and has a strict identifiable **modus operandi** (MO, or method of operation).

Contrast the organised serial killer with a disorganised one and the characteristics are very different. Personal characteristics of a disorganised serial killer include: sexually inadequate; poor hygiene; lives alone; lives and works near the crime scene; low IQ; unskilled work; anxious mood during criminal activity; and shows a change of behaviour. Crime scene characteristics include: victim known; spontaneous event with sudden violence; chaotic crime scene; depersonalises the victim; no restraints; sex after death; body not moved; weapon and physical evidence left at the crime scene. This criminal event is unplanned and has no identifiable MO.

There are problems with the organised/disorganised dichotomy which have been highlighted by Canter et al. (2004) and Taylor et al. (2012). Using statistical analysis (Smallest Space Analysis, or SSA), Canter et al. were able to show that most serial murders were organised and that many crime scene behaviours occurred across most serial murders. They concluded that behaviours classified as organised permeated most serial murders – hence, it is organised behaviour which encapsulates the essence of serial killing. Taylor et al. used a different statistical approach known as agglomerate hierarchical cluster analysis. This is also a multi-dimensional scaling technique designed to find traits that co-occur as clusters. This involves analysing a series of traits, such as restraints used and torture applied but little physical evidence left, to see which traits most commonly occur together across a sample of different crimes and crime scene details. If the FBI's organised/disorganised dichotomy is reliable then the clusters should support this divide by grouping together organised traits which are mutually exclusive from disorganised traits. Despite the many different clusters formed all contained 'rogue' traits belonging to the opposite typology. These findings supported the conclusions of Canter et al. that there is a generic organised element to serial murder. Taylor et al., however, also concluded that it might be more plausible to separate serial murders according to the presence of distinctive disorganised crime scene criteria.

One major problem for FBI profiling is highlighted by the case example of Albert Howard Fish (also known as the Thrill Vulture and Vampire Man). Fish was born in 1870 in Washington DC and spent an unhappy childhood in an orphanage where he witnessed the whipping of boys on a daily basis. He behaved rather oddly, and was seen dancing naked under the moon, eating his excrement and drinking his urine, sticking needles into his genitalia and setting fire to his rectum. In later years he heard voices and experienced hallucinations, at which point his wife and their six children left him. He killed children by strangulation and dismembered their bodies, saving the flesh for later consumption. His job as a house painter provided him with the opportunity to be geographically mobile and with a cellar in which to perform his crimes. Six years after murdering Grace Budd, Fish sent her parents a letter of confession. It is through this letter that police were able to locate him in a squalid room in a New York boarding house. He had murdered 30 children and was given a sentence of death by electrocution. It took two attempts to kill him because of the many needles he had swallowed in his life-time that resided in his body. As you can see, Fish is a contradiction. Many of his personal traits, such as poor hygiene, living alone, being an unskilled worker and sexually inadequate, fit the typology of a disorganised serial killer. Nevertheless, Fish managed to kill 30 children over a long period of time and avoided detection and capture. He must have been organised to be able to continue his serial killing for so long. Fish's MO resembles that of an organised serial murderer, in that there was planning, the use of his own torture and killing tools, and body disposal to evade detection. In effect, there was very little physical evidence left at the crime scene.

HOLMES AND DEBURGER'S FOUR TYPOLOGIES

Another profiling approach, based on the assumption that social and psychological experiences underlie the motivations for behaving in a certain way during a crime, was developed by Holmes and DeBurger (1985). Four typologies describe serial killers according to their relationship with the victim and how the victim serves to gratify their fantasy world.

- The visionary serial killer is compelled to murder as a consequence of what the voices in their head are telling them to do and what the hallucinations they see are showing them. In the U.S., David Berkowitz claimed he was told to kill people by his neighbour's dog.
- Alternatively, the mission serial killer's goal is to eliminate particular individuals. The Boston Strangler in the U.S., who murdered women out of hatred from 1962 to 1964, provides a good example of this.
- Hedonistic serial killers consist of lust-, thrill- and comfort-oriented types. The common element across these three subtypes is that they derive pleasure and self-gratification (i.e. hedonism) from murder. In the case of the thrill subtype, it is the thrill of murdering that provides hedonism. For lust-oriented types it is a sexual gratification, while for the comfort-oriented, murder is a way of achieving a goal such as gaining money. In the U.K., the GP Harold Shipman murdered his elderly patients so that he could alter their wills to obtain money.
- Power/control serial killers obtain gratification through controlling their victims, which gives them a sense of power. This feeling of domination occurs both during and after the crime. In the U.S., Theodore Bundy is a good example of this type of serial killer.

Although there appears to be support for the Holmes and DeBurger's typology approach, the empirical evidence against it somewhat reduces its reliability. Canter and Wentink (2004) demonstrated, using the statistical analysis of SSA, that these typologies were a modification of the organised/disorganised dichotomy. Taylor et al. (2012) also supported this conclusion using the cluster analysis approach.

Canter et al. (2004) used the SSA approach to obtain visual mappings of crime scene criteria. When all the crime scene criteria are entered into the analysis, a visual map is created which shows the most commonly occurring traits at the centre and the least commonly occurring ones at the periphery (see Figure 6.3 for an example of a map). For example, 'victim alive for sex' occurs in 50 per cent of serial killings and is placed at the centre. According to the FBI, this is an organised trait. Less common traits, such as 'ransacking', which occurs in 10 per cent of serial murders, are placed at the periphery of the map. Ransacking is classified as a disorganised trait by the FBI. Canter et al. used the Radex model to classify the role played by the victim during the crime. Three different themes were found: the victim as an object for the killer; the victim as a vehicle; and the victim as a person. When the killer perceives the victim as an object of their action, they find it easy to inflict horrific injuries. When the victim is the vehicle for the killer, the victim becomes a means of expressing the anger, aggression and desires of the killer. The anger directed towards the victim, for instance, might have its origins in the killer's childhood – perhaps symbolising the killer's mother or sister. Canter et al. claim that in this case the victim's humanity satisfies deeper needs of the killer, and that this can lead to extreme cruelty and venting of anger and hatred (this also explains why the victim is methodically targeted). When the killer considers the victim in the role of a person, the victim is considered to have feelings. Under these circumstances, the victim has something the killer wants, and the interaction between victim and killer becomes one of manipulation and violence used to achieve goal satisfaction.

British forensic psychologist David Canter used geographical pro-filing for his first ever profile. Canter assisted British police in their investigation of the 'railway murders' in 1986. The line of inquiry by the police was to establish if they were dealing with one culprit working alone or two working together. Using the crime scene data which was inputted to computer, Canter was able to develop a geographical profile. This was developed through a meticulous

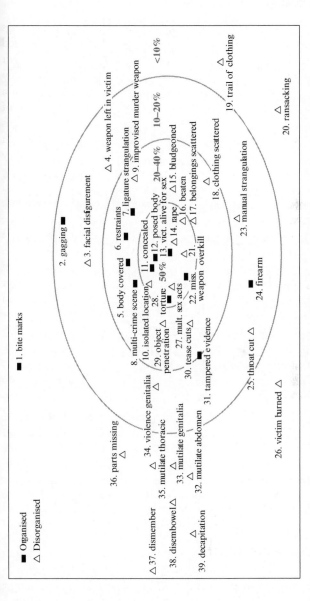

Figure 6.3 An example of a visual map configured by SSA. Adapted with kind permission of Professor David Canter (Canter et al. 2004).

process of comparing information for similarity and difference with regard to murder site locations, estimated times and the order in which these murders were committed. This procedure yielded findings demonstrating a high level of similarity only for some of the murders. Canter suggested that the murderer of the first three victims lived and worked near to the crime scene – the railway. He informed police that criminals have a mental map of an area in which they feel comfortable, which ultimately influences where they commit their crimes. Canter's profile led to the apprehension and arrest of John Duffy, who revealed that David Mulcahy was his partner in crime. The crime scene features of Mulcahy's murders were quite different from those exhibited at Duffy's crime scenes. Moreover, in line with Canter's predictions, Duffy was an employee of British Rail and so had extensive knowledge of the railway network.

The success of geographical profiling rests on the assumption that offenders operate in familiar hot-spot areas where they feel comfortable. There are similarities which parallel the Routine Activity Theory. This states that offenders often commit crimes where they and their target's paths meet. Hence, there has to be some convergence between the two, and when there is no convergence then no crime occurs.

The U.K. is generally considered to be the birthplace of geographical profiling during the 1980s, but some attribute its development to Detective Rossmo (2000) in the U.S., who used a computer program called RIGEL. The system operates in the same way as do other computerised programs like Dragnet – recording identified crime hot-spots, the timings of crimes and the chronological order of their occurrence. Armed with such computerised programs, police have a higher probability of finding where criminals live. Snook et al. (2005) showed that in Germany, as high a proportion as 63 per cent of 53 serial murderers lived within a six-mile zone of their crime scenes. There is no doubt that geographical profiling is an asset to police in their investigative work, but the disadvantage is that it is only as good as the information inputted.

TECHNIQUES OF IDENTIFICATION

Memory research in psychology has contributed towards our understanding of how we recognise and identify human faces. This, in turn, has helped police develop ways of prompting witnesses and victims to retrieve their memories of a perpetrator's face. These methods are labelled as system variables (Wells 1978) and are used to obtain information that can help locate the suspect. One method is to have a line-up, from which the witness selects the suspect if present. This has developed further, through the use of a computer where faces are presented sequentially to witnesses – this means that witnesses can avoid direct contact with the potential suspect. The modern approach introduced to British police forces uses the Video Identification Parade Electronic Recording (VIPER) system. VIPER line-ups have between five and eight faces which match the descriptions made by eyewitnesses. Eyewitnesses are then shown full face, head and shoulder footage of the person for 15 seconds, followed by a three-quarter profile, then returning to the full-face pose. The results obtained by using VIPER are promising – correct identifications have increased and misidentifications decreased. Technological development, however, has made even more strides in the construction of facial composites, which is where our attention will now focus.

There is a long list of different methods used in the construction of a reliable likeness of the suspect's face: PhotoFit, IdentiKit, Mac-A-Mug Pro, Compusketch, FaceKit, E-FIT, CD-Fit and EvoFIT. The early methods adopted involved piecing together features of a face by selecting from an array of individually presented face parts. In effect, the witness had to deconstruct their original memory trace of the perpetrator's face, only to then reconstruct it using the array of face parts. Facial memory research shows that faces are processed holistically, meaning that deconstructing the face into component features in this way is in direct conflict with the way facial information is originally encoded. It is not surprising, then, that methods such as PhotoFit and IdentiKit resulted in facial composites showing little resemblance to the suspect's appearance. Taylor et al. (2011) considered the effectiveness of E-FIT, a facial composite program that is consistent with the holistic cognitive style of constructing faces. In their study, participants were tested for their cognitive processing style – whether they were holistic, analytic or neither. Unlike the holistic cognitive style, analytic styles encourage the learning of individual facial features. After being shown a series of faces, participants were asked to complete a facial composite using E-FIT and it was found that those with a holistic cognitive style out-performed the other two groups (Taylor et al. 2011). Despite E-FIT relying on selecting features of a face, it works within a holistic facial framework, unlike PhotoFit and IdentiKit. By using E-FIT it is possible to develop a facial composite that could be accurately named 20 per cent of the time (Brace et al. 2000). Recent developments involving 'evolutionary systems', however, have increased the accuracy in the naming of facial composites therefore leading to suspect capture. The term 'evolutionary systems' is a metaphor derived from the approach's similarities to Darwinian evolution by **natural selection**. That is, these systems improve over time as a consequence of previous success in creating accurately recalled faces.

Both EFIT-V and EvoFIT operate using this evolutionary system. The way EFIT-V operates is arguably similar to DiPaola's (2002) research. He devised simple facial representations using 25 parameter vectors of a face (i.e. points of measurement of the face such as the spacing between mouth and chin) which then evolved through an interactive genetic algorithm. (In computer science a genetic algorithm is a search heuristic that mimics natural selection.) Kurt et al. (2006) later applied this approach to facial composite constructions. EFIT-V allows the witness to 'evolve' a facial image that resembles the target face they encoded in memory during the criminal event (Solomon et al. 2013). A facial composite is generated by presenting numerous faces each containing random features, from which the witness selects faces best resembling the suspect. These selected faces are then combined to produce another set of faces from which witnesses make more selections. The repetition of this process eventually leads to an 'evolved' composite. Developed in England, it has been reasonably successful, with a 40 per cent hit rate for naming the person depicted in the composite (Solomon et al. 2013), and is currently used in 75 per cent of U.K. police forces. However, it is EvoFIT, developed in the U.K., that has proved most successful, producing a 74 per cent hit rate for naming facial composites (Frowd et al. 2013). Frowd et al. (2012) found that using EvoFIT led to the successful conviction of the defendant in 29 per cent of cases. The reasons it is so successful rests on a system that is holistic, or global, in the way a likeness of the suspect is generated, and less reliant on witnesses' ability to accurately construct the separate features of a face (i.e. the eyes, nose and mouth).

SUMMARY

Forensic psychological research has been particularly helpful in different areas of police investigation such as interviewing witnesses and victims and interrogating suspects; in the recognition of deceit; in profiling offence and offender; and in techniques of identification. The Cognitive Interview has been implemented in many U.K. police forces as a successful tool for obtaining an abundance of good quality eyewitness information which can be used fruitfully in police investigations. It is a significant improvement on the standard police interview which interrupted eyewitness recall of events. The Cognitive Interview is based on sound empirical memory research and theory (i.e. multi-component theory of memory and encoding specificity theory), which is why it works so successfully. Interviewing vulnerable children who are victims of abuse can be difficult, which is why the Memorandum of Good Practice included a strategy for Achieving Best Evidence known as the ABE interview. The four-phased approach is focused on putting children at ease and allowing them to free-recall in a narrative style. Another interview protocol produced the National Institute of Child Health and Human Development, known as the NICHD, interview, which has a similar structure to the ABE interview but has three phases instead. Both approaches are based on empirical memory research. Interrogating suspects has also changed focus as a consequence of forensic psychological research. No longer is the obtainment of confessions the sole goal of interrogation; instead, the emphasis is on using ethical measures of interviewing suspects founded on the PEACE model (planning and preparation, engage and explain, account, closure, evaluation). In effect, this method probes the suspect's account and investigates any motives and defences used by the suspect. Knowing when a suspect is lying is important, and research from psychology has shown that there are tell-tale signs of deceit that police can be taught to recognise. Strömwall and Granhag (2003) have shown that police perceptions of what behaviours constitute lying are often in conflict with research findings. There are different types of offence and offender profiling, but those using the Radex model can offer insightful information about the offender's motivations and the role of the victim during the crime. Geographical profiling compares crime scene information for similarity and difference, which is useful for solving serial crimes. The assumption that offenders operate in hot-spot areas means that they commit their crimes in areas they know well and feel comfortable in. Forensic psychological research has also helped witnesses to improve their quality of facial composite reconstruction. Understanding that facial memory operates by using holistic strategies of facial construction, and not by a feature-by-feature approach, has meant new technologies such as EFIT-V and EvoFIT have helped to significantly improve the facial likeness of a composite.

RECOMMENDATIONS FOR FURTHER READING

Holmes, R.M. and Holmes, S.T. (2002). *Profiling Violent Crimes: An Investigative Tool*. Thousand Oaks, CA: Sage.

Vrij, A. (2004). Why Professionals Fail to Catch Liars and How They Can Improve. *Legal and Criminological Psychology*, 9, 159–81.

7

RESEARCH IN FORENSIC PSYCHOLOGY

Academic and practising forensic psychologists contribute towards the development of forensic psychology by undertaking scholarly activity in the form of research. It is therefore important that forensic psychologists are familiar with research design, methodology and the analysis and interpretation of results. In this chapter, research terminology will be explained and illustrated using examples of research undertaken within forensic psychology. Research generally follows the path of one of two different methodological approaches: quantitative and qualitative. The aims of quantitative and qualitative research are quite different, but each appropriately fills its own niche of problem solving. While quantitative researchers address specific questions and collect data in a numerical format, those adopting a qualitative approach obtain in-depth information increasing their understanding of human behaviour and why it has come about. There are ongoing debates concerning the divide between quantitative and qualitative approaches, but many researchers adopt the methodology that most appropriately solves the problem they are seeking to address; however, there is also an element of working within one's comfort zone. To understand the very nature of forensic psychological research it is necessary to explore the differences between quantitative and qualitative a bit further.

QUANTITATIVE RESEARCH

Broadly speaking, quantitative research follows a scientific methodo-logy which includes the experiment, epidemiological trials (measuring rates of illness in the population) and drug trials (measuring the effects of drugs), intervention studies (comparisons of effect across different techniques) and numerous types of survey. Quantitative research reduces information to numerical data that can be analysed statistically. This can be particularly useful in the quantification of behavioural and emotional states, opinions and attitudes. Due to its highly structured methodology, it is possible to measure, analyse and then generalise and apply findings to a larger sample of the population. This works particularly well when using questionnaires (see Box below, for an example of quantitative method).

WATCHING CRIME TV INCREASES FEAR OF CRIME

Taylor and Hartley (2009) were interested to see whether the amount of crime TV people watched had an effect on the level of fear of crime they displayed. They were also interested to see if age and gender had an impact on the person's fear of crime. These assumptions were based on previous research showing that fear of crime is influenced by the amount of crime TV viewed (Dowler 2003) and the age and gender of the person (Kershaw et al. 2007). A questionnaire containing statements about the type of crime television watched and a rating scale measuring the level of fear of crime experienced was dis-tributed to 45 males and 45 females grouped by age range (18–34, 35–54 and 55–74). The data obtained was numerical and analysed using a statistical test which uncovers any interactions (i.e. associations) between age, gender, fear of crime and the amount of crime TV viewed. All of the researchers' assumptions were supported. Crime TV does influence the amount of fear of crime exhibited. Female ratings for fear of crime were higher than male ratings, especially for the 18–34 and 55–74 age groups. This shows that we need to consider gender and age when examining the relation-ship between TV viewing habits and fear of crime.

It is to the experiment that we shall now turn, as it has been widely used in forensic psychology.

THE EXPERIMENT

The experiment has been described as a method consisting of prescribed stages: aim, hypothesis, participants, design, materials, procedure, analysis, results, discussion and conclusion. Hence, the question to be addressed is broken down into bite-sized aims which are redefined as statements that make predictions about the projected findings. These statements are called hypotheses. For example:

> Participants asked misleading questions about a car accident are more likely to recall incorrect information compared to those asked non-misleading questions.

In this case the hypothesis is making a prediction about the direction of difference in the outcome. Sometimes it is more appropriate to simply state that there will be a difference without predicting the direction of difference, as the following demonstrates:

> Participants in the misleading and non-misleading question conditions will recall information differently.

The hypothesis is an important starting point as it provides researchers with a structure for the design and procedure of the experiment. An experimental design can be defined as a method of research where a group of participants is subjected to specific treatment, the results of which can be compared with the results for participants in a control group. The specific treatment is known as the experimental variable. The researcher is interested to know the impact that this variable has on the participants. The control group, however, is not subjected to the same variable. This makes for a good control measure, for comparison's sake. There are different types of design depending on the nature of the experiment being conducted: related, unrelated, matched and single. These terms refer to the structure of the experiment and the variables that participants are subjected to (see Box, below).

DESIGN AND VARIABLES

In the case of a related design, all participants are allocated to all groups. For example, a participant is shown a video of a fight between two males and is asked to describe the incident immediately after viewing the footage and 30 days later. Hence, the participant recalls information under two time constraints: immediate and delayed recall. The variable defined by the researcher, such as when the participant recalls information from memory, is called the independent variable. How well the participant performs at immediate and delayed recall is known as the dependent variable (i.e. the results).

The participant in an unrelated design is subjected, in this same example, to either the immediate or the delayed timeframe. In using this design, researchers need to find double the number of participants.

A matched design is similar to the unrelated design, except that participants are matched for a host of factors that could influence results (such as age, gender and IQ), so that they can be paired across groups.

A single participant design measures the performance of one individual who is subjected to experimental variables alternating with control variables (a variable held unchanged or constant by the researcher to prevent it influencing the outcome, such as ensuring participants are alcohol free when taking part in an eyewitness study).

It is important that the materials used by the researcher measure effectively what the independent variable is trying to determine. Elizabeth Loftus' experiment on the adverse effects misleading questioning has on an individual's ability to remember information about a car accident highlights the importance of using an appropriate hypothesis, design and variables, and material (see Box, pp. 185–6).

THE EXPERIMENT HELPS TO INFORM EYEWITNESS RESEARCH

American memory researcher Elizabeth Loftus adopted the experimental approach to test for the effects of leading and misleading information on eyewitness memory. Loftus and Palmer (1974) used an ingenious experimental design which enabled them to isolate factors responsible for modifying, changing and even substituting the original event memory trace for a different one. This new memory trace was based on information presented after the witnessed event, known as post-event information. Participants were shown footage of a car accident which was followed by questions. They were randomly allocated into one of two conditions, where they were asked one of the two questions:

1. How fast were the cars going when they hit each other?
2. How fast were the cars going when they smashed into each other?

Interestingly, the two questions resulted in different estimations of car speed. The speed estimations were significantly higher when the word 'hit' was replaced with 'smashed' (34 mph versus 40.8 mph on average). When participants were asked whether they had seen any broken glass (none had been shown in the footage), 32 per cent in the 'smashed' condition responded that they had, compared to 14 per cent in the 'hit' condition. In another study, Loftus et al. (1978) showed a series of slides depicting stages of a car–pedestrian accident. The slides showed a pedestrian being knocked over by a red Datsun stopping at an intersection from a side street. Participants were divided into two conditions:

1. A stop sign was presented (i.e. you must stop before proceeding)
2. A yield sign was presented (i.e. give way to oncoming traffic, stop when necessary and proceed when safe).

The same question was asked to all participants: Did another car pass the red Datsun while it stopped at the stop sign? This meant that for half the number of participants the question was consistent with what they were shown, but for the remaining half (who had read the words 'yield sign') it was misleading. Slides previously presented were paired with new slides. In the case of participants asked the misleading question, the correct slide was selected in 41 per cent of cases, significantly lower than the result for the non-misled group, who correctly chose the slides in 75 per cent of cases. Loftus et al. concluded that misleading information reduces the accuracy of memory to below the 50 per cent chance level. Loftus explained these findings using the substitution hypothesis. This is where misleading post-event information transforms or displaces the original memory trace of an event. This original trace becomes irreplaceably lost. Hence, misleading information can be considered a destructive updating mechanism. In 2005, Loftus referred to post-event misleading information as the misinformation effect, the same phenomenon Robinson-Riegler and Robinson-Riegler (2004) previously called retroactive interference. This is when new information interferes with old information through distortion, substitution or loss of the original memory trace. The experiment has proven a successful method in the investigation of eyewitness memory.

In addition to Loftus' contribution to eyewitness memory, other areas of memory such as prospective memory have helped explain the workings of the witness's mind. Prospective memory plays an important role in our ability to monitor and keep track of our ongoing actions and planned future actions. For example, it helps us to remember where we parked our car and whether it is in a different place to the previous day. The amount of stress that we experience daily has an adverse effect on prospective memory. In the case of eyewitnesses who observe a stressful event, such as a bank robbery where the perpetrator threatens with a gun, then stress levels are likely to increase further. High stress levels during a violent crime can prevent eyewitnesses from attending to details of

:he perpetrator and instead lead to a focus on the weapon (Steblay 1992).

Another important area where the experimental method has proven to be successful is in the investigation of the effect of extra-legal defendant characteristics on juror decision making. Extra-legal defendant characteristics is a generic term describing a collection of social and physical information about a defendant that is irrelevant to the crime of which he or she is accused. In effect, this refers to non-evidential information that provides no factual evidence relevant to the case. Hence, such information should not be considered by the jurors. Jurors, however, like the rest of us, constantly process information about other people which helps in the construction of our own perceptions of their personality. These social perceptions are often arrived at through stereotyping and, despite lacking any validity in many cases, stereotypes are applied and believed to be true. The application of stereotypes by jurors in their decision making can be problematic and may lead to miscarriages of justice. There are many studies demonstrating the impact of non-evidential information on juror decision making (see Box, pp. 187–9).

EXTRA-LEGAL DEFENDANT CHARACTERISTICS THAT CAN MISLEAD JURORS

Extra-legal defendant characteristics are commonly divided into physical and social dimensions. Examples of physical characteristics include: physical attractiveness; scruffy versus clean shaven; bruising to the face; style of dress; and verbal diction. Examples of social characteristics include: community standing; churchgoer; work status; lifestyle; positive versus negative personality; and conformist versus non-conformist. Physical attractiveness and ethnicity are two factors commonly researched in 'mock jury' studies. Mock jury studies adopt an experimental design whereby a number of factors are manipulated by the researcher. Typically the manipulated factors are the type of crime and whether it has been committed by a physically attractive or unattractive defendant. Physical attractiveness is controlled by asking an independent group of individuals to rate a series of photographs using a scale of increasing attractiveness (1–10). The photos with the highest (most attractive) and lowest (least attractive) ratings are then attached to one of two fictitious transcripts, which participants read before making judgements of guilt, extent of guilt and sentence using an increasing scale of fine or length of imprisonment. There might be two or more versions of the transcript, depending on what the researcher is interested in. For example, if crime seriousness is being manipulated then there might be as many as three versions of events, where one element is changed – how serious the crime was. Or instead of crime seriousness, the type of crime committed could be controlled, for such as burglary versus swindle.

Participants, or mock jurors, receive one version of the transcript with either the attractive or unattractive photograph attached. Here's an example of two different crime scenarios:

1. Burglary with attractive photograph
2. Burglary with unattractive photograph
3. Swindle with attractive photograph
4. Swindle with unattractive photograph.

Research findings demonstrate that the physically attractive defendant was sentenced more leniently for burglary than for swindle. Also, the physically attractive defendant received shorter sentences for burglary than the unattractive defendant (Sigall and Ostrove 1975). Lenient sentencing for attractive defendants occurred even when participants were asked to give a sentence rating based on no information other than a photograph of the defendant who had been previously rated as physically attractive by an independent group of participants. Hence, the sentence and physical attractiveness ratings correlated highly, such that the higher the attractiveness the lower the sentence scores. It thus appears that participants inadvertently use this extra-legal defendant characteristic to decide an appropriate sentence when there is no other information to refer to (Leventhal and Krate 1977). Stewart (2001) also found this attraction-leniency effect, showing that defendant attractiveness correlated negatively with punitive sentence ratings. In 2007, Taylor and Butcher conducted a mock jury study where they tested three hypotheses:

1. Physically attractive defendants will be rated leniently for extent of guilt and sentence
2. Black defendants will be rated punitively for extent of guilt and sentence
3. An interaction between ethnicity of the defendant and the mock juror is influenced by the level of defendant physical attractiveness.

Their findings did not support an interaction (association) between defendant and mock juror ethnicity. Instead, an interaction was found for defendant ethnicity and physical attractiveness for sentencing only. Unattractive Black defendants received punitive sentence ratings, which occurred after they were rated guilty. This implies that attractiveness played little role in the early decision of a guilty verdict. Ethnicity had more influence after a guilty verdict was determined – that is, when mock jurors made decisions of sentence. It is then that ethnicity and attractiveness combined to have an interactive effect on secondary level decision making (i.e. on sentence instead of guilt). Taylor and Butcher (2007) concluded that two (or more) extra-legal defendant factors can affect jurors' decision making.

While experiments provide information about how defined variables impact on specific behaviour, the adoption of the survey method can enable researchers to obtain more wide-ranging information.

THE SURVEY

The survey method generally involves the use of questionnaires, self-assessment rating scales and standardised tests. The use of questionnaires has helped researchers to understand the relationship between emotional stress and memory recall for criminal events.

Some researchers have studied the relationship between emotional stress and memory in a 'real–world' setting. Christianson (1992), who has reservations about laboratory-based research, showed that memory for negative emotional events is superior to that for neutral events under natural conditions (see Box below).

NEGATIVE EMOTIONAL STRESS FOCUSES THE MIND

Christianson argued that attention increases when negative emotional events are experienced. This, he claimed, was good because it heightened the ability of witnesses to recall information, especially key details that are central to the observed event. Christianson and Hubinette (1993) asked 110 witnesses, who between them had seen 22 bank robberies, about their experiences. They also rated their own emotions during the event using a self-assessment rating scale. No correlation was found between emotionality ratings and recall. These real-life witnesses to criminal events were able to describe their ordeal with clarity and remembered vast amounts of information. Christianson and Hubinette concluded that contrived laboratory experiments produced contrived findings that did not reflect real-life experiences. These witnesses were able to retrieve both good quality and a large quantity of information describing their ordeal, despite it being highly stressful.

Self-rating scales have been used in another area of eyewitness investigation – the accuracy–confidence issue. Studies have shown that being confident does not necessarily equate to providing an accurate eyewitness testimony. Recently, however, Luna and Martin-Luengo (2010) showed that there is an incremental relationship between accuracy and confidence. After participants viewed footage of a bank robbery they were asked questions about the content of what they saw. They were also asked to rate how confident they were about each answer they gave. They found that if a participant gauged their confidence at 80 per cent then there was an 80 per cent probability that they were correct. Luna and

Martin-Luengo concluded that confidence estimations were a good index of an individual's level of accuracy.

QUALITATIVE RESEARCH

The qualitative approach is considered to be a method of exploratory research. Often, qualitative methods are employed to scan a problem area to gain insight into the underlying motivations or reasons why something occurs. This can be applied, for example, to understand plausible reasons why an offender behaves antisocially. Qualitative methods very often provide ideas for conducting quantitative research and, hence, can be considered to be a 'surveyor of the land'. There are different types of qualitative methods used, such as unstructured and semi-structured interviews, focus group discussions, analysis of media (spoken or written) and observation. Sample size in all of these examples is generally small, and participants are selected on the basis of a predefined characteristic (e.g. female or an ex-prisoner). Exploratory questions asked could include 'what it means to be a delinquent' or 'what it means to be a mother in prison away from her children'. Given that qualitative research rarely uses measurements or statistics, it is important to decide whether the objective of the task is to understand the meaning of something or to measure it. If understanding the meaning is the aim then the approach used is most likely to involve the in-depth descriptions that can be obtained through qualitative methods. Another important point to consider when deciding to use qualitative methods is whether the problem area has been researched before and whether there is any available information that could further the researcher's knowledge. In the case of obtaining information from eyewitnesses, the most appropriate method of inquiry is the interview – given that the information to be provided by the eyewitness is novel, it makes sense to have an exploratory approach. There are three types of interview that forensic psychologists use: structured, unstructured and semi-structured.

THE INTERVIEW

If the interviewer is interested in finding information about a specific topic then it is highly likely that an interview will be planned using a set of predetermined or standardised questions – a structured interview. This is similar to a questionnaire, with the difference that there is face-to-face interaction with the person of interest. There are likely to be specified criteria concerning who should be interviewed in this way. There is some question as to whether the structured interview should be classed as a qualitative method, as it is commonly used when conducting survey research. The unstructured interview, on the other hand, typifies the qualitative approach. It is commonly used in clinical forensic interviews, especially when evaluating sex offenders. Unstructured interviews, as the name suggests, have very little structure and the interviewer will ask open-ended questions in response to what the interviewee has said. The interviewee is given control over the interview and drives the direction of discussion. It has been criticised as being an unreliable method for assessing sex offenders, so the approach is often supplemented with various structured psychological tests. While it is good practice to enable witnesses to free-recall information about their ordeal, even the cognitive interview (CI) has some structure and the interviewer some control over how it is conducted. For this reason, it is probably fair to classify the CI as a semi-structured interview. There are set phases of approach when conducting the CI which interviewers adhere to. Nevertheless, during these phases the ball is in the interviewee's court. An example demonstrating the success of interviewing a victim using the CI can be seen in the Box, pp. 192–3.

STEPHANIE SLATER HELPED TO CAPTURE HER KIDNAPPER

In 1992, Stephanie Slater was kidnapped while showing a prospective buyer a property in Birmingham, England. She was gagged and blindfolded and transported to a make-shift coffin inside a wheelie bin located at her kidnapper's workshop in Newark. On numerous occasions she was threatened with electrocution via electrodes placed on her legs. A ransom of £175,000 was demanded from her boss. She was only allowed out in the morning to eat breakfast and to relieve herself. She was tortured and raped, as well as experiencing the constant psychological fear of being electrocuted. Despite her fear, she attempted to make conversation with her kidnapper, and they developed a rapport – she even asked him for a hug, a request which he obliged. She developed a rapport and wanted a hug so that she could gather more information about him such as his body and facial build, the way he smelled and the tone of his voice. When she was alone at night she listened for sounds, and could hear a distant train as well as hear rats running around. Surrounding noises and smells were indicative of a garage workshop. The ransom was paid and Stephanie was released, but her useful information, which was retrieved during the Cognitive Interview, meant that it was not long before Michael Sams, her kidnapper, was caught. Her memories were embellished with rich multi-model sensory information despite the absence of visual data. CI enabled her to free-recall her memories of her ordeal.

Another method of obtaining information in an exploratory way comes from the use of focus group discussions.

THE FOCUS GROUP DISCUSSION

Sometimes referred to as group interviews, in this method a group of individuals engage in guided conversations about a specified topic. One particular feature of the group interview relates to the fact that each individual is privy to what the others say. These statements and comments can facilitate memories of personal experiences linked with the topic discussed. In effect, each group member is interacting and engaging with each other, to produce a variety of interpretations and meaning relating to the topic discussed. A focus group was used by Miller et al. (2006) to explore the perceptions of therapeutic effectiveness among a group of therapeutic community residents in the U.K. Researchers were interested in the opinions held by the patients of the Triple C Programme, an intervention helping offenders to solve social problems using non-violent means. In particular, they wanted to know if the treatment received promoted psychological change. Psychiatric forensic inpatients of the programme were typically from deprived and dangerous social environments, dominated by inner city London gang culture. The objective of the programme was to teach offenders alternative ways of managing situations relating to offending behaviour. This might involve interventions which increase social problem solving, empathy and emotional stability while reducing cognitive distortions. Participants of the programme are expected to engage in role-play to practise their new-found social skills. On completion of the programme a focus group discussion was organised which allowed participants to talk freely, expressing their opinions of the programme's effectiveness. One of the main concerns expressed in the focus group was the less-than-real-life role-play situations used (Miller et al. 2006). Studies of this sort allow offenders to have a say in their own rehabilitation.

ANALYSIS OF MEDIA

One approach to analysing spoken or written information is to use discourse analysis, first introduced by sociologist Harold Garfinkel in 1967 as a method of deconstructing spoken language. Garfinkel claimed that analysing the content of what people say is an important way of understanding how people make sense of their social world. As a method, discourse analysis has helped forensic psychologists to investigate how people perceive criminality through the deconstruction of what they say. Worrall (1990) highlighted the differences in perception held by medical and legal professionals of women who commit offences. In particular, there were differences of opinion regarding the dimension of cognition. For example, psychiatrists attributed female criminality to mental illness or a mental state of helplessness, unlike magistrates, who considered these women as lacking common sense. In a very different study, Protess (1993) examined two very different Chicago newspapers: *The Tribune* and *The Sun Times*. Hate crime-related articles were analysed for sentences containing 'hate crime', 'inter-racial crime', 'racial disturbance' and 'racial crime'. These were compared with recorded hate crime data, only to find a significant discrepancy between what the newspapers suggested and what was actually the case. Actual hate crime figures showed that the majority of victims were from ethnic minority groups, but newspapers printed that most victims were White and most offenders were Black.

HE OBSERVATION

There are two types of observation method: participant and non-participant observation. Participant observation involves the observer entering the social world of those under investigation, and by doing so becoming both observer and participant. The true objective of the observer can be concealed from or revealed to those being studied. Non-participant observation means the observer keeps a distance from those being observed and is considered to be a 'fly on the wall' who watches but does not interact with the subject matter in any way. This type of observation method typically uses reporting of specified behaviour by way of tally counts (how often behaviours occur); observer narratives (notes taken which are used as a basis for collecting data at a later time); and audio or video recordings. In the context of forensic psychology, this method could be applied to observing risk-taking behaviour of offenders within a prison setting. While sociologists use participant observation more commonly in the study of deviant gang behaviour and other criminal cultures, in contrast, non-participant observation is frequently used by forensic psychologists under contrived experimental conditions such as observing and measuring behaviours. Such an experiment was undertaken by Zimbardo in 1971, known as the Stanford Prison Experiment, in which the participants were observed covertly by Zimbardo and his colleagues (see Box, pp. 195–6).

'PRISONER' AND 'GUARD' PARTICIPANT BEHAVIOUR WITHIN A SIMULATED AND CONTROLLED PRISON SET-UP

In a basement of the psychology department at Stanford University, a mock prison was devised consisting of three six-by-nine foot prison cells sleeping three mock prisoners, rooms accommodating mock guards, a room serving as a prison yard and an area used as a solitary confinement room. Twenty-four volunteers were randomly allocated to the role of prisoner or guard and were paid $15 daily over a 7-to-14 day period. The prisoners remained in the prison set-up for 24 hours a day during the study, while the guards worked in 8-hour shifts. When their shift was complete they could go home until the start of the next shift. Hidden cameras and microphones enabled Zimbardo and his researchers to observe the behaviour of the prisoners and guards and to monitor the interactions across the two groups. Unfortunately, the study had to be stopped after only six days. The reason for this was that the guards became hostile and dehumanised the prisoners, who became increasingly stressed and anxious. The aggression and abuse towards prisoners caused some to cry and suffer acute anxiety (those who did had to be released early). Zimbardo concluded that the situation plays a powerful part in influencing human behaviour. The guards had control and wielded power while the prisoners became passive and depressed. Zimbardo later likened the Stanford Prison Experiment to real-life examples of abuses taking place at Abu Ghraib towards Iraqi prisoners. However, it has been brought to light by Reicher and Haslam (2003) that the experiment had real flaws in its design – such as the fact that Zimbardo encouraged the guards to behave tyrannically. When Reicher and Haslam conducted the same experiment but remained uninvolved, the resulting observations were very different – the prisoners overthrew the guards. It is clear that observational methods that involve role-playing require tighter ethical guidelines and design.

Observing participants within an experimental set-up can be very enlightening and provide information useful in the understanding of criminal behaviour. For example, Zimbardo's observations can offer ideas about how serial killers can be so abusive towards their victims. It also demonstrates the important impact that situations can have on the behaviour of youngsters who find themselves caught up in delinquent gang culture.

Although quantitative and qualitative research methods have been discussed separately it is important to note that, very often, researchers adopt both as a strategy for studying and obtaining as much information as possible regarding the topic of interest.

SUMMARY

Conducting research helps increase knowledge and test existing theories for their validity. Within the context of forensic psychology, research helps inform practice and improve the understanding of offenders and offending. Research can be divided into two methodological approaches: quantitative and qualitative. Quantitative research typically follows a scientific methodology, using experiment and survey, for example. These methods produce numerical data lending itself to statistical analysis. In forensic psychology, many types of experiment have been conducted but the most popular area of investigation is memory. Loftus and Palmer's experiment on misleading information is a classic example showing how memory traces can be easily substituted by post-event information. Loftus demonstrated the destructive updating mechanism of misleading information. Prospective memory also plays a key role in monitoring and keeping track of our actions. Experiments also show how jurors find it difficult to ignore extra-legal defendant characteristics – traits such as physical attractiveness – and support concerns about jurors making judgements based on appearance, for example. Surveys are used to investigate opinions, attitudes and self-ratings of experiences relating to criminal events. Alternatively, qualitative research makes use of methods such as interviews, focus groups, analysis of media, and observation. The information obtained is non-numerical; therefore, statistical analysis is rarely performed. The depth of information obtained helps forensic psychologists bring meaning to the data. The interview approach has helped forensic psychologists develop the cognitive interview (CI) now used by many police forces in the U.K. Focus groups offer forensic psychologists insight into the effectiveness of intervention techniques such as the Triple C Programme. By enabling psychiatric forensic inpatients to discuss their experiences of the programme, the researchers were able to record their perspectives in detail. The analysis of media helps us to understand meaning, opinion and the perspectives of others based on what they say and write. Observation techniques enable forensic psychologists to view information they would find difficult to obtain using any other method – the Zimbardo Stanford Prison Experiment is one such example.

RECOMMENDATIONS FOR FURTHER READING

Huss, M.T. (2008). *Forensic Psychology: Research, Clinical Practice, and Applications*. Chichester: Wiley and Sons.

Langdridge, D. (2003). *Introduction to Research Methods and Data Analysis in Psychology*. Upper Saddle River, U.S.: Pearson Education.

8

RESPONDING TO NEW CHALLENGES

The work of the forensic psychologist is not carved in stone. Both academic and practising forensic psychologists need to be able to respond to developments in psychology and to technological advancements. In this final chapter we examine recent developments that forensic psychologists will need to respond to if the field is to remain a dynamic and proactive one.

Academic forensic psychologists, despite having a vast array of topics worthy of research within the subject area, are more restricted to a role of lecturer/researcher. Nevertheless, they too can be involved in providing police, social workers and the judiciary with information relevant to, for example, the investigative process or the reliability of evidence. Forensic psychologists have defined roles but they liaise with other professionals and work within the context of the legal system. Changes to the nature of their work occur as a consequence of new legislation both within the criminal justice system and within mental health services. New legislation influences the profession and the way forensic psychologists operate within it. Change also occurs within psychology per se. Changes in 2013 to the Diagnostic Statistical Manual (DSM), considered an encyclopaedia of psychological conditions, have had an impact on the assessment of certain conditions such as autism. No longer does Asperger Syndrome exist; instead, an umbrella term, clustering similar behavioural traits together under Autistic Spectrum Disorder, will be used in future. Given that some offenders were previously classified as having Asperger Syndrome under the old system of DSM-IV-TR (the revised fourth edition), the way they are classified and therefore assessed and treated now under DSM-5 (the fifth edition) is different. Attention Deficit Hyperactivity Disorder (ADHD) has also seen some changes, such as the recognition of the condition throughout the lifespan and the age at which symptoms first appear (which was 7 years, now increased to 12).

Coupled with changes in DSM-5, new mental health legislation, in the guise of the Mental Health Act (MHA) 2007 in the U.K., has meant forensic psychologists have to work within the confines of two masters. The MHA has, in many ways, increased ambiguity over definitions of what constitutes a mental health disorder. As discussed in Chapter 3, the MHA 1983 provided clearer guidance concerning what type of individual can be considered as mentally disordered and, in the case of offenders, the options available for assessment, treatment and rehabilitation and appropriate punishment. The problem becomes complicated when an offender has a mental disorder and is considered to be dangerous. In the MHA of 2007, the guidelines are less clearly defined, which muddies the waters as to which jurisdiction the offender now comes under – the MHA or criminal law.

Even though forensic psychologists working in the U.K. are restricted by the MHA, DSM-5 and the law (i.e. the Criminal Justice Act 2003 or CJA) they are free to choose their clinical approach and working paradigm. (Forensic psychologists working in the U.S. are bound by similar restrictions in terms of mental health and legal legislation.) The clinical approaches and working paradigms used are derived from a number of theoretical approaches within psychology, most of which have been previously discussed. Most theoretical approaches within psychology offer a working paradigm outlining how human behaviour can be understood, assessed and treated. Forensic psychologists normally subscribe to one or more of these theoretical frameworks which inform their clinical practice. For example, a behaviourist approach focuses on the triggers associated with the initialisation of the criminal behaviour. The stimulus-response trademark of **behaviourism** has led to treatment approaches such as aversion therapy and covert masturbatory satiation, often used to alter the sexual behaviour of sex offenders.

A cognitive approach focuses on the faulty thoughts, emotions and distorted thinking patterns lying at the core of sexual offending. It is through the amalgamation of behaviourism and cognitive psychology that forensic psychologists offer a robust treatment known as cognitive-behavioural therapy (CBT). The objective of CBT is to substitute deviant behaviours for appropriate and socially acceptable ones. In the case of sex offenders, this means the substitution of deviant thoughts about young children and sexually oriented behaviours towards them with more socially appropriate thoughts and behaviours.

Another factor influencing the way forensic psychologists work has been the recent developments in medical technologies such as brain scanning techniques. This has had a major impact and continues to do so, especially where the results of brain scans of murderers can be used as evidence in legal representation. This has brought about controversy concerning where a line should be drawn between what constitutes admissible and non-admissible evidence. More concerning still is the question of what happens to a murderer who is found to have a brain deficit or dysfunction. This opens a gateway to the whole philosophy of punishment, retribution and rehabilitation, which further impacts on other factors of law such as deterrence and public safety. These are important factors to consider as they lie at the heart of criminal law, which in turn is what the infrastructure of law rests upon. One deciding factor of a defendant's guilt is the extent to which they have free will over their behaviour. Brain scans showing deficits might be taken as evidence of a defendant having very little free will – so where does this leave jurors, if all other evidence shows the defendant to be guilty?

These three important influences on forensic psychology (i.e. MHA/CJA, DSM-5 and brain scanning) will be further explored in this chapter in the context of possible future changes to the role of the forensic psychologist. The way the MHA and CJA have influenced the work of forensic psychologists is considered first.

THE MHA AND CJA AND FORENSIC PSYCHOLOGISTS

In the U.K., individuals who have mental health issues are treated by mental health services. Contact with forensic psychologists occurs when an individual is considered to be at medium to high risk of causing harm to others. Under these circumstances they are managed within a secure mental health setting. Such individuals often have other problems, such as substance misuse perhaps coupled with a personality disorder, which combine to be the root of offending behaviour. This means their probability of having experienced the court and prison system is very high. As individuals are assessed as low, medium or high risk for harmful behaviour towards others, there are corresponding low, medium and high secure services designed to provide appropriate care and treatment and level of secure incarceration. As many individuals admitted to secure services have been charged with or convicted of violent acts, the court system will require advice from the professionals working with the offender to decide on the most appropriate service once sentenced. NHS England (2013) documented that there are currently about 680 inpatient beds in high secure mental health services, increasing to 2,800 and 2,500 in medium and low security provision respectively. Put into perspective, this translates to a population prevalence of 1.3, 5.3 and 4.6 per 100,000 respectively. A multidisciplinary approach is taken in which secure services are managed by professionals such as consultant forensic psychiatrists, clinical psychologists, forensic psychologists, mental health nursing staff and other specialists. Each professional service provides appropriate input where required so that the offender has a 'care pathway' operated under the Care Programme Approach. The way this operates in England is described below (the approach is slightly different across Wales, Scotland and Northern Ireland).

It involves:

1. Referral – maintains links with mental health services and advice to reduce future admission to secure forensic services.
2. Assessment and pre-admission – assessment determines the need for admission to a secure placement or the transfer to another. Placement and assessment information provided.
3. Admission, care and treatment – specialist provision provided for assessment, treatment and mental disorder management. Provision of treatment programmes relating to offending behaviour.
4. Forensic care pathway – liaison with relevant local services facilitating discharge.

5. Transition – a care plan is devised through the transition process, whether this is to a community or a prison setting. Forensic mental health teams are involved with implementing the care plan through treatment intervention and rehabilitation strategies based on level of assessed risk.

NHS England 2013

Forensic psychologists, as part of the forensic mental health team, are involved in assessing and implementing appropriate and clinically effective treatment packages. The context of working is within the guidelines of the MHA and CJA. Forensic psychologists also work within the stipulated professional codes of practice of the British Psychological Society and those of the Health and Care Professions Council.

In the U.K., the CJA 2003 provides forensic psychologists with legislation concerning issues relevant to legal practice. This most likely involves providing evidence in court concerning the defendant's mental health status, or risk assessments of predicted future dangerousness (see Box, pp. 203–4). In the U.S., expert forensic psychologists might more commonly be summoned to court to give expert opinion about the reliability of eyewitness testimony, especially if there is no other corroborating evidence.

DANGEROUSNESS IN THE U.K.

There is a set legal threshold of dangerousness and the task of forensic psychologists and other related professionals is to provide evidence to the courts that an individual has crossed it. The task, therefore, is to perform a risk assessment during court proceedings, or before an offender is eligible for release (in this case information is presented to the Parole Board). The risk assessment details are submitted to the court and used by the judge to inform his or her decision as to probable risk. The incarceration of dangerous offenders is a politically charged issue. For example, one political imperative is to keep the public safe by imprisoning those who are a danger and threat to others. This imperative drives a need for researchers (such as forensic psychologists) in both the U.K. and U.S. to develop increasingly sophisticated and accurate assessment tools. Unfortunately, there is a discrepancy in the definition of dangerousness between the CJA and those performing risk assessments. Forensic psychologists in the U.K. (excluding Scotland, who have CJSWs) are just one group of professionals working as part of the Offender Assessment System (OASys) which measures the risks and requirements of offenders. The system of risk assessment categorises the likelihood of reconviction as low, medium or high and the risk of serious harm as low, medium, high or very high. How these translate to CJA categorisations of dangerousness as 'significant risk of serious harm' (Criminal Justice Act 2003) is ambiguous.

As seen in the Box, p. 203–4, definitions used in law are not always consistent with definitions of the same issue used by other professions. This is one problem that is difficult to overcome. Another problem that can be to some extent overcome is the development of improved methods and tools of assessment. This is why conducting research is an important scholarly and clinical activity for forensic psychologists – it helps keep them informed and clinical approaches in forensic psychology up to date.

DSM-5 AND FORENSIC PSYCHOLOGISTS

The changes in DSM-5 will affect the way some individuals are assessed and diagnosed, which will ultimately impact on how offenders with specific mental health issues are considered for treatment. It is not uncommon for offenders to have specific mental health issues which, unless properly assessed and diagnosed, may go unnoticed. There are many prisoners with mental health problems who fail to receive the care and treatment required because they have slipped under the radar. NHS England (2013), for example, estimated that between 20 and 30 per cent of individuals in the criminal justice system in England and Wales have learning disabilities. Of these, one in a hundred has been diagnosed with Autistic Spectrum Disorder, making it as common as schizophrenia. NHS England also claims hat the preponderance of autism is higher in secure hospitals than among the general population. With the revision of DSM-5, the criteria for assessing behaviours considered to be similar to autism are now included under the classification of Autistic Spectrum Disorder. A new section on disruptive, impulse-control and conduct disorders has brought together disorders previously considered under infancy, childhood and adolescence. The conditions included here are oppositional defiant disorder, conduct disorder and intermittent explosive disorder, all of which have seen some changes to their definition but generally describe similar symptoms to those outlined in DSM-IV-TR. These conditions are commonly associated with delinquency. In particular, conduct disorder occurs between 23 and 87 per cent of youths incarcerated in detention facilities (U.S. Department of Justice 2006). In the U.K., Farrington (1995) found that 90 per cent of persistent adolescent offenders had conduct disorder when they were eight years old.

The major changes in DSM-5 have been to the classification of schizophrenia. Under DSM-IV-TR, schizophrenia was divided into five subtypes: catatonic (alternating states of excitement and immobility); disorganised (incoherent communication); paranoid (grandiose beliefs of the self and extremely suspicious); undifferentiated (a mixture of symptoms from other subtypes); and residual (presence of fewer symptoms). DSM-5 no longer has five subtypes of schizophrenia but instead uses a diagnosis of schizophrenia based on the presence of one or more symptoms over a six-month period. These symptoms include hallucinations, disorganised speech and behaviour, and delusions. The reasoning behind the exclusion of the five subtypes rests on the fact that symptoms observed in patients tend to overlap. Overlapping symptoms make it difficult for clinicians to justify the mutual exclusivity of the subtypes and therefore make a specific diagnosis of schizophrenia. In the context of diagnosing offenders with schizophrenia, it is sometimes necessary to include further information about the specific nature of the schizophrenic symptoms exhibited. This is especially pertinent when addressing symptoms of an offender with schizophrenia which could be potentially harmful and dangerous to other offenders incarcerated in a prison or hospital environment. Knowledge of an offender's paranoid and grandiose beliefs could go a long way towards ensuring that the right medical care and security (e.g. housing the offender away from specific other types of prisoner) are in place. Having a much detailed information as possible is more an advantage than a hindrance when it comes to offenders with mental health issues.

In DSM-5, as previously in DSM-IV-TR, personality disorder are classified according to three behavioural clusters:

1. Odd/eccentric
2. Dramatic/erratic
3. Anxious/fearful.

In each of these clusters lie specific personality disorders, as follows

Odd/eccentric – paranoid (hostile, suspicious, extreme sexua jealousy); schizoid (socially withdrawn, lack warmth toward others and indifferent); schizotypal (odd beliefs and use of magica thinking towards events and interpersonal difficulties)

Dramatic/erratic – histrionic (exhibit extreme emotions that in reality are shallow); borderline (erratic emotions, impulsive argumentative and unpredictable); narcissistic (self-centred, lack empathy, opinionated and grandiose view of abilities); antisocial (manipulative, irresponsible, destructive, aggressive and dishonest

Anxious/fearful – obsessive-compulsive (extreme drive for per fection which interferes with task completion, preoccupied with details and have difficulty giving up control); avoidant (extreme anxiety in social situations and oversensitive to any criticism) dependent (lack self-confidence and depend on other people).

A fundamental problem with defining personality disorders in this way using a 'top-down' approach is the assumption that each personality type is different. According to the American Psychiatric Association (APA), there is no conclusive evidence showing the existence of discrete personality types (American Psychiatric Association 2013). Furthermore, psychopathy as a personality disorder does not exist as a classification in any version of DSM. It is no clearly differentiated from Antisocial Personality Disorder (APD) As a diagnosis of APD is often associated with criminality, many inmates could have been diagnosed with this. This means that it is possible that a diagnosis of APD may have been arrived at using many different variations of symptom combination, thereby decreasing

ssessment and diagnostic accuracy. This can be particularly proble-
natic for forensic psychologists working within the U.S. legal system,
where in many states the death penalty is still used. A serious
offender diagnosed with APD is likely to be sentenced to death in a
tate that endorses capital punishment. Hence, in DSM-5, an alternative approach to assessing and diagnosing personality disorders was
developed, together with the introduction of the personality subtypes,
as a means of improving clinical practice. The inclusion of existing
personality disorder subtypes in DSM-5 maintains the continuity of
clinical practice, while the alternative approach helps reduce its short-
comings (American Psychiatric Association 2012). The alternative
approach rests on the assessment of impairments in personality func-
ioning (assessed under Criterion A) and the presence of personality
raits identified as pathological (assessed under Criterion B). Criterion
A is assessed using a scale based on levels of personality functioning,
0' representing little or no impairment and '4' representing extreme
impairment of self and interpersonal functioning. Criterion B is
assessed using five broad domains divided into different pathological
personality traits. With the introduction of Criteria A and B, forensic
psychologists can be more accurate in assessing and diagnosing an
offender with a personality problem.

There has also been change to the labelling of paraphilic disorders
n DSM-5 – a distinction between paraphilias and paraphilic disorders is specified. Criterion A specifies the nature of the paraphilia
e.g. sexual focus on children) and Criterion B the negative consequences of the paraphilia (e.g. harm to children). Only if both
Criterion A and Criterion B are met is the offender diagnosed with
paraphilic disorder. Individuals with the presence of Criterion A only
are considered to have a paraphilia but not paraphilic disorder. This
distinction allows forensic psychologists to separate individuals who
have non-normative sexual behaviours from those who have sexual
behaviours that are both non-normative and pathological. This is an
important distinction enabling forensic psychologists to identify
hose who are a potential danger.

BRAIN SCANNING AND FORENSIC PSYCHOLOGISTS

There are different ways of scanning the brain but the most popular
scanning technique is Magnetic Resonance Imaging (MRI), of

which there are two types: one that scans the structure of the brain and one that focuses on function (the latter known as fMRI). Interestingly, many studies using fMRI have detected differences of function in antisocial, violent and psychopathic criminals (Yang and Raine 2009). These criminals showed abnormally reduced prefrontal cortex activity in the brain. The prefrontal cortex is responsible for planning responses to complex and difficult problems and acts as a coordinator for decision making – in other words, it gathers information necessary for making an informed and appropriate decision. Deficits in decision making are common in psychopaths, especially in response to social and interpersonal situations. Other areas of malfunction in the brain of criminal psychopaths have been detected using fMRI. Studies show abnormal activity in an area of the brain called the amygdala (Adolphs et al. 1994; Aggleton 1992; Schiltz et al. 2007; Yang et al. 2009). This is involved in the regulation of our emotions and motivations, and is especially pertinent in emotions and motivations relating to survival. Hence, it is particularly active in processing fear and anger. One of the key behavioural facets of criminal psychopaths is that they experience little fear and little empathy (an emotion required to be able to understand and feel another's pain and anguish). Scans using fMRI are particularly informative in the identification of abnormal brain function in violent criminals, but their potential use as evidence in court for the defence has been debated. The technique was used by neuroscientist Kent Kiehl on prison inmate Brian Dugan in 2010. Dugan was already serving two life sentences in DuPage County Jail for two murders he committed in the 1980s, and was now facing the death penalty for a murder committed earlier. Dugan performed a series of tests while in the fMRI scanner. The scan showed that his brain function was abnormal and this was considered as admissible evidence in court for the first time in the history of legal representation (Kiehl cited in Hagerty 2010). However, another neuroscientist, Jonathan Brodie, presented persuasive evidence for the prosecution which convinced jurors that Dugan was guilty, resulting in his death sentence being restored.

This case highlights the debates around whether brain scans showing deficits should be admissible evidence and whether these deficits can truly be used to account for criminal culpability. As Professor Stephen Morse says, 'Brains don't kill people, people kill people' (cited by Hughes 2010).

In the Dugan case, the question was whether he should be put to death and not whether he was guilty of murder. In the end, despite the evidence of the fMRI scan, the murder he committed was considered dangerous enough to sanction his execution by the state and so his case was straightforward. But using fMRI scans as evidence in defence of having committed murder leads to numerous legal philosophical debates. If the defendant is guilty of having committed murder but is found to have abnormal brain function, how does the law punish such an individual? If the punishment is much more lenient than would be expected under a retributive approach, does this provide justice for the victim's family? The underlying philosophy of punishment is that the offender should receive a punishment that is in keeping with the seriousness and dangerousness of the crime and harm incurred by the victim. The ultimate harm is the victim's death; should a murderer receive unusually lenient treatment solely on the basis of an fMRI scan reading? Punishment also serves to protect the public from dangerous individuals; if the punishment is lenient such that the murderer serves less time behind bars, this theoretically offers future opportunity to kill again, leading to concerns over public safety. Finally, punishment acts not only as a deterrent to the individual (preventing them from reoffending during their incarceration) but also as a general deterrent to others; is this effect weakened in the light of a more lenient sentence? In conclusion, the use of fMRI scans in legal contexts is problematic and opens a whole can of worms. And in discussing murder cases, the debate has only just begun; this leads to discussion about where the law should draw the line regarding the admissibility in court of brain scans – in cases of burglary, mugging, robbery, drug-trafficking …

SUMMARY

Forensic psychologists perform a diversity of roles, many of which have to be contextualised within the restrictions of legal and mental health legislation. These pieces of legislation can sometimes be in conflict with definitions used in forensic psychology. A good example of this is the differences in the definition of dangerousness between the law and the teams of professionals (including forensic psychologists) which work together to perform offender risk assessments. In the U.K., the Criminal Justice Act of 2003 defines dangerousness as a 'significant risk of serious harm', and yet those professionals working as part of the Offender Assessment System (OASys) operate using the categorisation of likelihood of reconviction as low, medium or high, and of risk of serious harm as low, medium, high, or very high. The way forensic psychologists operate is largely defined by the British Psychological Society (in the U.K.) and the American Psychological Association (in the U.S.) Other countries throughout the world have their respective psychological associations which stipulate the running of the profession. Although forensic psychologists in the U.K. can choose the manner in which they deliver their therapeutic interventions, they often find that they are a part of a multidisciplinary team such as the Care Programme Approach and the OASys. In 2013, the classification of psychological disorders was updated in DSM-5. There are changes here which will have an impact on how some disorders are defined, assessed and treated. While some disorders are replaced by a single dimension, such as the incorporation of Asperger Syndrome into Autistic Spectrum Disorder, the classification of personality disorders is kept constant. DSM-5, however, also offers another method of assessing personality disorders by using Criteria A and B. This is claimed to bring more clarity to the assessment of overlapping symptoms of the different subtypes of personality disorder.

Brain scanning techniques is another area which has developed steadily over the past decade. Scanning the brains of criminal psychopaths using fMRI has demonstrated that activity in the prefrontal cortex, important for decision making, is significantly reduced. Furthermore, abnormal activity of the amygdala may help to explain how criminal psychopaths regulate their emotions and motivations (especially anger and fear) differently to most other people. Recently, there has been a shift towards using fMRI scans as evidence in defence of murderers. The reasoning behind this is that it is argued that they cannot help their affinity for harming and killing people if it is a result of abnormal brain functioning – this takes away their autonomy to behave appropriately and control a lust for murder. The use of fMRI in court has created much controversy, however, and prompts profound reflection on questions of what punishment is for. If a murderer is treated leniently in light of having abnormal brain function, is this a fair and just outcome?

RECOMMENDATIONS FOR FURTHER READING

American Psychiatric Association (2013). *Diagnostic and Statistical Manual of Mental Disorders (DSM-5)* (5th edn). Arlington, VA: American Psychiatric Publishing.

Kiehl, K.A., Smith, A.M., Mendrek, A., Forster, B.B., Hare, R.D. and Liddle, P.F. (2004). Temporal Lobe Abnormalities in Semantic Processing by Criminal Psychopaths as Revealed by Functional Magnetic Resonance Imaging. *Psychiatry Research*, 130, 297–312.

GLOSSARY

Adaptations: Characteristics selected for their positive outcomes in terms of reproduction and survival.

Behaviourism: An approach used in psychology placing emphasis on learning associations through stimulus–response reactions.

Cognitive overloading: The process by which, as a result of an increase in the amount of information a person has to attend to, memory and thought become overburdened.

Geographical mobility: Refers to changes in rural and urban populations due to people moving.

Interrogative suggestibility: Refers to the process of causing suspects to accept evidence presented to them during interrogation, and in some cases to confess to a crime they did not commit.

Mala in se: A Latin term used to describe criminal acts that violate the human moral code, such as murder.

Modus operandi: Refers to the specific method used by an individual to commit a crime; can often be used in relation to a specific serial killer.

Mutation: A change to genetic material resulting in the creation of a new characteristic found in the offspring.

Natural selection: A process described by Darwin allowing organisms to adapt optimally to their environment and so increase their likelihood of survival and reproduction.

Recombination: The process whereby genetic material (normally DNA) is broken and then joined with other segments of genetic material (also normally DNA). This process can occur with different areas of the same chromosome or across multiple chromosomes.

Remand: To place an accused person in custody until their court hearing.

Sexual selection: A mechanism described by Darwin as promoting evolutionary change by ensuring the survival of characteristics of those individuals who are more successful at finding a mate.

Socialisation: The learning of cultural values, mores and attitudes through nurturance.

Stimulus (pl. stimuli): An event or events causing a specific reaction which can be physical or psychological.

Suggestibility: The extent to which an individual is easily influenced by another person.

Tort Law: The section of law addressing cases of civil wrongs, where one person causes damage to another such as negligence and slander.

Tortious: Refers to an act of civil wrong, or a tort, that is considered by Tort Law.

BIBLIOGRAPHY

Abel, G.G., Mittelman, M.S. and Becker, J.V. (1985). Sex Offenders: Results of Assessment and Recommendations for Treatment. In M.H. Ben-Ron, S.J. Hucker and C.J. Webster (eds). *Clinical Criminology: The Assessment and Treatment of Criminal Behaviour*. Toronto: M and M Graphics.

Adolphs, R., Tranel, D., Damasio, H. and Damasio, A. (1994). Impaired Recognition of Emotion in Facial Expressions Following Bilateral Damage to the Human Amygdala. *Nature*, 372, 669–72.

Aggleton, J.P. (1992). *The Amygdala*. New York: Wiley-Liss.

American Psychiatric Association (2000). *Diagnostic and Statistical Manual of Mental Disorders (DSM-IV-TR)* (4th edn, text rev.). Washington, DC: American Psychiatric Association.

American Psychiatric Association (2012). *American Psychiatric Association Board of Trustees Approves DSM-5*. News Release, 1 December 2012. American Psychiatric Association.

American Psychiatric Association (2013). *Diagnostic and Statistical Manual of Mental Disorders (DSM-5)* (5th edn). Arlington, VA: American Psychiatric Publishing.

American Psychological Association (2002). *Code of Ethics of the APA*. Washington, DC: American Psychological Association.

American Psychological Association (2013). Public Description of Forensic Psychology. www.apa.org/ed/graduate/specialize/forensic.aspx.

Amir, M. (1971). *Patterns in Forcible Rape*. Chicago: University of Chicago Press.

Anderson, I. (2004). Explaining Negative Rape Victim Perception: Homophobia and the Male Rape Victim. *Current Research in Social Psychology*, 10(4).

Anderson, I. and Swainson, V. (2001). Perceived Motivation for Rape: Gender Differences in Beliefs about Female and Male Rape. *Current Research in Social Psychology*, 6(8).

Andrews, B., Brewin, C.R., Rose, S. and Kirk, M. (2000). Predicting PTSD in Victims of Violent Crime. *Journal of Abnormal Psychology*, 109, 69–73.

Andrews, D.A. and Bonta, J. (2006). *The Psychology of Criminal Conduct* (4th edn). Newark, NJ: LexisNexis.

Andrews, D.A. and Bonta, J. (2010). *The Psychology of Criminal Conduct* (5th edn). Newark, NJ: LexisNexis.

Archer, J. (2004). Sex Differences in Aggression in Real-World Settings: A Meta-Analytic Review. *Review of General Psychology*, 8, 291–321.

Art of Crimes (2013). Aileen Carol Wuornos. *Art of Crimes* blog, 11 August 2011. http://the-art-of-crimes.tumblr.com/post/58014133477/aileen-carol-wuornos-february-29-1956-october

ATSA (2001). *Code of Ethics of the ATSA*. Beaverton, OR: Association for the Treatment of Sexual Abusers.

Baddeley, A.D. and Hitch, G. (1974). Working Memory. In G.H. Bower (ed.). *The Psychology of Learning and Motivation: Advances in Research and Theory*, Vol. 8 (pp. 47–89). New York: Academic Press.

Bailey-Beckett, S. and Turner, G. (2009). Triangulation: How and Why Triangulated Research Can Help Grow Market Share and Profitability. White Paper, Beckett Advisors, Inc.

Barker, M. and Beech, T. (1993). Sex Offender Treatment Programmes: A Critical Look at the Cognitive-Behavioural Approach. *Issues in Criminological and Legal Psychology*, 19, 37–42.

BBC News (1999). *Mentally Ill Unlikely to Commit Murder*. BBC News Online, 5 January 1999. http://news.bbc.co.uk/1/hi/health/248841.stm

Beccaria, C. (1764/1986). *On Crimes and Punishments*. [Reprint (1986). Indianapolis: Hackett Publishing.]

Biggam, F. and Power, K. (1999). Suicidality and the State-Trait Debate on Problem-Solving Deficits. A Re-examination with Incarcerated Young Offenders. *Archives of Suicide Research*, 5, 27–42.

Billiald, S. (2009). *Crossing the Communication Divide: A Toolkit for Prison and Probation Staff Working with Offenders who Experience Communication Difficulties*. UK: National Offender Management Service.

Blackburn, R. (1996). What is Forensic Psychology? *Legal and Criminological Psychology*, 1(1), 3–16.

Blackburn, R. (2000). Treatment or Incapacitation? Implications of Research on Personality Disorders for the Management of Dangerous Offenders. *Legal and Criminological Psychology*, 5, 1–21.

Blair, R.J.R., Morris, J.S., Frith, C.D., Perrett, D.I. and Dolan, R.J. (1999). Dissociable Neural Responses to Facial Expressions of Sadness and Anger. *Brain*, 122, 883–93.

Blanchette, K. and Brown, L. (2006). *The Assessment and Treatment of Women Offenders: An Integrative Perspective*. Chichester: Wiley.

Bond, G.D. (2008). Deception Detection Expertise. *Law and Human Behaviour*, 32, 339–51.

Bonnie, R.J. and Grisso, T. (2000). Adjudicative Competence and Youthful Offenders. In R.G. Schwartz and T. Grisso (eds). *Youth on Trial: A Developmental Perspective on Juvenile Justice* (pp. 73–103). Chicago: University of Chicago Press.

Bottoms, A.E. and Brownsword, R. (1982). The Dangerousness Debate after the Floud Report. *British Journal of Criminology*, 22, 229–54.

Bowlby, J. (1958). The Nature of the Child's Tie to his Mother. *International Journal of Psychoanalysis*, 39, 350–73.

Boyd, N. (2000). *The Beast Within: Why Men Are Violent*. Vancouver, BC: Greystone Books.

Brace, N., Pike, G. and Kemp, R. (2000). Investigating E-FIT Using Famous Faces. In A. Czerederecka, T. Jaskiewicz-Obydzinska and J. Wojcikiewicz (eds). *Forensic Psychology and Law* (pp. 272–6). Krakow: Institute of Forensic Research Publishers.

British Psychological Society (2009). *Code of Ethics and Conduct: Guidance Published by the Ethics Committee of the British Psychological Society*. Leicester: The British Psychological Society.

British Psychological Society (2013). Careers: Forensic Psychology. http://careers.bps.org.uk/area/forensic

British Psychological Society (2015). Division of Forensic Psychology webpage. www.bps.org.uk/networks-and-communities/member-microsite/division-forensic-psychology

Brunner, H.G., Nelen, M., Breakefield, X.O., Ropers, H.H. and van Oost, B. A. (1993). Abnormal Behaviour Associated with a Point Mutation in the Structural Gene for Monoamine Oxidase A. *Science*, 262(5133), 578–80.

Bull, R. (1992). Obtaining Evidence Expertly: The Reliability of Interviews with Child Witnesses. *Expert Evidence*, 1, 5–12.

Bull, R. (2010). The Investigative Interviewing of Children and other Vulnerable Witnesses: Psychological Research and Working/Professional Practice. *Legal and Criminological Psychology*, 15, 5–23.

Bull, R. and Cherryman, J. (1995). *Helping to Identify Skills Gaps in Specialist Investigative Interviewing: Literature Review*. Home Office: London.

Bull, R. and Soukara, S. (2010). Four Studies of What Really Happens in Police Interviews. In G.D. Lassiter and C.A. Meissner (eds). *Police Interrogations and False Confessions: Current Research, Practice, and Policy*

Recommendations (pp. 81–95). Washington: American Psychological Association.

Buller, D. (2005). *Adapting Minds: Evolutionary Psychology and the Persistent Quest for Human Nature.* Cambridge, MA: MIT Press.

Burr, R.A. (2005). Mistaken Identification Leads to a Wrongful Conviction and Death Sentence: The Tony Ford Story. *Justice Denied*, 30. http://justice denied.org/issue/issue_30/jd_issue_30.pdf

Burton, D. and Smith-Darden, J. (2001). *North American Survey of Sexual Abuser Treatment and Models 2000.* Brandon, VT: Safer Society Foundation.

Buss, D.M. (2012). *Evolutionary Psychology: The New Science of the Mind* (4th edn). Boston: Pearson Allyn and Bacon.

Campbell, A. (2013). *A Mind of Her Own: The Evolutionary Psychology of Women* (2nd edn). Oxford: Oxford University Press.

Canter, D.V. (2012). *Offender Profiles.* www.davidcanter.com/professional-ser vices/offender-profiles/

Canter, D.V., Alison, L.J., Alison, E. and Wentink, N. (2004). The Organized/Disorganized Typology of Serial Murder: Myth or Model? *Psychology, Public Policy, and Law*, 10(3), 293–320.

Canter, D.V. and Wentink, N. (2004). An Empirical Test of Holmes and Holmes' Serial Murder Typology. *Criminal Justice and Behaviour*, 31(4), 489–515.

Christianson, S.A. (1992). Emotional Stress and Eyewitness Memory: A Critical Review. *Psychological Bulletin*, 112, 284–309.

Christianson, S.A. and Hubinette, B. (1993). Hands up! A Study of Witnesses' Emotional Reactions and Memories Associated with Bank Robberies. *Applied Cognitive Psychology*, 7, 365–79.

Civil Rights Act of 1866 (1866). 14 Stat. 27–30, 9 April 1866. United States Congress.

Clifford, B.R. and George, R. (1996). A Field Evaluation of Training in Three Methods of Witness/Victim Investigative Interviewing. *Psychology, Crime and Law*, 2, 231–48.

Cloward, R.A. and Ohlin, L.E. (1960). *Delinquency and Opportunity: A Theory of Delinquent Gangs.* New York: The Free Press.

Coccaro, E.F., Beresford, B., Minar, P., Kaskow, J. and Geracioti, T. (2007). CSF Testosterone: Relationship to Aggression, Impulsivity, and Venturesomeness in Adult Males with Personality Disorder. *Journal of Psychiatric Research,* 41(6), 488–92.

Cohen, M., Seghorn, T. and Calmas, W. (1969). Sociometric Study of the Sex Offender. *Journal of Abnormal Psychology*, 74, 249–55.

Coid, J., Wilkins, J., Coid, B. and Everitt, B. (1992). Self-Mutilation in Female Remanded Prisoners II: A Cluster Analytic Approach towards Identification of a Behavioural Syndrome. *Criminal Behaviour and Mental Health*, 2, 1–14.

Committee on Mentally Abnormal Offenders (1975). Report of the Committee on Mentally Abnormal Offenders (Chairman R. Butler). Cmnd 6244, London: HMSO.

Copas, J. (1983). Some Statistical Questions in the Prediction of Dangerous Offending. In J. Hinton (ed.). *Dangerousness: Problems of Assessment and Prediction* (pp. 133–45). London: George Allen and Unwin.

Copas, J. and Marshall, P. (1998). The Offender Group Reconviction Scale: A Statistical Reconviction Score for Use by Probation Officers. *Applied Statistics* 47, 159–71.

Cowburn, M. (1990). Work with Male Sexual Offenders in Groups *Groupwork*, 3(2), 157–71.

Crenshaw, M. (1985). An Organizational Approach to the Analysis of Political Terrorism. *Orbis*, 29(3), 465–89.

Crighton, D.A. (2000). Reflections on Risk Assessment: Suicide in Prisons *British Journal of Forensic Practice*, 2(1).

Crighton, D.A. and Towl, G.J. (1997). Self-Inflicted Deaths in Prisons in England and Wales: An Analysis of the Data for 1988–90 and 1994–95. In G.J. Towl (ed.). Suicide and Self-Injury in Prisons. *Issues in Criminological and Legal Psychology*, 28, (12–20).

Crime (Sentences) Act (1987). www.legislation.gov.uk/ukpga/1997/43/contents

Criminal Juctice Act (1991). www.legislation.gov.uk/ukpga/1991/53/contents

Criminal Justice Act (2003). www.legislation.gov.uk/ukpga/2003/44/contents

Dando, C.J. and Milne, R. (2009). The Cognitive Interview. In R. Kocsis (ed.). *Applied Criminal Psychology: A Guide to Forensic Behavioural Sciences* (pp. 5–9). Sydney: Charles Thomas Publishers.

Darwin, C. (1859). *On the Origins of Species by Means of Natural Selection*. Buffalo, NY: Prometheus Books.

Darwin, C. (1871). *The Descent of Man and Selection in Relation to Sex* (1st edn). London: John Murray.

Davies, G.M., Westcott, H.L. and Horan, N. (2000). The Impact of Questioning Style on the Content of Investigative Interviews with Suspected Child Sexual Abuse Victims. *Psychology, Crime and Law*, 6(2), 81–97.

Davis, R., Smith, B. and Henley, M. (1990). *Victim/Witness Intimidation in the Bronx Courts: How Common Is It, and What Are Its Consequences?* New York: Victim Services Agency.

Department of Health (2007). *Guidance on the Extension of Victims' Rights under the Domestic Violence, Crime and Victims Act 2004*. Department of Health, Mental Health Act Implementation Team/Ministry of Justice Mental Health Unit/NOMS Public Protection Unit.

DeValve, E.Q. (2005). A Qualitative Exploration of the Effects of Crime Victimisation for Victims of Personal Crime. *Applied Psychology in Criminal Justice*, 1(2), 71–89.

)iPaola, S. (2002). FaceSpace: A Facial Spatial-Domain Toolkit. In *Proceedings of the Sixth International Conference on Information Visualisation*, 2002.

)olan, B. (2004). Medical Records: Disclosing Confidential Clinical Information. *Psychiatric Bulletin*, 28, 53–6.

)olan, M. (2004). Psychopathic Personality in Young People. *Advances in Psychiatric Treatment*, 10, 466–73.

)onaldson (Lord) MR, ReD (A Minor) (Residence Order, 1992) 2 FLR 332, 336. CA.

)owler, K. (2003). Media Consumption and Public Attitudes toward Crime and Justice: The Relationship between Fear of Crime, Punitive Attitudes, and Perceived Police Effectiveness. *Journal of Criminal Justice and Popular Culture*, 10(2), 109–26.

)ugdale, R.L. (1877). *The Jukes: A Study in Crime, Pauperism, and Heredity*. New York: Putnam.

Egan, V. (2013). Are Terrorists Conservative? *The Psychologist*, 26(3), 226.

Eidin, M.N., Sheehy, N., O'Sullivan, M. and McLeavey, B. (2002). Perceptions of the Environment, Suicidal Ideation and Problem-Solving Deficits in an Offender Population. *Legal and Criminological Psychology*, 7(2), 187–201.

Ekman, P. (1992). Facial Expressions of Emotion: New Findings, New Questions. *Psychological Science*, 3(1), 34–8.

Ekman, P. (1996). Why Don't We Catch Liars? *Social Research*, 63(3), 801–17.

Evans, M. (2012). Sam Hallam's Murder Conviction Quashed by Seven-year-old Evidence. *The Telegraph*, 17 May 2012. www.telegraph.co.uk/news/uknews/crime/9272365/Sam-Hallams-murder-conviction-quashed-by-seven-year-old-evidence.html

Fallon, J. (2011). Horizon: Are You Good or Evil? BBC2, broadcast on 7 September 2011.

Farrington, D.P. (1992). Expanding the Beginning, Progress, and Ending of Antisocial Behavior from Birth to Adulthood. In J. McCord (ed.). *Facts, Frameworks, and Forecasts: Advances in Criminological Theory, Volume 3* (pp. 521–32). New Brunswick: Transactional Publishers.

Farrington, D.P. (1995). The Development of Offending and Antisocial Behaviour from Childhood: Key Findings from the Cambridge Study in Delinquent Development. *Journal of Child Psychology and Psychiatry and Allied Disciplines*, 36(6), 929–64.

Farrow, K., Kelly, G. and Wilkinson, B. (2007). *Offenders in Focus: Risk, Responsivity and Diversity*. University of Bristol: The Policy Press.

Fazel, S. and Danesh, J. (2002). Serious Mental Disorder in 23,000 Prisoners: A Systematic Review of 62 Surveys. *Lancet*, 359(9306), 545–50.

Fellner, J. (2006). A Corrections Quandary: Mental Illness and Prison Rules. *Harvard Civil Rights-Civil Liberties Law Review*, 41, 391–412.

Fine, C. and Kennett, J. (2004). Mental Impairment, Moral Understanding an Criminal Responsibility: Psychopathy and the Purposes of Punishment *International Journal of Law and Psychiatry*, 27(5), 425–43.

Fisher, R.P. and Geiselman, R.E. (1992). *Memory Enhancing Techniques fo Investigative Interviewing: The Cognitive Interview*. Springfield, IL: Charles C Thomas.

Fisher, R.P. and Price-Roush, J. (1986). *Question Order and Eyewitness Memory* Unpublished manuscript. Department of Psychology, Florida Internationa University, USA.

Floud, J. and Young, W. (1981). *Dangerousness and Criminal Justice*. London Heinemann Educational Books.

Foster, D. and Nicholas, L. (2000). Cognitive Dissonance, de Kock and Od Psychological Testimony. *South African Journal of Psychology*, 30(1), 37–40.

Freedman, M.D. (2001). False Prediction of Future Dangerousness: Erro Rates and Psychopathy Checklist-Revised. *Journal of the American Academy Psychiatry and Law*, 29(1), 89–95.

Frowd, C.D., Jones, S., Fodarella, C., Skelton, F., Fields, S., Williams A., Marsh, J., Thorley, R., Nelson, L., Greenwood, L., Date, L., Kearley K., McIntyre, A.H. and Hancock, P.J.B. (2013). Configural and Featura Information in Facial-Composite Images. *Science and Justice*, 54(3), 215–27.

Frowd, C.D., Pitchford, M., Skelton, F., Petkovic, A., Prosser, C. and Coates B. (2012). Catching Even More Offenders with EvoFIT Facial Composites In A. Stoica, D. Zarzhisky, G. Howells, C. Frowd, K. McDonald-Maier A. Erdogan and T. Arsian (eds). *IEEE Proceedings of 2012 Third Internationa Conference on Emerging Security Technologies* (pp. 20–6).

Gannon, M. and Mihorean, K. (2005). Criminal Victimization in Canada 2004. Juristat, Canadian Centre for Justice Statistics 25(7). In Ministry o Public Safety and Solicitor General (2009). *Victims of Crime: Victim Service Worker Handbook*. British Columbia: Victim Services and Crime Prevention division.

Gannon, T.A., Beech, A.R. and Ward, T. (2008). Does the Polygraph Lead to Better Risk Prediction for Sexual Offenders? *Aggression and Violent Behaviour* 13, 29–44.

Garfinkel, H. (1967). *Studies in Ethnomethodology*. Englewood Cliffs, NJ Prentice-Hall.

Garrido, E. and Masip, J. (1999). How Good are Police Officers at Spotting Lies? *Forensic Update*, 58, 14–21.

Geiselman, R.E., Fisher, R.P., MacKinnon, D.P. and Holland, H.L. (1985) Eyewitness Memory Enhancement in the Police Interview: Cognitive Retrieval Mnemonics versus Hypnosis. *Journal of Applied Psychology*, 70, 401–12.

General Medical Council (1993). *Professional Conduct and Discipline: Fitness to Practise*. London: GMC.

Gilbert, F. and Daffern, M. (2010). Integrating Contemporary Aggression Theory with Violent Offender Treatment: How Thoroughly Do Interventions Target Violent Behaviour? *Aggression and Violent Behavior*, 15, 167–80.

Glover, N. (1999). *Risk Assessment and Community Care in England and Wales*. Liverpool: Faculty of Law, University of Liverpool.

Glueck, S. and Glueck, E. (1950). *Unraveling Juvenile Delinquency*. New York: Harper and Row.

Goldstein, A.P. (2004). Evaluations of Effectiveness. In A.P. Goldstein, R. Nensen, B. Daleflod and M. Kalt (eds). *New Perspectives on Aggression Replacement Training* (pp. 230–44). Chichester: John Wiley and Sons.

Gray, N.S., Taylor, J. and Snowden, R.J. (2008). Predicting Violent Reconvictions Using the HCR–20. *The British Journal of Psychiatry*, 192, 384–7.

Greenwald, G. (2009). "Preventive Detention" and Prisoners of War. TalkLeft online magazine, 22 May 2009. www.talkleft.com/story/2009/5/22/112959/706/detainees/-Preventive-Detention-And-Prisoners–Of–War

Gregory, R.J. (2011). *Psychological Testing: History, Principles, and Applications* (6th edn). Boston, MA: Allyn & Bacon.

Griffin, R. (2012). *Terrorist's Creed: Fanatical Violence and the Human Need for Meaning*. Basingstoke: Palgrave Macmillan.

Griffiths, A. (2008). *An Examination into the Efficacy of Police Advanced Investigative Interview Training*. Unpublished PhD thesis, University of Portsmouth, UK.

Grimland, M., Apter, A. and Kerkhof, A. (2006). The Phenomenon of Suicide Bombing: A Review of Psychological and Nonpsychological Factors. *Crisis*, 27(3), 107–18.

Grubin, D. (1996). *Fitness to Plead in England and Wales*. Hove: Psychology Press.

Gudjonsson, G.H. (2003). *The Psychology of Interrogations and Confessions: A Handbook*. Chichester: John Wiley.

Gudjonsson, G.H. and Clark, N.K. (1986). Suggestibility in Police Interrogation: A Social Psychological Model. *Social Behaviour*, 1, 83–104.

Gudjonsson, G.H., Murphy, G.H. and Clare, I.C.H. (2000). Assessing the Capacity of People with Intellectual Disabilities to be Witnesses in Court. *Psychological Medicine*, 30, 307–14.

Gudjonsson, G.L. and Young, S. (2006). An Overlooked Vulnerability in a Defendant: Attention Deficit Hyperactivity Disorder and a Miscarriage of Justice. *Legal and Criminological Psychology*, 11(2), 211–18.

Gunn, J. and Buchanan, A. (2006). Paranoia in the Criminal Courts. *Behavioural Sciences and the Law*, 24, 373–83.

Hagerity, B.B. (2010). Inside a psychopath's brain: the sentencing debate. Special series: Inside the criminal brain. NPR. Online at www.npr.org/templates/story/story.php?storyId=128116806.

Halpern, D.F. (1997). Sex Differences in Intelligence: Implications for Education. *American Psychologist*, 52, 1091–1102.

Hamlyn, B., Phelps, A., Turtle, J. and Sattar, G. (2004). *Are Special Measure Working? Evidence from Surveys of Vulnerable and Intimidated Witnesses*. Home Office Research Study 283. London: Home Office Research, Developmen and Statistics Directorate.

Hanson, R.K. and Thornton, D. (2003). *Notes on the Development of Static-2002* Corrections Research User Report No. 2003/01. Ottawa: Department of the Solicitor General of Canada.

Hare, R.D. (1991). *Manual for the Psychopathy Checklist – Revised*. Toronto ON: Multi-Health Systems.

Harris, S. (2010). Toward a Better Way to Interview Child Victims of Sexua Abuse. *NIJ Journal*, 267, 12–15.

Hatz, J.L. and Bourgeois, M.J. (2010). Anger as a Cue to Truthfulness. *Journa of Experimental Social Psychology*, 46, 680–3.

Heilbrun, K., Hawk, G. and Tate, D.C. (1996). Juvenile Competence to Stand Trial: Research Issues in Practice. *Law and Human Behavior*, 20(5), 573–8.

Henderson, M. (1986). An Empirical Typology of Violent Incidents Reported by Prison Inmates with Convictions for Violence. *Aggressive Behaviour*, 12(1), 21–32

Hirschi, T. (1969). *Causes of Delinquency*. CA: University of California Press.

Hobson, J. and Shine, J. (1998). Measurement of Psychopathy in a UK Prison Population Referred for Long-Term Psychotherapy. *British Journal o Criminology*, 38, 504–15.

Hodge, S.A. (2000). Multivariate Model of Serial Sexual Murder. In D. Cante (ed.). Offender Profiling and Criminal Differentiation. *Legal an Criminological Psychology*, 5, 23–46.

Holmberg, U. and Christianson, S. (2002). Murderers' and Sexual Offenders Experiences of Police Interviews and their Inclination to Admit or Deny Crimes. *Behavioural Sciences and the Law*, 20, 31–45.

Holmes, R.M. and DeBurger, J. (1985). Profiles in Terror: The Seria Murderer. *Probation*, 49, 29–34.

Home Office (2002). *Achieving Best Evidence in Criminal Proceedings: Guidance fc Vulnerable or Intimidated Witnesses, including Children*. London: Home Office Communication Directorate.

Home Office (2007). *Achieving Best Evidence in Criminal Proceedings: Guidance on Interviewing Victims and Witnesses, and Using Special Measures*. London: Home Office Communication Directorate.

Horgan, J. (2005). *The Psychology of Terrorism*. USA: Routledge.

Hughes, V. (2010). Science in Court: Head Case. *Nature*, 464, 340–2.

Humes, E. (2004). Experts Say False Confessions Come from Leading Questions, Young Suspects, High-Pressure Interrogations. In R. Bell (ed.) *Coerced False Confessions during Police Interrogations*. True TV Crime Library Criminal Minds and Methods. Turner/Time Warner, Knight Ridder Tribune News Service.

nnes, M. (2002). The Process Structures of Police Homicide Investigations. *The British Journal of Criminology*, 42(4), 669–88.

ames, A. (1996). Suicide Reduction in Medium Security. *Journal of Forensic Psychiatry*, 7(2), 406–12.

ones, O.D. (2006). Behavioral Genetics and Crime, in Context. *Law and Contemporary Problems*, 69, 81–100.

Kahneman, D. and Tversky, A. (1979). Prospect Theory: An Analysis of Decisions under Risk. *Econometrica*, 4(2), 263–91.

Kebbell, M.R. and Hatton, C. (1999). People with Mental Retardation as Witnesses in Court: A Review. *Mental Retardation*, 377(3), 179–87.

Kebbell, M.R., Hurren, E. and Mazerolle, P. (2006). An Investigation into the Effective and Ethical Interviewing of Suspected Sex Offenders. In D. Walsh and R. Bull (eds). How do Interviewers Attempt to Overcome Suspects' Denials? *Psychiatry, Psychology and Law*, 19(2), 1–18.

Keen, J. (2000). A Practitioner's Perspective: Anger Management Work with Young Offenders. *Forensic Update*, 60, 20–5.

Kelly, J. and Lamb, M. (2000). Using Child Development Research to Make Appropriate Custody and Access Decisions. *Family and Conciliation Courts Review*, 38, 297–311.

Kendall, K.A. (2004). Anger Management with Women in Coercive Environments. *Issues in Forensic Psychology*, 2, 35–41.

Kennedy, L. (1989). Europe v England: The Advantages of the Inquisitorial over the Adversary System of Criminal Justice. In M. Schollum (ed.). *Investigative Interviewing: The Literature* (p. 22). Wellington, New Zealand: Office of the Commissioner of Police.

Kershaw, C., Nicolas, S. and Walker, A. (2007). Crime in England and Wales 2006/2007. *Home Office Statistical Bulletin*, London: HMSO.

Kesteven, S. (2002). *Women Who Challenge: Women Offenders and Mental Health Issues*. London: NACRO.

Kiehl, K.A., Smith, A.M., Mendrek, A., Forster, B.B., Hare, R.D. and Liddle, P.F. (2004). Temporal Lobe Abnormalities in Semantic Processing by Criminal Psychopaths as Revealed by Functional Magnetic Resonance Imaging. *Psychiatry Research*, 130, 297–312.

Kurt, B., Etaner-Uyar, A.S., Akbal, T., Demir, N., Kanlikilicer, A.E., Kus, M. C. and Ulu, F.H. (2006). Active Appearance Model-Based Facial Composite Generation with Interactive Nature-Inspired Heuristics. In B. Gunsel et al. (eds). *International Workshop on Multimedia Content Representation, Classification and Security*, 4105 of LNCS (pp. 183–90). Springer-Verlag.

Lamb, M.E., Hershkowitz, I., Sternberg, K.J., Esplin, P.W., Hovav, M., Manor, T. and Yudilevitch, L. (1996). Effects of Investigative Utterance Types on Israeli Children's Responses. *International Journal of Behavioral Development*, 19, 627–37.

Lamb, M.E., Orbach, Y., Hershkowitz, I., Esplin, P.W. and Horowitz, D. (2007). Structured Forensic Interview Protocols Improve the Quality and Informativeness of Investigative Interviews with Children: A Review of Research using the NICHD Investigative Interview Protocol. *Child Abuse and Neglect*, 31, 1201–31.

Lane, B. (1992). *The Encyclopedia of Forensic Science*. London: Headline Book Publishing.

Legal Aid, Sentencing and Punishment of Offenders Act (2012). www.legislation.gov.uk/ukpga/2012/10/contents/enacted

Leventhal, G. and Krate, R. (1977). Physical Attractiveness and Severity of Sentencing. *Psychological Reports*, 40, 315–18.

Loftus, E. (2005). Planting Misinformation in the Human Mind: A 30-Year Investigation of the Malleability of Memory. *Learning and Memory*, 12(4), 361–6.

Loftus, E.F., Miller, D.G. and Burns, H.J. (1978). Semantic Integration of Verbal Information into a Visual Memory. *Human Learning and Memory*, 4, 19–31.

Loftus, E.F. and Palmer, J.C. (1974). Reconstruction of Auto-Mobile Destruction: An Example of the Interaction between Language and Memory. *Journal of Verbal Learning and Verbal Behaviour*, 13, 585–9.

Lombroso, C. (1876). *The Criminal Man*. Milan: Ulrico Hoepli.

Lombroso, C. (1899). *Le Crime: Causes et Remèdes*. [English translation: *Crime, its Causes and Remedies* (1911). Boston, MA: Little Brown.]

Long, D.E. (1990). *The Anatomy of Terrorism*. New York: The Free Press.

Loucks, N. and Talbot, J. (2007). No One Knows. Identifying and Supporting Prisoners with Learning Difficulties and Learning Disabilities: The Views of Prison Staff. Prison Reform Trust.

Luna, K. and Martin-Luengo, B. (2010). New Advances in the Study of the Confidence-Accuracy Relationship in the Memory for Events. *The European Journal of Psychology Applied to Legal Context*, 2(1), 55–71.

McCauley, C. (1991). *Terrorism Research and Public Policy*. London: Frank Cass.

Maccoby, E.E. and Martin, J.A. (1983). Socialization in the Context of the Family: Parent–Child Interaction. In E.M. Hetherington (ed.). *Handbook of Child Psychology*, Vol. 4. New York: Wiley.

McCord, J. (1986) Instigation and Insulation: How Families Affect Antisocial Aggression. In D. Olweus, J. Block and M. Radke-Yarrow (eds). *Development of Antisocial and Prosocial Behavior: Research, Theories, and Issues*. New York: Academic Press.

McGuire, J. and Hatcher, R. (2001). Offence-Focused Problem Solving: Preliminary Evaluation of a Cognitive Skills Program. *Criminal Justice and Behavior*, 28, 564–87.

McKay, B. and McKay, K. (2009). So You Want My Job: Forensic Psychologist. The Art of Manliness. www.artofmanliness.com/2009/07/22/so-you-want-my-job-forensic-psychologist

McMurran, M. (2002). *Motivating Offenders to Change: A Guide to Enhancing Engagement in Therapy*. Chichester: Wiley.

Maden, A. (1998). Risk Assessment and Management in Psychiatry. *CPD Psychiatry*, 1(1), 8–11.

Mann, R.E. and Beech, A.R. (2003). Cognitive Distortions, Schemas, and Implicit Theories. In T. Ward, D.R. Laws and S.M. Hudson (eds). *Sexual Deviance: Issues and Controversies* (pp. 135–53). Thousand Oaks, CA: Sage Publications.

Martin, M.E. and Hasselbrock, M.N. (2001). Women Prisoners' Mental Health: Vulnerabilities, Risks and Resilience. *Journal of Offender Rehabilitation*, 34, 25–44.

Matza, D. (1969). *Becoming Deviant*. New Jersey: Prentice Hall.

Maynard-Smith, J. (1993). *The Theory of Evolution*. Cambridge: Cambridge University Press.

Mealey, L. (1995). Primary Sociopathy (Psychopathy) is a Type, Secondary is Not. *Behavioural and Brain Sciences*, 19, 579–99.

Mental Health Act (MHA) (1983). www.legislation.gov.uk/ukpga/1983/20/contents

Mental Health Act (MHA) (2007). www.legislation.gov.uk/ukpga/2007/12/contents

Merari, A. (2010). Driven to Death: Psychological and Social Aspects of Suicide Terrorism. Oxford: Oxford University Press.

Miller, S., Sees, C. and Brown, J. (2006). Key Aspects of Psychological Change in Residents of a Prison Therapeutic Community. *The Howard Journal*, 45(2), 116–28.

Milligan, R.-J. and Andrews, B. (2005). Suicidal and Other Self-Harming Behaviour in Offender Women: The Role of Shame, Anger and Childhood Abuse. *Legal and Criminological Psychology*, 10(1), 13–25.

Milne, R., Clare, I.C.H. and Bull, R. (1999). Using the Cognitive Interview with Adults with Mild Learning Disabilities. *Psychology, Crime and Law*, 5, 81–99.

Ministry of Public Safety and Solicitor General (2009). *Victims of Crime: Victim Service Worker Handbook*. British Columbia: Victim Services and Crime Prevention division.

Moffitt, T.E., Brammer, G.L., Caspi, A., Fawcett, J.P., Raleigh, M., Yuwiler, A. and Silva, P. (1998). Whole Blood Serotonin Relates to Violence in an Epidemiological Study. *Biological Psychiatry*, 43, 446–57.

Moffitt, T.E. and Caspi, A. (2001). Childhood Predictors Differentiate Life-Course Persistent and Adolescence-Limited Antisocial Pathways Among Males and Females. *Development and Psychopathology*, 13, 355–75.

Monahan, J., Steadman, H.J., Appelbaum, P.S., Robbins, P.C., Mulvey, E.P., Silver, B., Roth, L.H. and Grisson, T. (2000). Developing a Clinically Useful Actuarial Tool for Assessing Violence Risk. *British Journal of Psychiatry*, 176, 312–19.

Morrissey, C. and Towl, G.J. (1991). Psychologists' Assessment and Treatment of Lifers: Recommendations for Future Developments. *Proceedings of HM Prison Service Psychology Conference*. London: Home Office.

Mottram, P.G. (2007). HMP Liverpool, Styal and Hindley Study Report. Liverpool: University of Liverpool.

Mueller-Johnson, K. (2009) Elderly in Court. In A. Jamieson and A. Moenssens (eds). *Wiley Encyclopedia of Forensic Science*. Chichester, England: Wiley.

Murphy, G. and Mason, J. (2005). People with Intellectual Disabilities Who Are at Risk of Offending. In N. Bouras (ed.). *Psychiatric and Behaviour Disorders in Developmental Disabilities and Mental Retardation*. Cambridge: Cambridge University Press.

National Mental Health Association (2004). *Mental Health Treatment for Youth in the Juvenile Justice System. A Compendium of Promising Practices*. Alexandria, VA: National Mental Health Association.

Needs, A. and Towl, G.J. (1997). Reflections on Clinical Risk Assessment with Lifers. *Prison Service Journal*, 113, 14–17.

NHS England (2013). NHS Standard Contract for Medium and Low Secure Mental Health Services (Adults). *NHS England/CO3/S/a*.

Nicholas, L. (2000). An Evaluation of Psychological Reports Considered in the Amnesty Process of the Truth and Reconciliation Commission. *South African Journal of Psychology*, 30(1), 50–2.

Nieland, M.N.S., McCluskie, C. and Tait, E. (2001). Prediction of Psychological Distress in Young Offenders. *Legal and Criminological Psychology*, 6(1), 29–47.

Northern Ireland Prison Service (2007) *Population report*. Belfast: NIPS.

Ord, B., Shaw, G. and Green, T. (2004). *Investigative Interviewing Explained*. Australia: LexisNexis Butterworths.

Palmer, E.J. (2001). Risk Assessment: Review of Psychometric Measures. In D.P. Farrington, C.R. Hollin and M. McMurran (eds). *Sex and Violence: The Psychology of Crimes and Risk Assessment* (pp. 7–22). Reading: Harwood Academic Press.

Palmer, E.J. (2003). *Offending Behaviour: Moral Reasoning, Criminal Conduct and the Rehabilitation of Offenders*. Cullompton: Willan Publishing.

Parsons, S., Walker, L. and Grubin, D. (2001). Prevalence of Mental Disorder in Female Remand Prisoners. *Journal of Forensic Psychiatry*, 12, 194–202.

Pavlov, I.P. (1927). *Conditioned Reflexes*. London: Oxford University Press.

Peay, J. (2002). Mentally Disordered Offenders: Mental Health and Crime. In M. Maguire, R. Morgan and R. Reiner (eds). *The Oxford Handbook of Criminology* (3rd edn). Oxford: Oxford University Press.

Pfohl, S. (1979). From Whom Will We Be Protected: Comparative Approaches to the Assessment of Dangerousness. *International Journal of Law and Psychiatry*, 2, 55–78.

olice and Criminal Evidence Act (PACE) (1984). www.legislation.gov.uk/ukpga/1984/60/contents

ope, K.S. and Vetter, V.A. (1992). Ethical Dilemmas Encountered by Members of the American Psychological Association. *American Psychologist*, 47, 397–411.

'rins, H. (1996). Risk Assessment and Management in Criminal Justice and Psychiatry. *Journal of Forensic Psychiatry*, 7, 42–62.

'rotess, D. (1993). *Hate Crimes and the Press: A Refracted Mirror*. Chicago: North Western University.

Quetelet, A. (1831). *Recherches sur le Penchant au Crime aux Différents Âges*. Brussels: Hayez.

Raine, A., Buchsbaum, M. and LaCasse, L. (1997). Brain Abnormalities in Murderers Indicated by Positron Emission Tomography. *Biological Psychiatry*, 42, 495–508.

Raine, A., Meloy, J.R., Bihrle, S., Stoddard, J., LaCasse, L. and Buchsbaum, M.S. (1998). Reduced Prefrontal and Increased Subcortical Brain Functioning Assessed Using Positron Emission Tomography in Predatory and Affective Murderers. *Behavioural Science and the Law*, 16, 319–32.

Reicher, S.D. and Haslam, S.A. (2003). Social Psychology, Science, and Surveillance: Understanding the Experiment. *Social Psychology Review*, 5, 7–17.

Ressler, R.K., Burgess, A.W., Douglas, J.E., Hartman, C.R. and D'Agnostino, R.B. (1986). Sexual Killers and their Victims: Identifying Patterns through Crime Scene Analysis. *Journal of Interpersonal Violence*, 1, 288–308.

Rivera, E. (1993). Teen Sues Clinic Using Penis Device, *Newsday*, City edn, 12 November 1993. Excerpts available at www.ethicaltreatment.org/newsday.htm

Robertson, G. (1981). The Extent and Pattern of Crime Amongst Mentally Handicapped Offenders. *Journal of the British Institute of Mental Handicap*, 9, 100–3.

Robinson-Riegler, B. and Robinson-Riegler, G. (2004). *Cognitive Psychology: Applying the Science of the Mind*. Boston, MA: Allyn and Bacon.

Rossmo, D.K. (2000). *Geographic Profiling*. Boca Raton, FL: CRC Press.

Rutter, M. and Giller, H. (1983). *Juvenile Delinquency: Trends and Perspectives*. Harmondsworth: Penguin.

Safer Custody Group (2005). *Self-Inflicted Deaths: Trends Report 2005*. London: NOMS.

Schiltz, K., Witzel, J., Northoff, G., Zierhut, K., Gubka, U., Fellmann, H., Kaufmann, J., Tempelmann, C., Wiebking, C. and Bogerts, B. (2007). Brain Pathology in Pedophilic Offenders: Evidence of Volume Reduction in the Right Amygdala and Related Diencephalic Structures. *Archives of General Psychiatry*, 64, 737–46.

Scullin, M.H., Kanaya, T. and Ceci, S.J. (2002). Measurements of Individual Differences in Children's Suggestibility across Situations. *Journal of Experimental Psychology: Applied*, 8(4), 233–46.

Séguin, J.R., Boulerice, B., Harden, P.W., Tremblay, R.E. and Pihl, R.O. (1999). Executive Functions and Physical Aggression after Controlling for Attention Deficit Hyperactivity Disorder, General Memory, and IQ. *Journal of Child Psychology and Psychiatry*, 40, 1197–208.

Sentencing Guidelines Council (2008). *Dangerous Offenders: Guide for Sentencers and Practitioners* (Version 2). Sentencing Guidelines Council, Crown Copyright.

Shamay-Tsoory, S.G., Harari, H., Aharon-Peretz, J. and Levkovitz, Y. (2010). The Role of the Orbitofrontal Cortex in Affective Theory of Mind Deficit in Criminal Offenders with Psychopathic Tendencies. *Cortex*, 46(5), 668–77.

Sheldon, W.H. (1942). *The Varieties of Temperament: A Psychology of Constitutional Differences*. New York: Harper and Row.

Siegel, L. (2006). *Criminology* (9th edn). Belmont, CA: Thomson Wadsworth.

Sigall, H. and Ostrove, N. (1975). Beautiful but Dangerous: Effects of Offender Attractiveness and Nature of the Crime on Juridic Judgement. *Journal of Personality and Social Psychology*, 31, 410–14.

Singleton, N., Meltzer, H. and Gatward, R. (1998). Psychiatric Morbidity Among Prisoners in England and Wales. London: HMSO.

Skinner, B.F. (1953). *Science and Human Behavior*. New York: Macmillan.

Slack, J. (2009). Murders, Rapes … Shocking Crimes of the 65 Killers Released under Labour to Strike Again. *Daily Mail Online*, 5 March 2009. www.daily-mail.co.uk/news/article-1159477/Murders-rapes–shocking-crimes-65-killers-released-Labour-strike-again.html

Smith, C. and Borland, J. (1999). Minor Psychiatric Disturbance in Women Serving a Prison Sentence: The Use of the General Health Questionnaire in the Estimation of the Prevalence of Non-Psychotic Disturbance in Women Prisoners. *Legal and Criminological Psychology*, 4, 273–84.

Snook, B., Cullen, R.M., Mokros, A. and Harbort, S. (2005). Serial Murderers' Spatial Decisions: Factors that Influence Crime Location Choice. *Journal of Investigative Psychology and Offender Profiling*, 2, 147–64.

Solomon, C., Gibson, S.J. and Mist, J.J. (2013). Interactive Evolutionary Generation of Facial Composites for Locating Suspects in Criminal Investigations. *Applied Soft Computing*, 13(7), 3298–306.

Spry, W.B. (1984). Schizophrenia and Crime. In M. Craft and A. Craft (eds), *Mentally Abnormal Offenders* (pp. 125–37). London: Bailliere Tindall.

Steblay, N.M. (1992). A Meta-Analytic Review of the Weapon Focus Effect. *Law and Human Behavior*, 16(4), 413–24.

Stewart, J.E. (2001). Appearance and Punishment: The Attraction-Leniency Effect in the Courtroom. *Journal of Social Psychology*, 125(3), 373–8.

Strömwall, L.A. and Granhag, P.A. (2003). How to Detect Deception? Arresting the Beliefs of Police Officers, Prosecutors and Judges. *Psychology, Crime and Law*, 9, 19–36.

Sugg, D. (2000). *Wiltshire Aggression Replacement Training (ART): One-Year Reconvictions and Targeting*. (Unpublished report, RDS, prepared for the Correctional Services Accreditation Panel.) London: Home Office.

Taylor, A.J.W. (1979). Forensic Psychology: Principles, Practice and Training. In W.A.M. Black and A.J.W. Taylor (eds). *Deviant Behaviour* (pp. 3–8). Auckland: Heinemann.

Taylor, D.A., Turner, J., Groome, D. and Gardner, M. (2011). *Facial Composite Construction by Eyewitnesses: The Role of Holistic Cognitive Style*. In BPS Conference Proceedings.

Taylor, M. and Quayle, E. (1994). *Terrorist Lives*. London: Brassey's Publishers.

Taylor, P.J. (1986). Psychiatric Disorder in London's Life-sentenced Offenders. *British Medical Journal*, 289, 9–12.

Taylor, S.R. and Butcher, M. (2007). Extra-Legal Defendant Characteristics and Mock Juror Ethnicity Re-examined. In *Proceedings of the BPS*, 11(2), 272.

Taylor, S.R. and Hartley, R. (2009). Watching Crime TV Increases Fear of Crime. *BPS: Book of Abstracts*, Annual Conference 2009 (p. 81).

Taylor, S.R., Lambeth, D., Green, G., Bone, R. and Cahillane, M. (2012). Cluster Analysis Examination of Serial Killer Profiling Categories: A Bottom-up Approach. *Journal of Investigative Psychology and Offender Profiling*, 9, 30–51.

Taylor, S.R. and Maguire, M. (1992). *The Addictions Intervention Unit: Methods of Assessing Effectiveness*. Report to South Glamorgan Probation Service. Cardiff: Social Research Unit, Cardiff University.

Thornberry, T.P., Freeman-Gallant, A., Lizotte, A.J., Krohn, M.D. and Smith, C.A. (2003). Linked Lives: The Intergenerational Transmission of Antisocial Behavior. *Journal of Abnormal Child Psychology*, 31, 171–84.

Towl, G. (2002). Working with Offenders: The Ins and Outs. *The Psychologist*, 15(5), 236–9.

Towl, G. and Crighton, D. (2000). Risk Assessment and Management. In G. Towl, I. Snow and M. McHugh (eds). *Suicide in Prisons* (pp. 66–92). Leicester: BPS.

Trivers, R.L. (1972). Parental Investment and Sexual Selection. In B. Campbell (ed.). *Sexual Selection and the Descent of Man* (pp. 139–79). Chicago: Aldine.

Trivers, R.L. (1985). *Social Evolution*. Menlo Park, CA: Benjamin/Cummings.

US Department of Justice. (2006). *Psychiatric Disorders of Youth in Detention* (NCJ 210331) Washington, DC: US Government Printing Office.

van Goozen, S.H.M., Matthys, W., Cohen-Kettenis, P.T., Gispen-de Wied, C., Wiegant, V.M. and van Engeland, H. (1998). Salivary Cortisol and

Cardiovascular Activity During Stress in Oppositional-Defiant Disorder Boys and Normal Controls. *Biological Psychiatry*, 43, 531–9.

Vrij, A. (2004). Why Professionals Fail to Catch Liars and How They Can Improve. *Legal and Criminological Psychology*, 9, 159–81.

Vrij, A. and Mann, S. (2001). Telling and Detecting Lies in a High-Stakes Situation: The Case of a Convicted Murderer. *Applied Cognitive Psychology*, 15, 187–203.

Ward, T. and Beech, A.R. (2006). An Integrated Theory of Sexual Offending. *Aggression and Violent Behaviour*, 11, 44–63.

Ward, T. and Brown, M. (2004). The Good Lives Model and Conceptual Issues in Offender Rehabilitation. *Psychology, Crime and Law*, 10(3), 243–57.

Watson, J.B. (1913). Psychology as the Behaviorist Views it. *Psychological Review*, 20, 158–77.

Webster, C.D., Douglas, K.S., Eaves, S.D. and Hart, S.D. (1997). Assessing Risk of Violence to Others. In C.D. Webster and M.A. Jackson (eds). *Impulsivity: Theory, Assessment, and Treatment* (pp. 251–77). New York: Guilford.

Wells, G.I. (1978). Applied Eyewitness Testimony Research: System Variables and Estimator Variables. *Journal of Personality and Social Psychology*, 36, 1546–57.

West, D.J. (1982). *Delinquency: Its Roots, Careers and Prospects*. London: Heinemann.

West, D.J. and Farrington, D.P. (1973). *Who Becomes Delinquent?* London: Heinemann.

West, D.J. and Walk, A. (eds) (1977). *Daniel McNaughton: His Trial and the Aftermath*. Ashford: Gaskell Books.

Westcott, H.L., Davies, G.M. and Bull, R.H.C. (2002). *Children's Testimony: A Handbook of Psychological Research and Forensic Practice*. Chichester: Wiley.

Whitehead, T. (2011). Up to 2,000 Serious Offences Committed by Reoffending Criminals Every Year. *The Telegraph*, 18 March 2011. www.telegraph.co.uk/news/uknews/law-and-order/8388224/Up-to-2000-serious-offences-committed-by-reoffending-criminals-every-year.html

Wilkens, J. and Sauer, M. (1999). Haunting Questions: The Stephanie Crowe Murder Case. Part 2: The arrest. *San Diego Union Tribune*, 12 May 1999. http://legacy.utsandiego.com/news/reports/crowe/crowe2.html

Willner, P. (2011). Assessment of Capacity to Participate in Court Proceedings: A Selective Critique and some Recommendations. *Psychology, Crime and Law*, 17(2), 117–31.

Wilson, G. (2013). Psychologist: Mick Philpott is a "Psychopath". *ITV News*, 3 April 2013.

Wolfgang, M. (1958). *Patterns of Criminal Homicide*. Philadelphia: University of Pennsylvania Press.

Workman, L. and Reader, W. (2014). *Evolutionary Psychology: An Introduction* (3rd edn). Cambridge: Cambridge University Press.

Worrall, A. (1990). *Offending Women: Female Lawbreakers and the Criminal Justice System*. London: Routledge.

Xenitidis, K.I., Henry, J., Russell, A.J., Ward, A. and Murphy, D.G. (1999). An In-Patient Treatment Model for Adults with Mild Intellectual Disability and Challenging Behaviour. *Journal of Intellectual Disability Research*, 43, 128–34.

Yang, Y. and Raine, A. (2009). Prefrontal Structural and Functional Brain Imaging Findings in Antisocial, Violent, and Psychopathic Individuals: A Meta-analysis. *Psychiatry Research – Neuroimaging*, 174(2), 81–8.

Yang, Y., Raine, A., Narr, K.L., Colletti, P. and Toga, A.W. (2009). Localisation of Deformations within the Amygdala in Individuals with Psychopathy. *Archives of General Psychiatry*, 66, 986–94.

Yankowski, L. (1992). Testimony on the Phoenix Program. Provided to the Committee on Children's Psychological Treatment Programs of the Arizona Senate, 16 September 1992. www.ethicaltreatment.org/yankowski.htm

Zamble, E. and Porporino, F.J. (1988). *Coping Behaviour and Adaptation in Prison Inmates*. New York: Springer.

Zamble, E. and Quinsey, V.L. (1997). *The Criminal Recidivism Process*. Cambridge: Cambridge University Press.

Zapf, P.A. and Roesch, R. (2001). A Comparison of American and Canadian Conceptualisations of Competence to Stand Trial. In R. Roesch, R.R. Carrado and R. Dempster (eds). *Psychology in the Courts: International Advances in Knowledge*. London: Routledge (pp. 121–32).

Zigmond, A.S. and Snaith, R.P. (1983). The Hospital Anxiety and Depression Scale. *Acta Psychiatrica Scandinavica*, 67, 361–70.

Zimbardo, P.G. (1971). The Power and Pathology of Imprisonment. *Congressional Record, Serial No. 15, October 25, 1971*. Hearings before Subcommittee No. 3, of the Committee on the Judiciary, House of Representatives, Ninety-Second Congress, *First Session on Corrections, Part II, Prisons, Prison Reform, and Prisoners' Rights: California*. Washington, DC: US Government Printing Office.

INDEX

Note: Bold indicates boxed material.